KU-542-182

Qatar
The Complete **Residents'** Guide

Supported by

Qtel

Official telecom provider for Doha Asian Games 2006

Passionately Publishing... **EXPLORER**

Qatar Explorer 2006/1st Edition

ISBN 976-8182-53-9

Copyright © Explorer Group Ltd 2006.
All rights reserved.

Front Cover Photograph – Pete Maloney

Printed and bound by Emirates Printing Press, Dubai, United Arab Emirates.

Explorer Publishing & Distribution
PO Box 34275, Zomorrodah Bldg, Za'abeel Rd, Dubai
United Arab Emirates
Phone	(+971 4) 335 3520
Fax	(+971 4) 335 3529
Email	Info@Explorer-Publishing.com
Web	www.Explorer-Publishing.com

While every effort and care has been made to ensure the accuracy of the
information contained in this publication, the publisher cannot accept
responsibility for any errors or omissions it may contain.
No part of this publication may be reproduced, stored in a retrieval system,
or transmitted, in any form or by any means, electronic, mechanical,
photocopying, recording or otherwise, without the prior permission in
writing of the publisher.

Qatar Explorer 2006
The Complete Residents' Guide, 1st Edition

Also available in this series:
Abu Dhabi Explorer (5th Edition), Bahrain Explorer (1st Edition), Dubai Explorer (10th Edition)
Geneva Explorer (1st Edition), Kuwait Explorer (1st Edition), Oman Explorer (3rd Edition)

Forthcoming titles in this series:
Singapore Explorer (2006), Hong Kong Explorer (2006)

Contributing Authors
Heather Milbourn, Jeff Tynes,
Susie Sirri, Sylvia Symons

Publisher
Alistair MacKenzie
Alistair@Explorer-Publishing.com

Managing Editor
Claire England
Claire@Explorer-Publishing.com

Editors
Jane Roberts
Jane@Explorer-Publishing.com

David Quinn
David@Explorer-Publishing.com

Tim Binks
Tim@Explorer-Publishing.com

Sub Editor
Jo Holden-MacDonald
Jo@Explorer-Publishing.com

Editorial Assistant
Shelley Gibbs
Shelley@Explorer-Publishing.com

Production Assistant
Mimi Stankova
Mimi@Explorer-Publishing.com

Researchers
Helga Becker
Helga@Explorer-Publishing.com

John Maguire
John@Explorer-Publishing.com

Design Manager
Pete Maloney
Pete@Explorer-Publishing.com

Senior Designer
Ieyad Charaf
Ieyad@explorer-publishing.com

Project Designer
Jayde Fernandes
Jayde@Explorer-Publishing.com

Map Designer
Zainudheen Madathil
Zain@Explorer-Publishing.com

Designers
Noushad Madathil
Noushad@Explorer-Publishing.com

Varghese P.J
Varghese@Explorer-Publishing.com

Photography Manager
Pamela Grist
Pamela@Explorer-Publishing.com

Media Sales Manager
Alena Hykes
Alena@Explorer-Publishing.com

Media Sales Executive
Laura Zuffa
Laura@Explorer-Publishing.com

Corporate Sales Executive
Sue Page
Sue@Explorer-Publishing.com

PR & Marketing Executive
Marileze Jacobsz
Marileze@Explorer-Publishing.com

Office Manager
Andrea Fust
Andrea@Explorer-Publishing.com

Administrator
Wenda Oosterbroek
Wenda@Explorer-Publishing.com

Administration Assistant
Enrico Maullon
Enrico@Explorer-Publishing.com

Accounts Assistant
Cherry Enriquez
Cherry@Explorer-Publishing.com

Senior Software Engineer
Smitha Sadanand
Smitha@Explorer-Publishing.com

IT Support
Ajay Krishnan R.
Ajay@Explorer-Publishing.com

Distribution Manager
Ivan Rodrigues
Ivan@Explorer-Publishing.com

Distribution Executives
Abdul Gafoor
Gafoor@Explorer-Publishing.com

Mannie Lugtu
Mannie@Explorer-Publishing.com

Firos Khan
Firos@Explorer-Publishing.com

Ahmed Mainodin
Ahmed@Explorer-Publishing.com

Driver
Rafi Jamal
Rafi@Explorer-Publishing.com

Warehouse Assistant
Salithamby Nafayis
Nafayis@Explorer-Publishing.com

For general enquiries contact Info@Explorer-Publishing.com, for careers contact Jobs@Explorer-Publishing.com

Automobile Leaders of Qatar

Sole Agent in Qatar
ABDULLAH ABDULGHANI & BROS. CO. W.L.L.
Abdullah, Abduljaleel & Abdulghani Al-Abdulghani
TOYOTA **LEXUS**

Tel: (974) 4629222, Fax: (974) 4419660, P.O.Box: 1321, Doha-Qatar
www.aabqatar.com

A world of elegance, an unforgettable destination.

The Ritz-Carlton, Doha

© 2005 The Ritz-Carlton Hotel Company, L.L.C.

Experience the hospitality of The Ritz-Carlton, Doha. The exquisite cuisine in our nine restaurants and lounges is complemented by the opulence of our rooms and suites. From the beautifully appointed spa to a fitness centre with gymnasium, jacuzzi, pools, tennis and squash courts, a world of recreational facilities awaits the discerning traveller.

THE RITZ-CARLTON®
DOHA
الدوحة

P. O. Box 23400, Doha, State of Qatar
Tel: (974) 484 8000, Fax (974) 484 8484, Email: info.doha@ritzcarlton.com
Website: www.ritzcarlton.com

it's not just sports   it's

it's not just sports

The 15th Asian Games Doha 2006 welcomes 45 countries
and regions from across all of Asia to compete in 39
sports, and 423 events. Be prepared for breathtaking
athletic performances, and a celebration of humanity
that will captivate hearts worldwide.

Be prepared for the Games of your Life.
1-15 December 2006

www.doha-2006.com

©DAGOC 2006

Corporate Family Days
Theme Decoration • Birthday Parties

Tel: 00 971 4 347 9170   www.flyingelephantuae.com

A smooth ride even when you're not driving.

From the minute you walk in to fill-up the rental forms, to the time you drive out of our parking lot on any of our superbly maintained vehicles, the only problem you'll have is parting with such a customer-friendly, hassle-free rent-a-car company.

Al Muftah Rent-A-Car, First-rate cars, First-rate service.

MITSUBISHI MOTORS

AL MUFTAH
RENT A CAR SINCE 1971

P.O. Box 1316, Doha, Qatar Main Office, C Ring Road: Tel: 4328100/4442003 Fax: 4414339
herib Branch Office: Tel: 4426649/4326840 Fax: 4312899 • Ras Laffan Industrial City (RLC complex) Tel:/Fax 474884
E-mail: rac@qatar.net.qa Website: www.rentacarqatar.com

Enrico Maullon
AKA: The Crooner
Frequently mistaken for his near-namesake Enrique Iglesias, Enrico decided to capitalise and is now a regular stand-in for the Latin heart-throb. If he's ever missing from the Explorer office, it usually means he's off performing to millions of adoring fans on yet another stadium tour of America.

Firos Khan
AKA: Big Smiler
Previously a body double in kung fu movies, including several appearances in close up scenes for Steven Seagal's moustache (to save the indignity of revealing his stick-on). He also once tore down a restaurant with his bare hands after they served him a mild curry by mistake.

Ieyad Charaf
AKA: Fashion Designer
When we hired Ieyad as a top designer, we didn't realise we'd be getting his designer tops too! By far the snappiest dresser in the office, you'd be hard pressed to beat his impeccably ironed shirts.

Helga Becker
AKA: Fantasy Foodist
From alfresco eateries to burger joints, and cocktail bars to nightclubs, Helga has been around the Dubai block a few times (in the culinary sense of course). A walking restaurant and bar guide, Helga is the goddess of going out and makes Explorer look good enough to eat.

Jane Roberts
AKA: The Oracle
After working in an undisclosed role in the government Jane brought her super sleuth skills to Explorer. And lucky she did because whatever the question she knows what, where, who, how and when. In fact Jane's so deep undercover as a resident spy that even Alistair still doesn't know who she is.

Ivan Rodrigues
AKA: The Aviator
After making a mint in the airline market, Ivan came to Explorer out of the goodness of his heart. Distributing joy across the office he is the man with the master plan – if only we could understand his spreadsheets.

Jo Holden MacDonald
AKA: Eagle Eye
With better vision than a hawk, but about the same wingspan, her gift of spotting even the minutest mistakes means we have to manually put some back in just to give the competition a chance. Jo can spit a tiepo a myle away xxx insert text here xxx

Jayde Fernandes
AKA: Pop Idol
When not secretly listening to Britney or writing to McFly to become their fifth member, Jayde actually manages to get a bit of designing done (in between spells singing to himself in the bathroom mirror). He's The Man, and all because the ladies love his in-tray!

Abdul Gafoor
AKA: Ace Circulator

After a successful stint on Ferrari's Formula One team Gafoor made a pitstop at our office and decided to stay. As Explorer's most cheerful employee, he's the only driver in Dubai yet to succumb to road rage.

Alena Hykes
AKA: Sales Supergirl

A former bond girl, Alena speaks more languages than we've had hot dinners and she's not afraid to be heard. She dresses to kill and has a sales pitch to die for with everything she touches turning to gold - must be that Goldfinger!

Alistair MacKenzie
AKA: Media Mogul

If only Alistair could take the paperless office one step further and achieve the officeless office he would be the happiest publisher alive. Remote access from a remote spot within the Hajar mountains would suit this intrepid explorer. The only problem could be staffing - unless he can persuade Pizza Hut to deliver.

Andrea Fust
AKA: Mother Superior

Although already in a successful career as Head Nun in a Swiss convent, with a penchant for ruling with an iron fist, she shrugged off her habit to run away with a gold smuggler. Now settled in Dubai, she now runs the Explorer office like clockwork and we all go cuckoo.

Sue Page
AKA: Wheeler Dealer

Sue drives such a hard bargain that she has been barred for life from all souks, and even Spinneys (because she convinced the cashier to give her a 70% discount). We never have to pay full price for lunch when she's around.

Cherry Enriquez
AKA: Bean Counter

With the team's penchant for sweets and pastries, it's good to know we have Cherry on top of our accounting cake. The local confectioner is always paid on time, so we're guaranteed great gateaux for every special occasion.

Claire England
AKA: Whip Cracker

No longer able to freeload off the fact that she once appeared in a Robbie Williams video, Claire now puts her creative skills to better use - looking up rude words in the dictionary! A child of English nobility, Claire is quite the lady - unless she's down at Jimmy Dix.

David Quinn
AKA: Sharp Shooter

After a short stint as a children's TV presenter was robbed from David because he developed an allergy to sticky back plastic, he made his way to sandier pastures. Now that he's thinking outside the box, nothing gets past the man with the sharpest pencil in town.

On your marks, get set, go! The Qatar Explorer is out of the blocks and sprinting ahead to bring you the inside track on living life to the full in Qatar.

Whether you're here to work, here to live, here to play, or here to explore, the Qatar Explorer will be your first and last point of reference. In their quest for accuracy and invaluable info, our roving resident reporters have left no stone unturned to bring you the ultimate fact-filled guide to this interesting and emerging country.

The General Information chapter tells you everything you ever wanted to know about Qatar, covering its history, geography, economy, and culture, plus you'll find details of the country's hotels and places to stay. The Residents chapter is for people who intend to make Qatar their home, with page after page of vital advice on visas, documents, work, housing, health, education, transport and more. The Exploring chapter helps residents and visitors to get their bearings and discover what Qatar has to offer, while Activities features no end of clubs, societies, and sports and leisure facilities for those precious free time moments. Spenders big and small should head for the Shopping chapter for info on what to buy and where to buy it, and when the day is done, the Going Out chapter has reviews of every restaurant, cafe and bar worth knowing about. To cap it all, the detailed satellite image maps at the back of the book provide the most accurate aid to navigation available.

By getting your hands on this prized publication you've backed a real winner, because the Qatar Explorer is miles ahead of the competition and always first past the post for insider info.

The Explorer Team

Now it's over to you...

Just because you didn't get involved in the making of this book doesn't mean you can just sit on your laurels. We've done our best to uncover all the facts about living in Qatar, but we accept – and it hurts to say this – that we might have left things out. Which is where you come in. We want to know what we've done

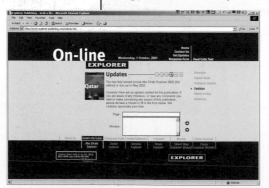

wrong, who we've missed and where we can improve. Have we left out your ice-sculpting club or dissed your favourite restaurant? Tell us! And don't forget that compliments are also gratefully received, so feel free to send in as many expressions of unadulterated praise as you want.

Visit our website to fill in our Reader Response form, and tell us exactly what you think of us.

www.Explorer-Publishing.com

Bods Behind the Book...

A lot goes into the production of our Complete Residents' Guides.
Sweat, tears, late nights, laughter, talents, tantrums, dedication,
prayers, moral support and a colourful collection of vocabulary have
all been offered selflessly by members of the Explorer family over
the last few months. They all deserve a shake of the hand, a pat on
the back, and copious air kisses for their contributions.

Our creative genius aside, there's a whole extended Explorer family to thank. A big
shout goes out to the tireless efforts of our roving reporters and backstage hands.
These are the people who work just as hard as us (sometimes harder), and yet still
manage to hold down their day jobs. Thank you to everyone who had a hand in
the creation of this masterpiece – here they are:

Asela Jayaweera, Gail Rundle, Karen Roche, Sue Farrow – they deserve medals for
their contributions to food and drink research.

Thanks also to the following for lending a hand: Anand and Tony from Emirates
Printing Press, Maher and Peter (maps), Jassim
Al Mansoori, Abdulla Ali Khamis Al Kuwair,
Fadi Barakeh, Mustafa Jamel Al-Qatami, Mr.
Saed Al Darmaki (Director of Censorship – Abu
Dhabi), Mr. Ahmed Al Shamsi, Ms. Maha Shams
Al Kelani, Ms. Lamiya Ali Al Shamsi, Mr. Ibrahim,
Mr. Nadawi, Mr. Juma Obaid Alleem (Director of
Censorship – Dubai).

Extra special thanks to long-suffering partners
Alan, Alex, Arnel, David, Dominik, Felicitas,
Fraser, Grace, Greg, Justin, Jodie, Marjan, Nijula,
Peter, Raihanath, Raji, Robert, Sadanand,
Sadhiya, Sajithkumar and Sunitha: well done
for putting up with our bad moods, late
nights and general deadline frenzy. And to
the youngest Explorers – Caitie, Dylan, Fiza,
Hannah, Kanyon, Lauren E, Lauren G, Louise-
Alodia, Lourdes-Amely, Mohammed Shaaz,
Peter-Vincent, Sean, Shahaha, Shahhina, and
Shahinsha – your mummies and daddies will
be home soon!

**Come on then if you think
you work hard enough...**
If you fancy yourself as an
Explorer and want a piece of
the action send your details
to Jobs@Explorer-Publishing.
com and mark the email
subject with one of the
following: Food Reporter (if
you want to write for your
supper), Freelance Writer (if
you think you have insider
info to contribute), Editorial
(if you want to join the ranks
of our esteemed production
team), Design (if you have
professional creative skills),
Research (if you think
you could be an Explorer
investigator).

xi

Rafi Jamal
AKA: Soap Star

After a walk on part in The Bold and the Beautiful, Rafi swapped the Hollywood Hills for the Hajar Mountains. Although he left the glitz behind, he still mingles with high society, moonlighting as a male gigolo and impressing Dubai's ladies with his fancy footwork.

Salithanby Nafayis
AKA: The Shadow

None of us have ever met Salithingymebob – the closest we've come is the fleeting footsteps we hear whenever we open the warehouse door. The place is run with baffling efficency though, and that's good enough for us.

Shelley Gibbs
AKA: Queen of Clubs

After a few close calls, Shelly decided that running an underground casino in Mirdif was too risky, and came to work for Explorer. And we've quickly learnt that when the stakes are high, and the chips are down, she always has an ace up her sleeve.

Smitha Sadanand
AKA: Pocket Rocket Scientist

Despite her placid appearance, IT genius Smitha is actually a power-crazed megalomaniac obsessed with taking over the world, but since joining Explorer, she's managed to curb her fiery temperament and now writes computer programs to assist with Explorer's domination plans.

Varghese P.J.
AKA: Spiderman

After spotting an open window while scaling our building using only paper clips and fridge magnets, he climbed in and we haven't been able to get rid of him. But he comes in useful for doodling and casting his web over design decisions.

Tim Binks
AKA: Cookie Monster

After flying the Explorer nest at the beginning of the millennium in search of sushi, Tim eventually tired of egg rolls and flew back with the promise of a more calorific career. When the cookie crumbles Tim is the man to gather the pieces – as long as it's chocolate chip of course!

Wenda Oosterbroek
AKA: Ink Monitor

Wenda has been in Dubai so long it was only a matter of time before she ended up working for us here at Explorer. Coming from a family of dhow traders, her contacts among the Iranian merchant set have proved invaluable in acquisitions for the office.

Zainudheen Madathil
AKA: Map Master

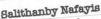

Often confused with football star Zinedine Zidane because of his dexterous displays with his digits, Zain tackles design with the mouse skills of a star striker. Maps are his goal and despite getting red-penned a few times, when he shoots, he scores.

John Maguire
AKA: Coffee Bean

Concerned that the average employee age was creeping above 25, Explorer hired John to inject a little youthful vigour. Although aged just six and only able to talk baby language, he keeps himself buzzing with constant coffee top-ups and makes sure the office wrinklies are always on their toes.

Laura Zuffa
AKA: Travelling Salesgirl

Laura's passport is covered in more stamps than Kofi Annan's, and there isn't a city, country or continent that she won't travel to. With a smile that makes grown men weep, our girl on the frontlines always brings home the beef bacon.

Marileze Jacobsz
AKA: General Idealist

Stop the press! Marilieze may be a marketing whizz but unfortunately for the boys she is now off the market. After walking down the aisle at the end of 2005 she has left a string of broken hearts behind her, but still seems to have the city's media wrapped round her little finger.

Mannie Lugtu
AKA: Distribution Demon

When the travelling circus rode into town, their master juggler Mannie decided to leave the Big Top and explore Dubai instead. He may have swapped his balls for our books but his juggling skills still come in handy.

Mimi Stankova
AKA: Mind Controller

A master of mind control, Mimi's siren-like voice lulls people into doing whatever she asks. Her steely reserve and endless patience mean recalcitrant reporters and persistent PR people are putty in her hands, delivering whatever she wants, whenever she wants it.

Ajay Krishnan
AKA: Web Wonder

Ajay's parents knew he was going to be an IT genius when they found him reconfiguring his Commodore 64 at the tender age of three. After a successful run as the technology consultant on all three Matrix movies Ajay joined Explorer – there's fewer celebrities, but it's just as slick.

Pamela Grist
AKA: Happy Snapper

If a picture can speak a thousand words then Pam's photos say a lot about her - through her lens she manages to find the beauty in everything - even this motley crew. And when the camera never lies, thankfully Photoshop can.

Pete Maloney
AKA: Graphic Guru

Image conscious he may be, but when Pete has his designs on something you can bet he's gonna get it! He's the king of chat up lines, ladies – if he ever opens a conversation with 'D'you come here often?' then brace yourself for the Maloney magic.

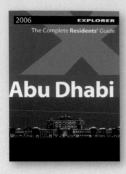

Residents' Guides

Activity Guides

Practical Guides

Lifestyle Guides

Map Guides

Visitors' Guides

Photography Books

Contents   General Info

Residents

Everything you need to know for life in Qatar; from finding a job, a place to live and setting up home when you first arrive, to all the essentials such as driving licences, a new car or getting married, or just sourcing the medical facilities, schools and services you'll need along the way.

Contents   Exploring

An in-depth look at the areas worth exploring in Qatar and all the attractions to be found there, including museums, heritage sites, parks, beaches and amusement centres, and what can be found in Qatar's neighbouring countries.

Activities

With enough to keep everyone busy, from beach lovers and theatre players up to even the most ardent extreme sports enthusiasts, Qatar has a variety of sports and activities to keep you busy. Comprehensive listings for all the sports, activities, clubs and relaxation available.

From large and flash malls to traditional, atmospheric souks, there's a massive range of shopping opportunities in Qatar. There are reviews on each mall and shopping area and sections on where to find whatever you want to buy.

Whether you love fine dining or street-side shawarma, this chapter opens up Qatar's culinary delights with independent reviews of all the 'must-do' places. You'll also find details of cinemas and live entertainment venues.

Qatar Today قطر اليوم

EVERYTHING ELSE IS ORDINARY

No other magazine in Qatar gives the reach and quality that the combination of Qatar Today & Qatar Al Yom does.

As Qatar's only monthly news and business magazine it reaches more decision makers and opinion leaders than any other title.

It is the first choice of premium international and regional brands targeting an up market, affluent audience. So if you want your brand to stand out of the ordinary, be in a medium that is not ordinary!

To find out more call us at +974-4550983 or email ravi@omsqatar.com

Oryx Publishing & Advertising Co.
Suite #4, Al Khalejia Bldg No 18, 930 Al Wafa St, Al Hilal Area No 41, PO Box 405 Doha - Qatar
Tel: (+974) 4672139, 4550983, Fax: (+974) 4550982, 4672511

The fastest way to get free flights every year.

Earn more than 100,000 bonus Qmiles

Introducing CbClass cards

- Up to 20,000 *Qmiles* up on joining

- 100,000 *Qmiles* or more on balance transfers

- First flight bonus - up to 4,000 *Qmiles*

- 1.5 *Qmiles* for every 1 Wafapoints Transferred

- Guaranteed free flights every year with renewal bonus *Qmiles*

- Earn *Qmiles* twice on Qatar Airways ticket and holiday packages

- Double *Qmiles* on all fees and charges

Plus many more card benefits and privileges

Call 4440012

* Terms & Conditions Apply

QATAR AIRWAYS القطرية
Privilege Club

For more information, please visit the nearest branch
www.cbq.com.qa

البـنك التـجاري
Commercial bank

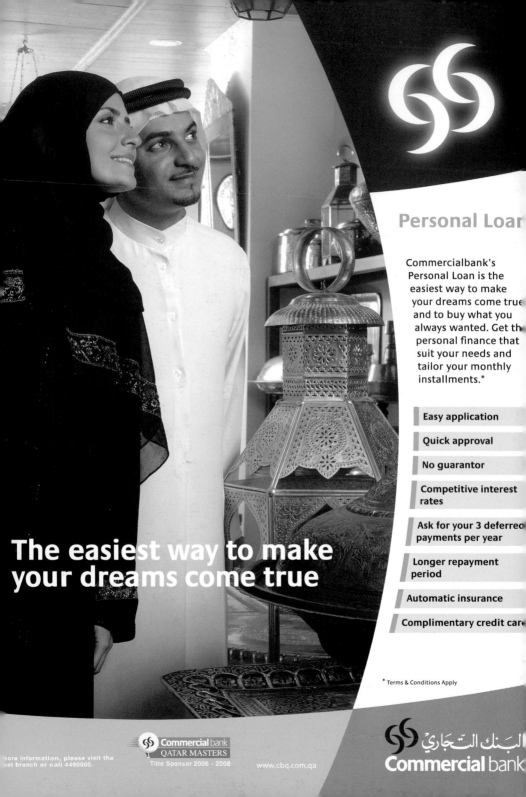

General
Information
EXPLORER

General Information

Highlights...

A Burgeoning Horizon
p.6

Qatar is currently undergoing rapid expansion with all manner of shiny new developments under construction. With the Asian Games in December 2006 the country has invested billions of dollars in creating world-class sporting facilities, while various island developments and tourist resorts are set to change the face of Qatar.

A Full Calendar
p.35

Although the Asian Games might be the biggest thing to happen in Qatar since oil was discovered in 1939, there are plenty of other exciting events on the annual calendar worth checking out too. Whether it is the Qatar International Tennis Tournaments or the Qatar Masters Golf Tournament, if it is sport you're after then you won't be disappointed.

Geography

The Gulf state of Qatar is a peninsula that is surrounded by the waters of the Arabian Gulf and anchored to the mainland at its border with Saudi Arabia. The country is about 11,437 square kilometres, running roughly 85km wide and 180km long and located in the centre of the Gulf Cooperation Council (G.C.C). Mud flats make up a large portion of the shoreline which is dotted with inlets and coves. The interior terrain is mostly flat, varying from just 6m to 103m above sea level at Qurayn Abu al-Bawl. Some rocky limestone outcrops are found in the most southern parts of the country.

The country also includes several islands such as Sheraouh, Al Aliyah, Al Bushayriyah, Al Safiliyah and, about 80 km northeast of the capital, is Halul. This island, operated by Qatar Petroleum, is of particular importance as it serves as the export terminal for marine crude oil produced from Qatar's offshore oilfields.

The majority of the population of Qatar resides in the capital city, Doha, however the other major towns include Mesaieed, Dukhan, Al Khor, Al Shamal and Al Wakrah.

Qatar's subtropical desert means it becomes very hot and humid from June to August when many residents make the summer exodus to their home country to escape the oppressive heat. During the Qatari winter months from November through February, however, the country's weather is extremely pleasant. Average rainfall is 81 mm per year with an average high temperature of 31 C and lows touching some 22 C. The country is quite dusty and the occasional sandstorms manage to bury grains of sand into the most difficult nooks and crannies around your home.

Qatar is also on the humid side with average humidity highs in the mid 70+% range, although there is a slight dip in the evening. With limited amounts of fresh water from ground wells, rain offers the only respite. But rainfall is very rare, though not as unheard of as some locals might suggest. Due to its extremely sporadic occurrence of rain there are no real gutters on the roads so they can get flooded with standing water when the skies do finally open. Rural wadis fill during the infrequent rainfall satisfying the scarce vegetation. The lack of rainfall means only about one percent of the country is arable, with permanent crops registering barely a blip in the yearly agricultural output.

Archaeologists have uncovered evidence of human habitation in Qatar possibly dating back to the fourth and fifth millennia BC. In the fifth century BC the Greek historian Herodotus referred to the ancient Canaanites as the original inhabitants of Qatar, and the country features on old maps of the region suggesting that Qatar was known to seafarers and traders of the time. As Islam swept the region in the 7th century AD, the inhabitants of Qatar are said to have aided the formation of the first Islamic naval fleet. The country also became well known for the quality of its textile manufacturing (especially Qatari cloaks) and for the making of arrow heads.

Around the 13th and 14th centuries Qatar enjoyed a favourable relationship with the caliphates (successors of the Prophet Mohammed) in Baghdad and it became an important centre for pearl trading. Evidence from this Abbasid era (caliphate rule) can be seen in the architecture of Murwab Fort on Qatar's west coast. In the 16th and 17th centuries the Portuguese were a powerful force throughout the Gulf region, and to protect the country from occupation and aggression Qatar aligned with the Turks. This saw the start of over three centuries of rule by the Ottoman Empire, although throughout this period the real power in Qatar remained with local sheikhs.

The ancestors of today's ruling family, the Al Thanis, arrived in Qatar in the early 18th century. Originating from a branch of the Bani Tamin tribe from Najd in modern-day Saudi Arabia, they first settled in southern Qatar before moving to the north of the peninsula in the mid 1700s. Qatar, and especially the northern town of Zubara, continued to be a key centre for the pearl trade. The Al Khalifa family of Bahrain (now the ruling family) exercised a degree of control over the pearling industry and this caused serious tensions with the Al Thani family whose influence was growing in the country.

In the mid 19th century Sheikh Mohammed bin Thani established Al Bidda, the modern city of Doha, as the capital and seat of power and a treaty negotiated with the British in 1868 recognised him as the first official Emir of Qatar. This treaty signed with the British also recognised Qatar's independence, and Sheikh Mohammed exercised this independence when in 1871 he signed another treaty, this time with the Turks, accepting protection against external attack. A Turkish garrison was established in Doha, but the relationship was an uneasy one and the Ottomans were forced to abandon Doha in 1915. In 1916 Sheikh Abdullah al Thani signed a further treaty with the British promising not to enter into relations with any other power without prior consent. In return, Britain guaranteed the protection of Qatar 'from all aggression by sea.'

A number of factors, including the worldwide economic depression and the introduction of cultured Japanese pearls, led to the almost complete collapse of the Gulf's pearling industry in the 1930s. Pearling had been the mainstay of Qatar's economy for generations, and while life for the country's inhabitants had never been easy, this sudden development dealt a desperate blow. The region was plunged into dire poverty, and disease was rife amongst the undernourished people. In the midst of despair there was hope though. Bahrain had become the first Gulf state to discover oil earlier in the decade and in 1935 Shaikh Abdullah signed the first Oil Concession Agreement with the Anglo-Persian Oil Company. Drilling began and oil was discovered in Dukhan in 1939. The onset of World War Two halted production almost immediately however, and the first oil wasn't exported from Qatar until ten years later. This new found wealth transformed the lives of the small population almost beyond recognition, as the rulers set about modernising the country's infrastructure and creating healthcare and education facilities. The wealth generated from oil exports, and the discovery and exploitation of what is believed to be the world's largest single reservoir of natural gas, means that Qatar today enjoys one of the highest levels of income per capita anywhere in the world.

Historic Qatar

In 1968 Great Britain announced its intention to withdraw from the Gulf region. Qatar entered into talks with Bahrain and the Trucial States with the intention of forming a federation, but agreement could not be reached and after Bahrain withdrew from the discussions Qatar followed suit. When the British left on September 3rd 1971, Qatar became officially independent. The ruler at the time was Sheikh Ahmed bin Ali al Thani, but he was succeeded the following year by his cousin Khalifa bin Hamad al Thani, with the full support of the ruling family, the Qatari people and the armed forces. Sheikh Khalifa led Qatar into a period of continued prosperity, especially thanks to the huge rises in oil and gas prices during the 1970s. He also went some way to diversify Qatar's economy by establishing facilities for producing goods such as steel and fertiliser.

In June 1995, Sheikh Khalifa was succeeded as Emir by his son and heir, the Crown Prince and Minister of Defence, Sheikh Hamad bin Khalifa al Thani. On coming to power, Sheikh Hamad continued with the modernisation and liberalisation programmes he had started as Crown Prince. Press freedom was extended and in 1997 the state-funded satellite TV news channel Al Jazeera was launched, quickly gaining a reputation for its outspoken coverage of sensitive topics. 1999 saw the country's first steps towards democracy, when free elections for the Central Municipal Council were held. Women were allowed to stand for office as well as vote. Sheikh Hamad is seen as a progressive ruler and is widely respected by Qatar's citizens, who benefit from the country's wealth in the form of free or subsidised healthcare, education and housing.

Oil and gas: Qatar's main export

Timeline

7th century AD	-	Islam sweeps the Arabian peninsula. Residents of Qatar help form the first navel fleet
13th century	-	Qatar an important pearling centre
16th century	-	Qatar aligns with the Ottomans as protection against the Portuguese
Early 18th century	-	ancestors of the al Thani arrive in Qatar
Mid 18th century	-	Mohammed al Thani establishes al Bidda (now Doha) as the capital
1868	-	treaty signed with the British, recognises Qatar's independence, and Mohammed al Thani as the first Emir
1871	-	treaty signed with the Turks, accepting protection against external attack
1915	-	the Ottomans abandon Doha
1916	-	a further protection treaty signed with the British
1930s	-	pearl industry collapses
1939	-	oil found in Dukhan
1949	-	first oil exported from Qatar
1971	-	discovery of the world's largest single concentration of natural gas
Sept 3rd 1971	-	Qatar declares independence
June 27 1995	-	Sheikh Hamad al Thani succeeds his father Sheikh Khalifa as Emir of Qatar

Economy

Qatar Overview

Thanks mainly to its abundant reserves of oil and gas, and the high prices these have commanded in recent years, Qatar has one of the strongest and fastest growing economies in the world. Analysts predict that in the near future, the country's Gross Domestic Product (GDP) per capita will overtake that of Switzerland, effectively making Qatar the richest nation on earth.

Qatar's GDP for 2004 was over QR 103 billion, a 20.5% increase on the previous year. The sector officially referred to as Mining and Quarrying

Doha's picturesque corniche

(which covers the extraction and production of oil and gas) accounted for 62% of the GDP, proving that Qatar's economy is very much reliant on hydrocarbons. The other significant contributors to GDP were Government Services (9.6%), Manufacturing (7.7%), Finance, Insurance, Real Estate & Business Services (6.7%), Building & Construction (5.2%), Trade, Restaurants & Hotels (4.2%), Transport & Communications (2.8%), and Electricity & Water (2.2%).

In an effort to boost oil production, significant sums have been invested to locate additional oil fields and to prolong the productive life of existing ones. Proven oil reserves currently stand at 15 billion barrels. However, in order to become less reliant on oil and diversify the economy to some degree, Qatar is investing heavily in its liquefied natural gas (LNG) industry. The country's natural gas reserves stand at 910 trillion cubic feet, ranking Qatar third in the world behind Russia and Iran. In 2004, Qatargas exported 9.3 million tons of LNG, but they hope to increase exports to 17.3 million tons per annum by 2009 and 25.2 million tons by 2012, by which time Qatar will be the world's largest producer of LNG.

To achieve this, Qatar Petroleum is set to invest $75 billion in its hydrocarbon industries in the next five years. This expansion will lead to an increase in the number of staff working in the industry, who in turn will need more housing, healthcare, retail, leisure and entertainment facilities. In addition, $15 billion will be spent on the country's infrastructure.

Qatar's main exports are crude oil, natural gas and petroleum, with the main export partners being Japan, South Korea, Singapore and more recently India. Qatar's main import partners are the US and Japan.

In 2004, Standard & Poor's updated their outlook on Qatar from stable to positive. Their credit rating for the country's currency is A+.

Tourism Developments

While Qatar's economy is dominated by its hydrocarbon industries, the country is attempting to diversify into other areas. With year-round sunshine, golden beaches, exciting outdoor activities and a fascinating culture and history, this is a prime tourist destination that remains relatively undiscovered. Qatar doesn't necessarily want to attract mass tourism, but aims to become known as a high-quality destination appealing to high-income sectors such as the MICE market (meetings, incentives, conferences and exhibitions). To help achieve this the government is investing a massive $15 billion to develop Qatar's infrastructure, including a new airport to cater to the growing number of tourists – currently numbering 400,000 a year but estimated to top one million a year by 2010.

While most of the major international hotel chains are already represented in Qatar, the investment in infrastructure will also see a host of new hotels and resorts to cater to the anticipated growth in visitor numbers. By summer 2005 Qatar had approximately 3,700 hotel rooms, but with 37 new hotels either under construction or in the advanced planning stage that number is set to soar. As well as stand-alone hotels, there are a number of projects currently under way that will include facilities for tourists, such as the Lusail development, the Al Fareej Resort and of course the Pearl Qatar.

In a further boost for the tourism sector, Doha is set to host the Asian Games in December 2006, an event that will bring many first-time visitors to Qatar and undoubtedly raise the country's profile around the world. The Games has prompted a number of multi-million dollar projects that will bring Doha's infrastructure up to premium international standards. These developments include new roads, transportation systems, hotels, and sports and leisure facilities that are either finished or well underway.

Key Qatar Projects

As part of Qatar's massive investment in its infrastructure, many new and exciting projects are planned or already under construction. A selection of these key projects is featured below.

Al Sharq Village Resort & Spa

The five-star Al Sharq Village Resort and Spa overlooks Doha's corniche, and claims to be the first resort to portray the architectural style and culture of Qatar. As the name suggests, the resort will be arranged like a village, with the 160 guest rooms housed in a number of villas. The resort will also feature a traditional Qatari souk, leisure and entertainment facilities, and a Six Senses Spa. Opening is scheduled for May 2006.

www.qnhc.com

Asian Games

Doha will host the 15th Asian Games from 1 to 15 December 2006. In preparation for this prestigious sporting event, Qatar is investing huge sums (estimated at over $2.8 billion) to provide state of the art facilities, accommodation and infrastructure. Many new sports venues and stadia are being built or renovated, including the redeveloped Sports City. Over 10,000 athletes from 45 countries and regions will be housed at the new 'Athletes' Village', which has been designed so it can be converted into a modern medical facility once the Games are over.

www.doha-2006.com

Dubai Towers, Doha

Located on the corniche near the Diplomatic District, Dubai Towers is the first overseas development by Dubai International Properties. At 80 storeys high it will be the tallest tower in Qatar. This multi-purpose project will contain offices, a shopping arcade, a hotel, and serviced and unserviced apartments. The overall cost is in excess of QR 1 billion, and the complex is expected to be partly open in time for the Asian Games, and be fully completed by early 2007.

www.dubaitowers-doha.com

Education City

Developed by the Qatar Foundation for Education, Science and Community Development, Education City is already home to a number of institutions and international university campuses, but its growth continues. Projects currently at the

Key Qatar projects

planning stage or under construction include a 350-bed teaching hospital, a conference and convention centre, and the Qatar Science and Technology Park. Upon completion (scheduled for 2008) the site will house 30 buildings, including a museum, sports and recreational facilities, a shopping centre, a mosque, and accommodation for students and staff.

www.qf.edu.qa

Lusail

Launched at the end of 2005, this mixed use development will eventually cover 35 square kilometres and be home to 200,000 people. Occupying a strip of coastline north of Doha, the project will have ten districts featuring marinas, hotels, entertainment and leisure, office towers, lots of shopping, two golf courses, and housing in the shape of apartment buildings and exclusive gated communities. With an estimated $5 billion price tag, the work is scheduled for completion by 2010.

www.lusail.com

Museum of Islamic Art

The 45,000 square metre Museum of Islamic Art will showcase one of the region's most impressive art collections. Designed by renowned architect I.M. Pei, the museum will feature exhibition halls, a library, study areas, a gallery and a restaurant. Situated on Doha's corniche, construction is progressing well and the museum will open in 2006.

New Doha International Airport (NDIA)

Construction is well under way on Doha's new airport, a few kilometres east of the exisiting airport and located partly on reclaimed land. With two runways, and designed to cater to the growing number of visitors expected over the coming years, the airport will be built in three phases.

New Doha International Airport

Phase one will open in 2008, with an annual capacity of 12 million passengers. When complete in 2015 the airport will be equipped to handle 50 million passengers a year and will also feature a separate Emiri Terminal for visiting VIPs and Heads of State. The airport will serve as a global hub for Qatar Airways, which by 2006 plans to serve 70 destinations and has a multitude of aircraft on order. Before the new airport is completed, the existing one will be upgraded to cope with the increase in visitor numbers.

www.ndiaproject.com

Oil and Gas

Qatar Petroleum is investing billions of dollars in the country's oil and gas facilities and infrastructure. Projects include the expansion and upgrading of facilities at Dukhan City (Qatar's first oil centre), Mesaieed Industrial City, and Halul Island. Ras Laffan Industrial City is already the world's largest Liquefied Natural Gas export facility, and a new $1.6 billion plant will soon process gas to be pumped over 370km through a dedicated pipeline being laid between Qatar and Abu Dhabi. In time, Qatar hopes to supply gas throughout the UAE and Oman.

www.qp.com.qa

Pearl Qatar

Perhaps the best-known of Qatar's current development projects, the Pearl is a new island complex built on reclaimed land off the shore of the West Bay Lagoon. It will feature apartments, town houses and villas, plus retail outlets, restaurants, entertainment venues, and three five-star hotels. The design of the Pearl means it will have four separate marinas with berths for 700 boats. It will eventually be home to 35,000 residents, and significantly it was the first development in Qatar to offer freehold property to non-Locals. All owners will be issued with a residency visa. The cost of the project is around $2.5 billion, and the first homes are scheduled to be handed over in late 2006.

www.thepearlqatar.com

Qatar – Bahrain Causeway

The so-called 'Friendship Causeway' will be a 40 km road link between Qatar and Bahrain. It will consist of bridges and highways built on reclaimed land. To allow shipping to pass beneath, some of the bridges may have to be 40 metres above the sea. To some it is seen as an extension of the King Fahd Causeway that connects Bahrain to Saudi Arabia, and when complete it will be the longest fixed link in the world. A Danish consortium carried out feasibility studies and the causeway is expected to take four or five years to complete. Estimates for the cost of the project vary from $2 billion to $4.7 billion.

Qatar National Library

More good news for the country's culture-lovers comes in the shape of the Qatar National Library. The tall, bold design, by Japanese architect Arata Isozaki, will become an unmistakable landmark on the Doha corniche. The library will have the capacity for up to two million books and will feature an art gallery, a natural history museum, a science museum, lecture halls, and conference facilities. Opening is scheduled for 2007.

Qatar Photography Museum

The Photography Museum, also on the corniche in Doha, will include 11,000 square metres of gallery space for both photographs and photographic equipment. Designed to house the government's collection of over 15,000 items, the museum will also feature the work of local artists. An aspect of the building that will perhaps attract the most publicity is the 'smart' walls that will open and close to control the amount of light that can enter. The museum will open in 2007.

International Relations

Qatar is committed to the support of Arab unity, but also enjoys strong international relations. In the 1990s the country upset its Arab neighbours when discussions took place with Israel regarding the possible supply of natural gas. Qatar is a founding member of the Gulf Cooperation Council (GCC). With its five other members – Saudi Arabia, Kuwait, Oman, UAE and Bahrain – the objective of the GCC is to encourage integration and coordination between member states. Presidency of the GCC rotates yearly between its members. All major embassies and consulates are represented in Qatar and the country is a member of the International Monetary Fund (IMF), the Organisation of Petroleum Exporting Countries (OPEC), the United Nations (UN), the World Health Organisation (WHO) and the World Trade Organisation (WTO).

Government & Ruling Family

Qatar is governed by hereditary rule. The head of state is the Emir, His Highness Sheikh Hamad bin Khalifa al Thani, who came to power in 1995. He has introduced many reforms and steered the country towards a more open and democratic system of government. The Emir's brother, His Highness Sheikh Abdullah bin Khalifa al Thani, is the Prime Minister, and the Emir's son, His Highness Sheikh Tamim bin Hamad al Thani, is the Crown Prince and Heir Apparent.

Qatar's permanent constitution was overwhelmingly approved by the local people in a 2003 referendum. As outlined in the constitution, the Emir holds legislative and executive powers and he appoints the Council of Ministers by an Emiri decree. The Council of Ministers recommends laws, after consultation with the Advisory (or Consultative) Council, the Majlis Al Shura. Laws require consent from the Emir before being enacted. The constitution promises freedom and equality, and provides for a 45-member Majlis Al Shura, two thirds of which would be elected by the public with the remaining members appointed by the Emir (the Majlis al Shura currently has 35 members, all appointed by the Emir). Changes in constituency boundaries have led to the first Shura Council elections being delayed – they are now expected to take place sometime in 2006 or 2007.

Qatar did hold historic democratic elections in 1999 (and again in 2003) for the Central Municipal Council (CMC), made up of 29 councillors representing the country's municipalities. Women were eligible to vote and stand for election, although a female candidate has yet to be elected. The CMC has consultative powers and is aimed at improving services in the municipalities, but it has no executive powers.

Facts & Figures

Population

In 2004 Qatar's population stood at 744,029. Local Qataris account for around 20% of the total population, with the remainder made up of expatriates, mostly from the Indian subcontinent, but also from other Arab countries, Europe, and the US. The growth rate is very high, at around nine or ten per cent, and the July 2005 population estimate (according to the CIA World Factbook) was over 850,000.

Population Age Breakdown

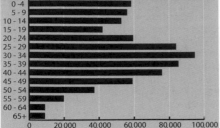

Age	
0 - 4	
5 - 9	
10 - 14	
15 - 19	
20 - 24	
25 - 29	
30 - 34	
35 - 39	
40 - 44	
45 - 49	
50 - 54	
55 - 59	
60 - 64	
65+	

0   20,000   40,000   60,000   80,000   100,000

Population By Area

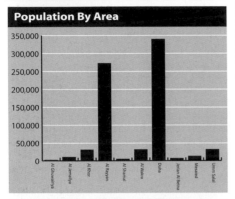

350,000
300,000
250,000
200,000
150,000
100,000
50,000
0

Al Ghuwairiya, Al Jemaliya, Al Khor, Al Rayyan, Al Shamal, Al Wakra, Doha, Jerian Al Betna, Mesaied, Umm Salal

Education Levels

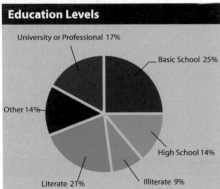

- University or Professional 17%
- Basic School 25%
- Other 14%
- High School 14%
- Literate 21%
- Illiterate 9%

Source: The State of Qatar Planning Council

National Flag

The Qatari flag is maroon with a white serrated band that has nine points on the hoist side. The flag was adopted in 1971 – the year that Qatar declared its independence.

According to the Qatari Foreign Ministry, the white colour of the flag reflects the internationally recognised symbol of peace while the maroon colour symbolises the bloodshed during the several wars Qatar had undergone, particularly in the second half of the 19th century.

The nine-point serrated line indicates that Qatar is the ninth member of the 'reconciled emirates' of the Arabian Gulf in the wake of concluding the Qatari-British treaty in 1916.

The flags of Bahrain and Qatar are very similar, with only a slight deference in colour, depicting the two countries' historical links. The Qatari flag can be seen mainly on public and governmental buildings, schools, ships and private cars. More flags can be seen hoisted around the city during sports events, national celebrations or major diplomatic meetings.

Local Time

Qatar local time is three hours ahead of UCT (Universal Coordinated Time – formerly known as GMT). It is fixed across the country and there is no summer time saving. So when it is 12:00 in Doha, it is 13:00 in the UAE, 09:00 in London, 04:00 in New York, 18:00 in Tokyo, and 14:30 in New Delhi (not allowing for any daylight saving in those countries).

National flag

Social & Business Hours

The working week in Qatar runs from Sunday to Thursday with Friday (the holy day for Muslims) and Saturday off. However, some business offices choose to take only Friday off, or give just a half day on Thursday. Government offices recently amended their working hours to 06:00 to 14:00, matching those of Qatar Petroleum and most of the oil, gas and petrochemicals companies. Banks open from 07:30 until 13:00 although some branches, especially those located in shopping malls sometimes open in the evenings.

Commercial offices have two shifts. The first from 07:30 to 12:00 and then from 15:30 to 19:30, though this may vary. As a result, siesta is a common practice among locals and residents who tend to stay up late and then have to wake early for their first shift, making that afternoon nap a necessity.

Major shopping malls are usually open from 10:00 until 24:00 but the majority of them close on Friday mornings. Timings for independent shops vary but are generally from 08:30 to 12:30 and 16:00 to 21:00. Many are closed all day Friday, although some do open late afternoon.

Timings change during the holy month of Ramadan with government offices working two or three hours less and commercial shops usually closing during Iftar (the breaking of the fast just after sunset) and re-opening later in the evening. Shopping malls that remain open during the day (without serving any food or beverage between dawn and dusk) usually close later than usual – sometimes as late as 02:00. Late shopping and hanging out in malls for evening coffee during Ramadan is very common, so don't be surprised if you can't find a place to park at midnight.

Public Holidays

The two major public holidays in Qatar are religious ones: Eid al Fitr and Eid al Adha. Eid al Fitr marks the ending of the fasting month of Ramadan, which is the ninth month of the Islamic calendar (Hijri calendar). During this month, Muslims are required to abstain from food, drink, cigarettes, sexual acts and unclean thoughts from dawn until dusk.

The Islamic calendar is based on the lunar months, thus the beginning and the ending of Ramadan is not fixed but instead is decided on the sighting of the moon. As a result, holidays will only be determined 24 hours in advance.

Eid al Fitr is usually marked by a three-day celebration where almost every business in the country shuts down for the occasion. In this month many Muslims pay Zakat al Fitr (charity of Ramadan).

Eid al Adha, the festival of the sacrifice, commemorates Ibrahim's willingness to sacrifice his son to God. It follows Eid al Fitr by around 70 days and is marked by a four-day celebration. Many mark this religious occasion by carrying out the Hajj, the pilgrimage to Mecca. On the occasion of this Eid, some Muslims slaughter sheep and distribute the meat to the poor.

Besides these two religious celebrations there are two other fixed holidays: Accession Day and Independence Day.

Public Holidays – 2006	
Eid al Adha	Jan 10[Moon]
Accession Day	June 27[Fixed]
Independence Day	Sep 3[Fixed]
Eid al Fitr	Nov 3[Moon]

Electricity & Water

Other options → Electricity & Water [p.74]

Electricity and water are provided by the state-operated corporation, Kahramaa. The electric supply operates at 220 – 240 volts and 50 Hz. As both old and new construction still exist in the capital, both two and three-pin plug mains are found, but adapters are available in most supermarkets and other corner shops. Most people tend to drink bottled water either purchased from grocery stores or delivered in large bottles for a water dispenser. Kahramaa also offers online services such as bill payment and account balance at either www.kahramaa.com.qa or via the Qatar e-government website, www.e.gov.qa.

Photography

Tourist photography is generally acceptable but some care must be taken when photographing people, particularly women. On the whole photographs of local women should be avoided and most photos taken of people should be preceded by a polite request for permission. Photography of government facilities is generally frowned upon and it is legally prohibited to photograph defence facilities. Mosques and airports carry a general sensitivity to photography and you may be requested to refrain from taking your holiday snaps with these backdrops.

Climate

Qatar's climate is characterised by mild winters and very hot summers with temperatures reaching over 40 degrees Celsius, 104 Fahrenheit. Many residents choose to leave the country during the months of July and August as these are the hottest months of the year as well as the most humid. A piece of advice is if you're coming to Qatar any time soon, try to avoid these two months as much as possible. If you are planning to reside here for some time then it is advisable to plan your annual vacation between the months of July and August.

In recent years the government has been trying to encourage people to stay in the country during the hot summer season by organising summer festivals that include shopping promotions and entertainment for families.

During the summer the humidity sometimes reaches over 80%, however, this Gulf emirate doesn't really experience the continuous oppressive high humidity found in some of the other Gulf countries.

Doha's winter from late October until late March is extremely pleasant both during the day and evening. Rainfall is scarce, averaging 70mm per year, and falling on isolated days in the winter season. According to Qatar's Tourism Authority, the temperatures during the summer range from 38°C (100.4 F) to 42°C (107.6 F) during the day and fall to 18°C (64.4 F) at night. Winter temperatures can reach 34°C (93.2 F) during the day, dropping to 10°C (50 F) at night.

Flora & Fauna

As you would expect in a country with such an arid climate the variety of flora and fauna in Qatar is somewhat limited. Much of the country consists of sand dunes, rocky hills, gravel plains and expanses of sabkha (salt flats) with little or no vegetation. Qatar has no rivers or lakes, although after heavy rainfall water may gather in wadis. There are some greener areas with plants, grasses, flowers, shrubs and trees (mostly acacia trees and lycium bushes) though, and after a spell of rain a previously barren stretch of desert can spring to life. There are also coastal wetland areas, with extensive mangrove woodlands.

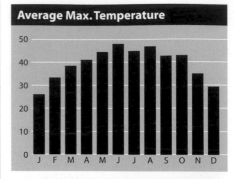

Average Max. Temperature

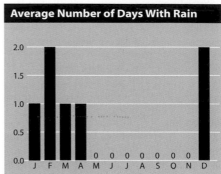

Average Number of Days With Rain

Creatures that may be encountered in the wild include the Ethiopian Hedgehog, the Arabian Red Fox, jirds, jerboas, and various species of reptiles including snakes, geckos, and the Spiny-tailed Lizard (or Dhab). Qatar also has a number of resident and migratory bird species, including gulls, cormorants, herons, flamingos, egrets and terns. A number of uninhabited offshore islands act as important breeding grounds for birds.

Date palms

The warm waters of the Arabian Gulf are home to a rich variety of marine life. Studies have recorded around 150 species of fish, in addition to dolphins, whales, and porpoises. The region is home to Green and Hawksbill turtles and a significant population of the endangered Dugong, or sea-cow.

Protection

The Supreme Council for the Environment & Natural Reserves (SCENR, www.qatarenv.org) was set up in 2000 with the purpose of protecting the environment, conserving endangered species of wildlife, and protecting their natural habitats. With the continuing population growth and the country's massive investment in hydrocarbon industries, Qatar's environment is clearly under threat. These threats include spillage of oil, gas and hazardous chemicals, and production facilities damaging the marine environment. However, while Qatar currently has no national parks or protected areas officially designated for nature conservation, the SCENR and the gas and oil companies do have programmes in place to monitor the local environment and minimise their impact on it. Qatargas achieved ISO 14001 certification (for environmental protection and management) in 2000, and Qatar Petroleum has initiated schemes to conserve Qatar's mangroves and protect the sea turtle population.

Qatar is a signatory to a number of environmental conventions, including the Bio-diversity Convention and the 1969 Kuwait and 1971 Brussels conventions.

Culture & Lifestyle

Culture

Qatar's culture is very much based on Islamic tradition. Islam is more than just a religion, it is a way of life that influences day to day living, from the clothes Muslims wear to what they eat and drink. In parts of the world, Islamic fundamentalism has unfortunately shrouded the Muslim religion in negativity. However, in contrast to this image Qatar is a fairly tolerant and welcoming country, with few restrictions placed on foreigners living or visiting here. Women are able to drive and walk around unescorted, and alcohol is available in licensed hotels. Among the most highly prized virtues of Islam are courtesy and hospitality, and visitors are sure to be charmed by the genuine warmth and friendliness of the local people.

Language

Other options → Learning Arabic [p.78]
Language Schools [p.142]

The official language in Qatar is of course Arabic. It is used by locals and the relatively big Arab community residing here. The Arabic dialect used in Qatar is commonly dubbed as the 'Khaleeji' accent in reference to the Gulf or Al Khaleej.

English is widely spoken in everyday life in Qatar and most road signs are written in both English and Arabic. English is also used in the work place, especially at private companies which are capable of completing transactions and services in English . English is also widely used in tourist areas, hotels and malls.

You might get by using English in governmental buildings, but you may find it a struggle so if possible an interpreter will help to make sure that you grasp fully the ins and outs of the bureaucratic system here. Also all official documents such as visa and resident permits should be translated into Arabic. Urdu and Hindi are also commonly used languages in Qatar due to the huge community of Asian workers.

Religion

For Qataris, Islam is more than just a religion, it is a way of life. Qataris in general are conservative and almost all practise their religion. The basis of Islam is that there is only one God and that Prophet Mohammed is the messenger of God. Islam is based on five pillars: profession of faith or al-Shahada, praying, fasting, pilgrimage to Mecca (or Makkah) in Saudi Arabia, and giving charity or Zakat. Muslims' holy book is the Quran.

Islam requires believers to pray five times a day. Locals and residents pray at home, at work or at a mosque. Calls to prayer, which are reminders of the prayer times, are broadcast from loudspeakers installed on the minarets of mosques . Mosques can be found almost everywhere in Qatar, which is a way of making sure Muslims do not miss the prayer time. Praying must be preceded by ritual cleansing, thus washing facilities can be found in buildings and public places.

There are two main forms of Islam: Sunni and Shia. Almost 90% of Qataris are Sunni Muslims.

ⓘ

Pilgrimage

In Islam there is the pilgrimage, or Hajj, and there is also the lesser pilgrimage, or Umra. Muslims who are physically and financially fit are required to do Hajj at least once in their lifetime, as it is one of the five pillars of the faith. Hajj is the trip to Mecca in Saudi Arabia during the lunar month of Zul Hija. The lesser pilgrimage, or Umra, is also performed in Saudi Arabia but it can be done any time of the year. In both Hajj and Umra, Pilgrims wear plain white cloth garments, so as to stand equally in front of God, without class or wealth distinction.

Women are not obliged to cover up in public, however, they are expected to dress conservatively, especially during the fasting month of Ramadan. Public displays of affection are considered immoral and thus are not allowed. Friday is the holy day of the week. Mosques are usually packed with mostly male worshippers on a Friday, when they get to listen to a sermon or 'Khotbeh' given by a preacher or imam.

Fasting is observed for a whole month during Ramadan, which is the ninth month of the Islamic calendar and determined by the moon. Believers are required to fast from dawn until dusk. Eating in public is prohibited during the fasting period. Restaurants are closed, except for some in major hotels. Alcohol is never served or sold during the holy month. A religious celebration, Eid al Fitr, follows the month of fasting. Around seventy days after Eid al Fitr, Muslims celebrate Eid al Adha, which translates as the festivity of sacrifice, in which Muslims slaughter sheep and distribute part of their meat to the poor.

Qatar is a fairly tolerant country. Christian churches are not yet officially sanctioned in the country, but there are resident chaplains and priests who hold regular services.

National Dress

On the whole, the national population always wear their traditional dress in public. For men this is the dishdash(a) (or khandura, or thobe) – a white full length shirt dress, which is worn with a white, or red and white checked, headdress called a gutra. This is secured with a black cord (agal). Sheikhs and important businessmen may also wear a further robe with fine embroidery called a bisht, or mishlah, over their dishdasha at important events. Qatar has a tradition of producing quality embroidered textiles and clothing.

In public, women wear the black abaya – a long, loose black robe that covers their normal clothes – plus a headscarf called the sheyla. The abaya is often of very sheer, flowing fabric and may be open at the front. Some women also wear a thin black veil hiding their face and/or gloves, and older women sometimes still wear a leather mask, known as a burkha, which covers the nose, brow and cheekbones. Underneath the abaya, women traditionally wear a long tunic over loose, flowing trousers (sirwall), which are often heavily embroidered and fitted at the wrists and ankles. However, these are used more by the older generation and modern women will often wear the latest fashions from international stores underneath.

Dress Code

Qatar is a Muslim country, and as such you should respect the local customs by dressing conservatively whenever out in public. Skirts or shorts above the knee should be avoided, as should sleeveless tops that expose the shoulders or upper arms. Very tight or revealing clothing is a no-no (for men and women!). It's not that you'll get into heaps of trouble, you'll just attract a lot of unwelcome attention and possibly some remarks. The best bet is to cover up.

Mosques can be found all over Qatar

Basic Arabic

General

Yes	na'am
No	la
Please	min fadlak (m) / min fadliki (f)
Thank you	shukran
Please (in offering)	tafaddal (m) / tafaddali (f)
Praise be to God	al-hamdu l-illah
God willing	in shaa'a l-laah

Greetings

Greeting (peace be upon you)	as-salaamu alaykom
Greeting (in reply)	wa alaykom is salaam
Good morning	sabah il-khayr
Good morning (in reply)	sabah in-nuwr
Good evening	masa il-khayr
Good evening (in reply)	masa in-nuwr
Hello	marhaba
Hello (in reply)	marhabtayn
How are you?	kayf haalak (m) / kayf haalik (f)
Fine, thank you	zayn, shukran (m) / zayna, shukran (f)
Welcome	ahlan wa sahlan
Welcome (in reply)	ahlan fiyk (m) / ahlan fiyki (f)
Goodbye	ma is-salaama

Introduction

My name is	ismiy ...
What is your name?	shuw ismak (m) / shuw ismik (f)
Where are you from?	min wayn inta (m) / min wayn inti (f)
I am from ...	anaa min
America	ameriki
Britain	braitani
Europe	oropi
India	al hindi

Questions

How many / much?	kam?
Where?	wayn?
When?	mata?
Which?	ayy?
How?	kayf?
What?	shuw?
Why?	laysh?
Who?	miyn?
To/ for	ila
In/ at	fee
From	min
And	wa
Also	kamaan
There isn't	maa fee

North	
South	
East	
West	
Turning	
First	
Second	
Road	
Street	
Roundabout	
Signals	isha...
Close to	qarib...
Petrol station	mahattat...
Sea/ beach	il bahar
Mountain/s	jabal / jibaal
Desert	al sahraa
Airport	mataar
Hotel	funduq
Restaurant	mata'am
Slow Down	schway schway

Accidents

Police	al shurtaa
Permit/ licence	rukhsaa
Accident	haadith
Papers	waraq
Insurance	ta'miyn
Sorry	aaslf (m) / aasifa (f)

Numbers

Zero	sifr
One	waahad
Two	ithnayn
Three	thalatha
Four	araba'a
Five	khamsa
Six	sitta
Seven	saba'a
Eight	thamaanya
Nine	tiss'a
Ten	ashara
Hundred	miya
Thousand	alf

Taxi / Car Related	
Is this the road to ...	hadaa al tariyq ila
Stop	kuf
Right	yamiyn
Left	yassar
Straight ahead	siydaa
	shamaal
	januwb
	sharq
	garb
	mafraq
	awwal
	thaaniy
	tariyq
	shaaria
	duwwaar
	...ara
	...in
	...betrol

...eer in a shopping mall ...that is not attached to ...ub. Residents can get a ...ome consumption but ...ated aisle in your local ...will have to visit the ...quor Licence on p.45 ...152.

...an important part of

Eating Arabic Style

Eating in the Middle East is traditionally a social affair. Whether eating at home with extended families, or out with large groups, the custom is for everybody to share a feast of various dishes, served in communal bowls. Starters, known as mezze, are usually enjoyed with flat Arabic style bread, and main courses are often eaten with the fingers.

Culture & Lifestyle | General Info

...milder effect.

Arabic Coffee

Coffee in this part of the world is more than just a quick shot of caffeine, in fact it is an important ritual of hospitality. Traditional coffee (or 'gahwa') is mild with a distinctive taste of cardamom and saffron. It is served black without sugar, although dates are served at the same time to sweeten the palate. It is polite to drink about three cups if offered (the cups are very small, so it's similar to drinking a shot of espresso). To refuse the coffee is seen as a refusal of the host's generosity, although if you have had your fill you can shake the cup as a sign that you don't want another refill.

Pork

Muslims do not consume pork and you won't see it used at all in local cooking. Pork is outlawed in Qatar, so cannot be bought anywhere, and it is illegal to bring into the country.

Pork aside, Muslims are forbidden to eat the meat of an animal that has not been slaughtered in the correct manner. The meat of animals killed in accordance with the Islamic code is known as halaal.

Entering Qatar

Visas

Other options → **Entry Visa [p.40]**
Residence Visa [p.42]

Rules and regulations concerning the issuing of visas vary depending on nationality, and because details can change with little warning it is worth checking before travelling. However, in order to promote tourism and international business the government is determined to make things easier for visitors. Citizens of the 33 countries listed below can get a visit visa (or tourist visa) on arrival, valid for two weeks, for QR 55. Nationals of other GCC countries (Bahrain, Kuwait, Oman, Saudi Arabia and the UAE) can also get a two-week visa on arrival, for QR 105. These visas may be extended for a further two weeks. Citizens of those countries not listed may be able to arrange a tourist visa prior to travel, sponsored by a Qatar-based hotel or tour company. Visitors on such a tourist visa must use Qatar Airways to enter the country.

Other visas include a businessman visit visa, an official visit visa and a work visa. The businessman visa can be applied for in advance by eligible Qatari companies, allowing businessmen to visit them from overseas. It is valid for two weeks and can be extended for a further two. An official visit visa allows ministries and government agencies to sponsor official visitors free of charge (valid for one month), and a sponsor will apply for a work visa for their potential employees.

Visitors may also obtain a joint visa valid for visiting Qatar and Oman. Costing QR 55, it is valid for 21 days and can be extended for a further seven, but the visa holder must visit Qatar first.

The e-government initiative means that these visas can be applied for online – visit www.e.gov.qa, but you will need to register through the site's home page before you can access any application. Qatari residents will need their ID number while people outside Qatar will have to submit their passport number.

Visa on Arrival

Andorra, Australia, Austria, Belgium, Brunei, Canada, Denmark, Finland, France, Germany, Greece, Hong Kong, Iceland, Ireland, Italy, Japan, Liechtenstein, Luxembourg, Malaysia, Monaco, Netherlands, New Zealand, Norway, Portugal, San Marino, Singapore, South Korea, Spain, Sweden, Switzerland, the UK (with the right of abode), USA, and the Vatican.

Meet & Greet

Al Maha (465 6386) is a meet and greet service offered by Doha International Airport for arriving, departing, and transit passengers. The service includes the use of a lounge offering refreshments and Wi-Fi internet access. Passengers will enjoy a fast-track passage through passport control and immigration, as well as assistance with baggage reclaim and customs. The arrival and departure service costs QR 70 per passenger, and QR 45 for each additional passenger travelling together. There is an Al Maha desk in the arrivals terminal, but bookings must be made 24 hours in advance – visit www.dohaairport.com or email almahaservice @qatarairways.com.qa for more details.

Customs

Customs duties will not normally be levied on general household items and effects being brought into the country. Cigarettes and tobacco do carry a customs charge, so you are advised to wait until you are in the country where most cigarette brands are freely available at reasonable prices. Visitors are permitted to bring in 'a reasonable amount' of perfume. Items that are prohibited by customs include weapons and ammunition, fireworks, pornographic or obscene material, narcotics, counterfeit money, pork products, and alcohol. While alcohol is sold in the duty free shop in Doha International Airport, it can only be bought by passengers departing the country.

Leaving Qatar

Visitors are free to leave the country, but will be liable to penalties if they have overstayed the validity of their visit visa. Residents holding a work visa must obtain an exit permit from their employer or sponsor in order to leave, but this is not necessary for their dependents.

Check-in desks at Doha International Airport generally open two hours before the flight and close one hour before, so don't be too late. Qatar Airways offers an express telephone check-in (465 6676) for passengers with hand luggage only. Telephone as early as six hours before your flight, or as late as 90 minutes before, with your flight details, then just turn up at the desk 45 minutes before the flight and collect your boarding card. The airline also offers a service for unaccompanied children, taking care of the child both during the flight and in the airports at either end of the journey.

Qataris display their national pride

Health Requirements

No health certificates are required for entering Qatar, except for visitors arriving from cholera or yellow fever infected areas. Some overseas government and medical websites recommend that visitors to Qatar are immunised against typhoid and hepatitis A, and vaccinations for diphtheria, hepatitis B, polio, TB and rabies are sometimes recommended although these diseases are virtually unheard of in Qatar. There is no real risk of malaria in the country.

Health Care

Other options → General Medical Care [p.68]

The quality of healthcare in Qatar is generally very high. The state provides heavily subsidised medical care, although the rapid growth of Qatar's population has put a strain on resources and the government is encouraging the private sector to provide increased facilities. There are now many private health clinics and dentists operating alongside the government practices, including the American Hospital, Al Ahli Hospital and the Doha Clinic Hospital. While the standard of care is very good in the state hospitals and clinics, many visitors and expat residents arrange private health insurance.

The Hamad Medical Corporation currently manages three state hospitals; the Hamad General Hospital, The Rumailah Hospital, and the Women's Hospital. When completed in 2007, Hamad Medical City in Doha will feature three new hospitals, adding over 600 beds. Plans are also in place for a number of additional hospitals in Doha and throughout the country, including a nursing home, a cardiology hospital, and a new teaching hospital as part of Education City.

The emergency services telephone number is 999.

Travel Insurance

Despite the good quality healthcare provided by the state at very reasonable prices, visitors are recommended to arrange private medical insurance before travelling to Qatar. You should make sure that the policy covers repatriation to your home country, should that be necessary.

Embassies/Consulates

Embassy	Telephone	Map Ref.
Algeria	483 1186	17-B1
Bahrain	483 9360	6-C3
China	493 4203	9-D2
Egypt	483 2555	8-E1
France	483 2283	8-E1
Germany	487 6959	7-D4
Hungary	493 2531	6-A2
India	467 2021	11-D4
Iran	483 5300	8-D1
Italy	466 7842	13-A3
Japan	483 1224	8-E1
Jordan	483 2022	8-E1
Kuwait	483 2111	8-D1
Lebanon	493 3330	8-C1
Oman	493 1910	13-C3
Pakistan	483 2525	8-D1
Romania	498 3777	15-D1
Saudi Arabia	483 2030	8-E1
South Africa	485 7111	3-E4
Syria	483 1844	8-C1
Thailand	455 0715	16-C1
UK	442 1991	10-B3
United Arab Emirates	483 8880	8-E2
USA	488 4101	9-A1

Female Visitors

Women visitors will face few problems or restrictions while in Qatar and are allowed to drive and travel freely (accompanied or alone) within the country. Harassment is uncommon, but as with anywhere, local customs should be respected and women should avoid tight or revealing clothing, especially when in traditional areas. No matter what, most females will find that they occasionally receive some unwanted stares, but it's best to ignore it if possible.

Travelling with Children

Doha offers plenty to keep children amused, and most hotels, shopping malls, restaurants and visitor attractions are child-friendly.

Aladdin's Kingdom next to the InterContinental Hotel has rides and amusements for kids (see page 110), and Winter Wonderland in City Center has an ice rink, a water park and a bowling alley (also on page 110). The annual Qatar Summer Wonders is a month-long festival, running between July and August, that has entertainment and leisure attractions especially geared towards families and children.

Business...

Or leisure?

The dedicated multinational team at Mannai Air Travel prides themselves on their attention to detail and personalised customer service. Providing expert advice on business and leisure travel, the Mannai team is always ready to be of assistance.

For over 25 years, Mannai has been reaching out to its customers from its head office in Doha and its well-positioned branch offices located outside the capital city. With this extensive network and its commitment to quality, Mannai Air Travel provides excellence in customer service.

Mannai Air Travel – with you all the way. That's the Mannai Way.

Mannai Air Travel

Address: 13 Wadi Musheireb Street 339 Telephone: +974 444 2402, Fax: +974 436 7935, E-mail: manair@mannai.com.qa, Website: www.mannaicorp.com

Physically Challenged Visitors

Facilities for handicapped travellers are not as advanced as they are in some western countries but they are improving. Some hotels, such as the InterContinental, Four Seasons, Movenpick, Ramada, Rydges Plaza, Sheraton and Ritz Carlton have rooms and facilities adapted for disabled guests, and the airport has ramps and chair lifts available. Doha International Airport's meet and greet service, Al Maha (465 6386), will also offer assistance to physically challenged visitors.

Dress Code

Qatar is not as strict as some of its neighbours in the region, but expatriate visitors and residents should still show respect for the local customs and sensibilities. Women are not required to cover their hair, but should avoid tight or revealing clothing. When out in public, both men and women should wear garments that cover the shoulders and knees, as vests, shorts, and short skirts are not really appropriate. It's fine to wear shorts at a sports club, and swimming costumes are perfectly acceptable at the swimming pools and beaches (although women should never sunbathe topless).

Perhaps most importantly, you should cover up in the strong summer sun. Hats and sunscreen are a must and it is not uncommon to see people carrying umbrellas to act as parasols!

Shopping malls, restaurants and cinemas can be a little cold due to the air conditioning, so it's worth taking along a sweater or cardigan.

Dos and Don'ts

When you come to Qatar, although tolerance of other cultures is apparent you should still remember that it's a Muslim country. In order to respect the culture and not offend the locals make sure you dress conservatively. For women, tight clothes, sleeveless shirts and short skirts are frowned upon, so avoid wearing them in public. Public displays of intimacy between men and women are a no-no and can lead to arrest. Also, handshakes (or any form of contact) between unmarried men and women is viewed unfavourably, so if in doubt when meeting a local of the opposite sex don't offer your hand unless the other person offers theirs first.

If you enter the home of an Arab you should first remove your shoes, and if you sit down you should never show the soles of your feet as it is considered rude. Also, never sit with your back to other guests.

When it comes to alcohol, it is served here in very limited places and should never be drunk openly in public places. You should not carry alcohol with you, even in your car, except to take it on the day of collection from the distribution centre to your home. There is zero tolerance for drinking and driving. Depending on the circumstances, offenders may face detention, a substantial fine, a prison sentence or even deportation.

Penalties for possession of, or trade in, drugs are severe, often resulting in prison sentences. As for smoking, it is banned in government offices and major shopping malls.

Safety

Qatar is considered a safe country both for visitors and residents. The crime rate is much lower than in some western countries for example, but you should still take sensible precautions with valuables and cash, and avoid unfamiliar areas especially when alone or at night. Perhaps the biggest danger to the safety of visitors is the standard of driving on Qatar's roads. Accidents are commonplace, so make sure you're expecting the unexpected when driving, and be especially careful if out and about on foot.

Qatar's police force

Police

The telephone number for the police (and all emergency services) is 999. The police are usually fairly quick to respond to a call. If you are involved in a traffic accident you should remain at the scene and not move your vehicle until the police arrive. Obviously though, if someone is injured they must get to a hospital as soon as possible. Police officers are generally courteous and professional, and always willing to offer assistance to visitors.

Lost/Stolen Property

If your belongings are lost or stolen you should contact the local police. In the event of theft you should obtain a police statement which may be required when making an insurance claim. If bank and credit cards go missing you should contact the bank to have the cards cancelled, and if you lose your passport your embassy or consulate should be able to help. For contact numbers see the table on p.18. As always, it is a good idea to keep copies of your essential documents (tickets, passport etc) in a safe place, in case of such an emergency.

Doha Tourist Info Abroad

Qatar's overseas offices dedicated to promoting tourism are currently confined to a few European countries, but more are planned. For an up to date list check the Tourism Authority website – www.experienceqatar.com. Qatari embassies and consulates around the world may also be able to provide basic information.

Doha Tourism Overseas Offices		
France	Marseilles	+33 680406469
Italy	Milan	+39 393 4411555

Places to Stay

Qatar is committed to promoting itself as a high-quality destination, appealing to well-off tourists, business travellers, and the lucrative MICE market (Meetings, Incentives, Conferences and Exhibitions). Luxury four and five-star hotels dominate the accommodation options, although there are also a number of reasonable lower-class hotels out there. Another alternative is serviced hotel apartments, which tend to work out cheaper than hotels for longer stays. At the moment there are no hostels to speak of, or camp resorts, although camping is a popular pastime in the cooler winter months.

Qatar currently has 3,700 hotel rooms (summer 2005), but with 37 new hotel projects either under construction or at the advanced planning stage, that number is set to increase to 5,400 by the time of the Asian Games in December 2006.

Hotels

Other options → **Weekend Breaks [p.114]**

The majority of five-star hotels are located in the West Bay area as it is the perfect location for direct access to the beach. Occupancy rates in Doha's hotels are very high, as visitor numbers (both business visitors and tourists) are increasing faster than new hotels can be built, so remember to always book in advance. New hotels are being constructed to accommodate the influx of visitors to the Asian Games in 2006. The rack rate for a double room ranges between QR 300 and 2000. The more expensive hotels usually provide direct access to the beach and comprehensive sports activities, along with a spa and a wide range of restaurants.

Ritz-Carlton Doha

Al Bustan Hotel
Map Ref → 11-A4

In close proximity to the main areas of Doha, including the Diplomatic District and the corniche, and just a few minutes' drive from the airport, the Al Bustan is popular with both business travellers and visitors who want to be close to the buzz of the city. Home to one of Doha's favourite restaurants, The Albatross, the hotel also has a recreation centre and the standard rooms are comfortable and affordable.

Mövenpick
Map Ref → 11-A3

This modern hotel boasts the breathtaking corniche as its vista, where guests can enjoy a morning jog or afternoon stroll. Close to both the airport and the National Museum, the hotel recently won the Silver Award for Best 4 Star Business Hotel in The Spirit of Hospitality Awards, thanks to its wireless internet service and excellent business rooms. This boutique-style hotel also attracts tourists with its excellent restaurants and leisure facilities.

Intercontinental Doha
Map Ref → 6-D3

Tucked away in the West Bay Lagoon area, the Intercontinental Doha is best known for having the longest beach and largest free form pool in town. This 245-room, six-floor hotel has an architecture that combines modern design with traditional Arabic elements. Out of the city, it is about 25 minutes away from the airport, giving it a relaxing and serene atmosphere. With its friendly staff and a variety of top-notch restaurants this hotel is suitable for both business and pleasure.

Grand Regency
Map Ref → 9-E3

Grand by name and grand by nature, this impressive hotel is situated in the Al Sadd area, 15km from the airport. It has 192 rooms including 21 suites, all with cable TV, direct-dial telephones and high speed internet access. The hotel has four restaurants and a coffee shop. Guests can also make use of the business centre and a meeting and conference room, plus a gymnasium and fat burning studio featuring Hypoxi training machines.

Marriott Doha
Map Ref → 11-D4

Located just a few minutes away from the airport, this modern hotel is favoured by business travellers as it provides a wide range of facilities including guest rooms equipped with dual line data port system and high speed internet access. Its restaurants are also among the most favourite in town including Salsa and Asia live. The 350-room hotel has a well-maintained spa and fitness centre, and the panoramic view of Doha from the rooftop is worth a photo or two.

Ramada Hotel Doha
Map Ref → 13-B2

Situated in a convenient, central location, this large capacity hotel has 273 rooms and 47 suites, all with cable TV and high speed internet access. Leisure facilities include a large swimming pool, a gym with sauna and steam room, and tennis and squash courts. The hotel also has a business centre and meeting rooms. The Ramada is home to a number of popular restaurants, offering Italian, Japanese, and Indian cuisines.

Mercure Grand Hotel Doha
Map Ref → 10-D4

While its location in the heart of the business district dictates that a large number of guests at the Mecure Grand are in town on business, holidaymakers are also attracted to this grand hotel. The 172 rooms, three suites and three large conference rooms, as well as the swimming pool, fitness centre with sauna, tennis courts, squash courts, nearby golf course and mini shopping centre, guarantee occupancy throughout the year.

Ritz-Carlton Doha
Map Ref → 4-D2

A deluxe hotel, located 20 minutes from the airport, all of the 374 rooms and suites are exquisitely decorated, with breath-taking views over the sea or marina. The beach club provides a great selection of water sports while the luxurious spa has every pampering treatment imaginable. The hotel has a variety of restaurants, serving both international and Arabic cuisine and it also houses the Admirals Club, a very popular upscale night club.

Qatar Main Hotels

Rydges Plaza Map Ref → 10-C3

The recently opened Rydges Plaza Doha has an impressive atrium and striking architecture that makes it a welcome addition to the Doha skyline. The hotel houses 136 guest rooms and suites (the suites have kitchenettes), the excellent Garden Court and Il Rustico restaurants, and the popular Aussie Legends Bar, as well as boasting a high standard of recreational facilities.

Sheraton Doha Hotel and Resort Map Ref → 8-E3

Overlooking Doha's attractive corniche, the Sheraton is one of Qatar's oldest hotels and is often used as a landmark when promoting the country. It has a good range of sports facilities and restaurants, and there is often a cultural or business event taking place in the hotel. Standing amid 70 acres of landscaped gardens, the 363 room hotel has direct access to the beach.

Sealine Beach Resort Map Ref → 1-C3

About 55km from Doha Airport, the Sealine Beach Resort is the perfect getaway from the buzz of Doha's metropolis. Great for business conventions as well as romantic weekends or family holidays, the resort has regular guest rooms, intimate chalets for two, and villas that sleep up to six people. Situated on the beach, each chalet and villa has its own private car park and the resort is set in picturesque gardens.

The Four Seasons Map Ref → 8-E2

This world-class hotel, located in the Diplomatic District, has an exclusive beach and marina curved at its feet. With its high reputation and its excellent location, the 232-room Four Seasons is vying for the finest hotel in Qatar crown. The restaurants, facilities, decor and service are all of a very high standard and should certainly impress business travellers and cosmopolitan visitors.

Hotels

Five Star	Beach Access	Phone	Map	Website
Doha Marriott Hotel	No	429 8888	11-D4	www.marriotthotels.com
Four Seasons Hotel	Yes	494 8888	8-E2	www.fourseasons.com
Grand Regency P.183	No	434 3333	9-E3	www.grand-regency.com
InterContinental Doha	Yes	484 4444	6-D3	www.ichotelsgroup.com
Ritz-Carlton Doha P.v	Yes	484 8000	4-D2	www.ritzcarlton-doha.com
Sheraton Doha Hotel & Resort	Yes	485 4444	8-E3	www.starwoodhotels.com
Four Star				
Al Bustan Hotel	No	432 8888	11-A4	www.qatar.net.qa/albustan
Mercure Grand Hotel Doha	No	446 2222	10-D4	www.mercuredoha.com
Mövenpick Hotel Doha	No	429 1111	11-A3	www.moevenpick-hotels.com
Oasis Hotel & Beach Club	Yes	442 4424	11-C4	www.oasishotel-doha.com
Ramada Doha P.191	No	441 7417	13-B2	www.ramada-doha.com
Rydges Plaza	No	438 5444	10-C3	www.rydges.com
Sealine Beach Resort	Yes	477 2722	1-C3	www.qnhc.com
Three Star				
Al Sadd Merweb Hotel	No	447 1111	13-A1	www.merweb-hotel.com
Doha Tower Hotel	No	435 4646	10-E4	na
Gulf Horizon Hotel	No	443 2525	10-E4	www.gulfhorizonhotel.com
Qatar Palace Hotel	No	442 1515	11-A4	www.qatarpal.com.qa
Regency Hotel	No	436 3363	10-E4	www.hotel-regency.com
Two Star				
New Capital Hotel	No	444 5445	10-D4	na
Safeer Hotel	No	435 3999	11-A4	na
Shezan Hotel	No	486 5225	7-E1	www.freewebz.com/shezanhotel

Hotel Apartments

The cost of renting a furnished hotel apartment can be cheaper in the long term than a standard hotel room. The daily rate for a one-bed apartment is around QR 400, while the monthly rate for a two-bed should be between QR 8000 and 12,000. Most buildings have some kind of leisure facilities for guests, although perhaps not as comprehensive as the big hotels.

Hotel Apartments	
Al-Muntazah Plaza Hotel	435 5677
Gulf Paradise	432 2212
Royal Wings	421 1333
Sahara Hotel	432 7771

Campsites

Other options → **Camping [p.123]**

Camping is not a regulated activity in Qatar. As such there are no official campsites with facilities. However, camping takes place on a regular basis by residents and locals and is indeed part of local tradition. However, for expatriates living in Qatar, it is perhaps best to take a cautionary approach unless invited by a local. A number of local tour operators provide organized camping trips that include meals and entertainment amongst the sand dunes.

Getting Around

Other options → **Maps [p.210]**
Exploring [p.86]

In Qatar the car is king. A good road network, and the absence of buses, trams and trains, means that getting from A to B means getting behind the wheel. A series of north-south ring roads follow the shape of Doha's corniche, while major routes head off north, south, and west to link the capital with the rest of the country. A bus service does exist between Doha and the neighbouring towns, but there are no actual bus routes within the city itself.

Air

Other options → **Meet & Greet [p.17]**

With Doha as its hub, the national carrier Qatar Airways has been expanding rapidly in recent years and now serves 65 destinations worldwide. In

Airlines	
Air France	432 0802
Air India	432 4111
Biman Bangladesh	441 3422
British Airways	432 1434
Cyprus Airways	441 8666
Delta Airlines	483 0725
Egypt Air	445 8458
Emirates	438 4477
Gulf Air	445 5444
KLM	432 1208
Kuwait Airways	443 5340
Pakistan International Air	442 6290
Qatar Airways	449 6666
Royal Jordanian	443 1431
Saudi Arabian Airlines	432 2991
SriLankan Airlines	444 1217

2005 the airline placed orders for up to 80 new aircraft and will be among the first to take delivery of the new Airbus A-380 'super-jumbo.' Doha International Airport accommodates over 20 passenger airlines and is currently undergoing an expansion programme to cater to the growing number of visitors to Qatar. Just a few kilometres away, the new airport is being constructed, ready

Doha Airport accommodates over 20 airlines

ONCE UPON A TIME...

Learn what life was like before gleaming skyscrapers and traffic jams, when Dubai was no more than a sandy fishing village. These memories, shared by locals who have seen the city change immeasurably, offer a fascinating glimpse into life in simpler, and yet infinitely more difficult, times.

Supported by

بنك دبي الوطني
National Bank of Dubai

TELLING TALES

Phone (971 4) 335 3520 · **Fax** (971 4) 335 3529
Info@Explorer-Publishing.com · www.Explorer-Publishing.com
Residents' Guides · Photography Books · Activity Guidebooks · Practical Guides · Maps

EXPLORER

Passionately Publishing...

to offer state of the art facilities to airlines and passengers. (see p.8).

The existing airport has a well-stocked duty free shop selling the usual array of electronics, perfumes and alcohol (for departing passengers only).

Airport Bus

Most of the five-star hotels in Doha offer some variation of return bus service for the airport. Arrival bus pickups are not currently in use. The available services do change on a regular basis but are free and quite flexible in their timings. The best advice is to contact the concierge to verify the schedule or to request a drop-off for your specific flight.

Boat

With so much coastline there is plenty for boat owners to see and do, but there are no regular passenger services linking coastal towns and cities. There was previously a ferry service between Iran and Qatar, operated by the Qatar National Navigation Company, but this has been indefinitely halted. However, it is possible to take a boat ride to some of the offshore islands, such as Palm Tree Island, or to cruise the bay aboard a traditional dhow. The best bet is to contact one of the local tour operators for island tours, see p.109.

Bus

Presently no public bus system exists in Qatar, although plans for a public bus service that will operate in the downtown area have been in play for some time. In all likelihood, the bus will not be readily available that soon, but should be operating at some level when the Asian Games come to Qatar in December 2006. Work developing the new taxicab system, which operates at a generous fare, is the current priority. The buses, small and large, that are visible throughout the city are privately owned and used to transport workers to and from work sites.

Bus to the Games

The organisers of the Asian Games have announced that a special bus service will operate during the games to transport the thousands of officials, athletes and guests. The transport company Mowasalat has promised that up to 600 buses will run every day.

Car

Other options → Transportation [p.78]

In Qatar the preferred method of transport is definitely the car. The country has a good network of roads and highways, generally in a good state of repair, but Doha's many roundabouts can be daunting and confusing, and the burgeoning population is leading to increased congestion and traffic delays in the capital. Signposts are almost always in English as well as Arabic.

Petrol stations can be found throughout Doha and along the main roads in Qatar, and most visitors will be pleasantly surprised to find the price of fuel is a lot lower than elsewhere in the world. This means that many motorists can afford to run gas-guzzling 4WDs, of which there are many on Qatar's roads.

Driving Habits & Regulations

The quality of driving in Qatar leaves a lot to be desired, although the standard is perhaps a little higher than in some other Gulf countries. If you intend to drive in Qatar you must have your wits about you and remain alert at all times, as speeding, tail-gating, and sudden lane-changing are all too common. The best advice is to expect the unexpected. Be careful to contain your frustration though, as obscene gestures and examples of road-rage can result in severe penalties. Driving is on the right, and seatbelts are mandatory for the driver and front seat passenger.

Zero Tolerance

Qatar has a strict zero tolerance policy when it comes to drinking and driving. The penalties for drink-driving can include a hefty fine, a jail term, and even deportation. Also, if you are involved in an accident and are found to have been drinking, your insurance will be invalidated. If you have had anything at all to drink then get a cab or a lift. Don't take the risk - it just isn't worth it.

Speed Limits

Speed limits in Qatar range from 50kmph on some roads in towns and cities to 120kmph on the highways. Radar speed cameras are becoming more common, both fixed and mobile, and drivers will be fined for breaking the limit. Cameras also feature at major junctions and traffic lights. In spite of the prescence of cameras, many motorists pay little attention to the legal limits and speeding is all too common.

Driving Licence

If you are a visitor to Qatar, you may be able to drive on your existing licence (depending on your nationality) but only for seven days after arrival. (However, expats from other GCC countries who hold a valid resident's licence may drive in Qatar for up to three months.) You must then get a temporary Qatar licence from the traffic department. For this you'll need your original licence, four passport photos, QR 150, and you will have to take an eye test. If you are hiring a car, the hire company will be able to advise you on the process. A separate licence is required if you plan to ride a motorbike in Qatar.

Blood Money

If you're driving and have an accident in which someone dies, you may be liable to pay 'blood money' to the family of the deceased (regardless of whether you were at fault or not). This should be covered by your insurance, but you should check your policy carefully to make sure. However, the insurance company will not pay if you are found to have been driving without a licence or under the influence of alcohol.

Accidents

The standard of driving in Qatar is a cause for concern and traffic accidents are a common occurrence. If you are unfortunate enough to be involved in an accident, call the police and leave all vehicles where they are, even if blocking the traffic. None of those involved should leave the scene of the accident (unless of course someone is injured and requires urgent medical attention). The police will survey the scene and apportion blame to the driver at fault (hopefully). It's a good idea to carry your driving licence with you at all times, and perhaps keep a copy of your insurance papers in the vehicle.

Non Drivers

As if dealing with Qatar's erratic drivers was not enough, you will also encounter pedestrians and cyclists with little or no regard for the rules of the road and their own safety. Pedestrians often step into the road seemingly oblivious to oncoming vehicles, and cyclists tend to ride towards the flow of traffic. You should be especially careful if you see a bus or taxi at the side of the road, as people may be trying to cross from the other side to reach it. A further hazard to be aware of when driving outside the towns is camels crossing the road.

Parking

Car parking is widely available around Qatar and in most parts of Doha, although some areas of the capital have become increasingly congested, prompting the introduction of new parking meters that have recently appeared on many of the city's streets. Most shopping centres, office blocks and residential buildings have car parks, and parking can often be found on the street or on areas of waste ground between buildings.

Car Hire

Most of the internationally known car-hire firms are represented in Qatar, with offices at the airport and some of the big hotels. There are a number of local firms offering car rental too, with competitive prices to match the recognised companies. Rental can be for just one day or for weeks or months at a time, and a wide range of cars is available. Expect to pay from around QR 120 per day for a small car to QR 250+ for a luxury model or 4WD.

Car Rental Agencies		
AAB Rent-A-Car Company P.iv		443 7000
Al Muftah Rent a Car P.ix		
C Ring Road		432 8100
Musheirib		432 6840
Ras Laffan Industrial City		474 8840
Alfardan Automobiles		460 1177
Avis		466 7744
Budget Rent-A-Car		468 5515
Europcar		443 8404
Hertz		462 2891
Mannai Autorent P.79		455 8640
Prestige Rent a Car		483 8500

Beware of dangerous driving

Cycling

Other options → Cycling [p.123]

While cycling the 7km of the Corniche is popular, especially in the cooler months, there are no cycle tracks around the city. As a mode of transport to get you from A to B cycling is not a preferential choice. Thanks to the somewhat aggressive driving habits and oppressive heat, hopping on your bike to get to work is not an activity that is, or will likely ever be, commonplace. There is however a cycling federation for those who are keen to get peddling for a hobby, see Cycling in the Activities section on p.123.

Taxi

If you're planning to stay in Doha for a long visit or you are a new resident then relying on taxis may be a pain. With the increasing number of people visiting or moving to Doha it is becoming harder to find an empty taxi. At times it seems like there are not enough taxis to accommodate all the residents and if you're unlucky you may end up waiting for over 40 minutes for a taxi

At the moment there are two types of taxis, the run-down orange and white ones and the new (more expensive) blue cars. The newer blue cars are run by the private taxi service, 'Karwa' which was launched in 2004. The future plan is that the Karwa taxis will eventually replace the orange and white ones which are being withdrawn from the market gradually. The good news is that Karwa is steadily increasing the number of their taxis, so hopefully the problem of finding a cab will be solved soon.

Karwa taxis' meters start at QR 3 and run at QR 1 per kilometre. To save yourself the headache of flagging a taxi, you can always order one in advance for an extra charge of QR 1 by calling 458 8888. As for the old orange and white taxis, there is no central dispatch to order a car from, so your only option is to flag one from the side of the road.

Illegal Pickups

Don't be surprised if while you are waiting for a cab, an unmarked car stops and shouts "taxi" in your direction. These are regular drivers who are looking for ways to make extra money by driving people around. It is advisable not to bother with these unlicensed public drivers especially if you are a female.

Taxi drivers (especially those who drive the orange and white cabs) know the city pretty well although street names are not commonly used and most drivers navigate using landmarks.

Taking a taxi from the airport, you have the option of either an orange and white taxi whose driver will refuse to take you anywhere for less than QR 20-30, but you can always bargain, or taking a blue taxi which uses meters, but has a higher pick-up charge from the airport.

Taxi Companies	
Mowasalat – Karwa (blue taxis)	458 8888
National Taxi (orange taxis)	441 3190

Walking

Perhaps because of the summer heat, or perhaps because everybody can afford a luxury car, walking is not really a common mode of transport in Qatar. Modern roads, ample parking and cars equipped with super-cool air-conditioning make driving a much more pleasant way to get around. However, there are plenty of areas suitable for walking for those who do it for pleasure – the famous corniche, which runs a 13km stretch from the Sheraton to Ras Abu Abboud, is always busy with active people striding, biking, rollerblading or pram-pushing up and down.

Money

Cash is still the preferred method of payment in Qatar, especially in smaller shops and the souks, but major stores, hotels and restaurants do accept credit and debit cards. Cheques, however, are not widely accepted.

Local Currency

The monetary unit of Qatar is the Qatar Riyal (QR). It is divided into 100 Dirhams (not to be confused with the UAE Dirham which has almost the same value as the Qatari Riyal). Banknote denominations include QR 1, QR 5, QR 10, QR 50, QR 100, and QR 500.

The coins that are most commonly found are 25 and 50 Dirhams. One, five, and 10 Dirhams coins are still legal tender but are rarely seen. The Riyal is pegged to the US dollar at a mid rate of 3.65. Exchange rates of all major currencies are published daily in the local newspapers.

Exchange Rates

Australia	0.36	2.77
Bahrain	0.103	9.65
Bangladesh	17.51	0.057
Canada	0.345	2.89
Cyprus	0.126	7.88
Denmark	1.64	0.6
Euro	0.22	4.53
Hong Kong	2.138	0.46
India	11.96	0.08
Japan	29.67	0.033
Jordan	0.194	5.13
Kuwait	0.08	12.46
Malaysia	1.044	0.957
New Zealand	0.386	2.59
Pakistan	16.38	0.061
Philippines	14.95	0.066
Saudi Arabia	1.03	0.97
Singapore	0.456	2.19
South Africa	1.825	0.547
Sri Lanka	27.46	0.036
Sweden	2.023	0.49
Switzerland	0.34	2.93
Thailand	11.09	0.09
UAE	1.009	0.99
UK	0.15	6.627
USA	0.274	3.638

* Rates valid at the time of print

Banks

Qatar is fairly well represented by various national banks and a number of international banks, including HSBC and Standard Chartered. The main branches are concentrated along Grand Hamad Street in Doha, with smaller branches throughout the city and elsewhere in the country. Doha Bank even has a Mobile Banking Unit, or bank-on-

Main Banks

Ahli Bank QSC	432 6611
Arab Bank	438 7777
Bank Saderat Iran	441 4646
BNP Paribas	437 8378
Doha Bank Ltd.	445 6600
Grindlays Qatar Bank	441 8222
HSBC Bank Middle East Limited p.IBC	438 2100
Mashreq Bank	441 3213
Qatar Industrial Development Bank	447 3700
Qatar International Islamic Bank	433 2600
Qatar Islamic Bank	440 9409
Qatar National Bank	440 7407
Standard Chartered Bank p.51	465 8555
The Commercial Bank of Qatar (QSC) p.xxi	449 0000
United Bank Ltd.	443 8666

wheels, that visits different locations. All banks offer money exchange and transfer services. Opening hours are generally 07:30 – 12:00 Sunday to Wednesday, and 07:00 – 11:30 on Thursday, but many branches now open for longer, as well as on Saturday and in the evenings.

Pearl monument

ATMs

The capital city has a fairly large number of automatic teller machines (ATMs or cash points). All local banks provide them onsite but many local shopping malls also have the odd ATM. Many of the larger hotels have cash machines in the lobby, as do some supermarkets. Outside Doha, ATMs are less prevalent with fewer banks and retail establishments. Qatari banks do not charge transaction fees for withdrawals from remote banks, but remote banks may charge a fee. The systems accepted in most ATMs are American Express, Cirrus, Plus, Visa Electron, MasterCard and Visa.

Money Exchanges

Major hotels do offer exchange services for some of the main currencies, however, independent money exchanges tend to offer better rates and a broader number of currencies. Banks also provide exchange services but again the rates may be slightly higher and the range of currencies more limited than the independent money exchanges. Most exchange centres follow similar timings of 08:00 to 12:00 then 16:00 to 20:00 on weekdays, with some open from 16:00 to 20:00 on Friday. The majority are located within shopping malls.

Exchange Centres	
Al Fardan Exchange & Finance	440 8214
Al-Jazeera Exhchange	436 3595
Almana Exchange	442 4226
City Exchange	443 5060
Habib International Finance	432 8853
National Exchange	432 3359

Credit Cards

Qatar is becoming more and more accustomed to plastic, with credit cards accepted at the majority of outlets. Most retailers in the capital and major retailers in the suburban communities accept credit and debit cards. Some smaller shops in the souk area of Doha take credit cards but may prefer cash and offer a better bargained price for those cash buyers. No surcharge should be levied by retailers taking credit cards. Qatar is eager to employ electronic transactions, with banks providing online accounting and usage notification via mobile telephone. Visa, Mastercard, American Express and Diners Club are widely accepted.

Tipping

Tipping is not as regimented in this part of the world as it has become in Europe. Tips are most common in restaurants, averaging 10%, although some establishments automatically add a 10% service charge but this should be stated on the menu. Taxi fares are generally minimal, so tips for rounding out dirhams or riyals are quite common although there is no hard and fast rule. Tipping for tour guides is subjective, but is good practice considering the average salary of most guides.

Media & Communications

Newspapers/Magazines

The two main English newspapers here are Gulf News and The Peninsula. They are published every day except for Friday and cover a range of international and local issues with a focus on the activities of the Asian community in Qatar. Each paper costs QR 2 and both are widely available. You can find them in supermarkets, stores, hotels, bookshops, and they are also sold by street vendors at traffic lights. Alternatively, you can get a subscription so that your paper will be delivered to your residence or office.

Some UAE-based English publications like Khaleej Times and Gulf News are also available on the day of publication. Foreign newspapers, mostly British, American and Asian, are also available but they usually arrive 24 hours after the publication date. They can be found in supermarkets, hotels and some shops, but are more expensive than their places of origin. There are three local Arabic dailies issued from Qatar, Al-Raya, Al-Sharq and Al-Watan, which all cost QR 2.

English language magazines published in Qatar include Qatar Today which focuses mainly on business issues but also covers news, motoring, travel, and technology. Woman Today is a recent entrant to the market, with articles and features aimed at working women in Qatar. Abode is a locally published lifestyle magazine that features English and Arabic text side by side.

Imported English language magazines are often more expensive than at home, and are mostly hobby magazines featuring photography, sports, film and computing. Many are censored using a black marker pen to cover exposed parts of women's bodies (for example in beauty product adverts). Also don't be surprised if you find some pages missing from the magazines as tearing whole sections is a another form of censorship here.

Further Reading

Other options → **Websites [p.32]**

A listing of monthly events that are happening in Qatar can be found in a free booklet called Qatar Happening which is usually distributed in malls, hotels, and some DVD rental stores.

There are very few travel guides on Qatar, but the locally published booklet Marhaba provides comprehensive information about Qatar in addition to giving tips for new residents. Published three times a year, Marhaba also runs social, business and entertainment features about Doha and publishes a listing of events happening around town. Another guidebook about Qatar is a business travellers' handbook entitled simply 'Qatar' published by Gulf Agency Qatar.

Post & Courier Services

Other options → **Postal Services [p.67]**

Postal services in Qatar are provided by Q-Post with their headquarters and main post office on the corniche and further branches across Doha and throughout the country. Q-Post offers a variety of services, including regular letter and parcel postage both locally and internationally, bill payment, money transfers, and even renewal of dependents' residency visas and ID cards.

Postage rates for letters to addresses in Qatar start at 50 Dirhams, and QR 3 to Europe, and QR 3.5 to the US and Australia.

Qatar doesn't have a regular home delivery postal service, so most people either use their company PO Box address or take a PO Box of their own. Most branches have PO Boxes, and the main post office has 25,000 'electronic boxes' operated with a key-card. The initial cost for a medium 'lock and key' box at a branch is QR 165, with an annual subscription charge of QR 105. A similar size electronic box costs QR 235 initially, then QR 175 a year. Q-Post does offer a service to have your box checked regularly, and the mail delivered to your home or workplace (www.qpost.com.qa).

Courier Companies

Aramex International	442 6101
DHL	462 1202
Federal Express	466 1722
Skynet	443 1122
TNT	462 2262
United Parcel Service	432 2444
WGA	441 2881

Radio

There are only a few Qatar-based radio services available. Qatar Radio (QBS) is the main station, which operates both in English and French on 97.5 and 102.6 FM, although the French broadcast operates only from 13:15 to 16:00. A new Arabic service, Voice of the Gulf, has also been launched on 100.8 FM.

Television/Satellite TV

Other options → Television [p.67]
Satellite TV & Radio [p.67]

Qatar has three terrestrial television channels - Channel 1 and 2 and Al Jazeera Satellite Channel. Channel 1 broadcasts local programmes exclusively in Arabic while Channel 2 provides predominantly English entertainment programming. Al Jazeera has its famous news channel and a well-respected sports channel,

although it is currently expanding with an English channel on the horizon as well as a documentary channel and a children's channel.

Satellite TV is available via Qtel's Cable Vision (QCV) decoder, which combines a mix of international satellite channels with selections from Orbit and Showtime satellite services providing English and American sitcoms, documentaries, movies and sports. There is also Orbit direct (www.orbit.net) with online billing and local distributors that provide printed schedules, service and installation. Showtime satellite, based in the UAE, is making inroads into Qatar. Check out www.showtimearabia.com for a list of dealers in Qatar.

Telephones

Other options → Telephone [p.65]

Telecommunications in Qatar is operated by Qtel (www.qtel.com.qa), a recently privatised local company. Customer Service Centres are located all over the capital and throughout the country, providing a variety of services for both landline and mobile users. Rates locally and internally remain fairly competitive despite their monopoly of the market. Local calls from landlines, both business and residential, are free, while long distance and mobile calls from a landline phone require a deposit or a guarantee from a sponsor. Public phones are not that prevalent, however, those that are available operate on pay cards purchased from Qtel offices and many grocery and convenience stores. Calls from hotel rooms are somewhat higher than private lines (even local calls incur a charge so using the lobby phone may be better). Qtel also offers a prepaid mobile service, Hala Plus, which requires no guarantor and is therefore a good option for visitors.

Useful Telephone Numbers

Airport – general enquiries	465 6666
Airport Immigration/Passport Control	462 1276
Al Mowasalat (Taxi)	458 8888
Al Rayyah Transport (Limousine)	444 2111
Directory Assistance	180
Hamad Hospital	439 2111
International Phone Call Enquiry	190
Local Call Assistance	100
Police, Fire, Amblance	999
Qtel Main Office	440 0400
Speaking Clock (English)	140
Weather	465 6590

...et

Other options → Internet [p.66]
Internet Cafes [p.202]

Internet availability and usage are becoming increasingly commonplace in Qatar, most notably in the capital with a surge of internet cafes and a greater number of tempting offers of ADSL broadband internet packages via Qtel. Internet cafes are found in most high traffic areas, with two easily accessible in Doha's City Center shopping mall, and a growing number of Qtel wireless HotSpots are becoming available in hotels, cafes and restaurants. Qtel regulates all internet traffic and you may find that access to certain unsuitable sites is blocked. The Qatari domain is '.qa', prefixed primarily by the '.com' domain. Qtel offers a number of packages giving internet access, with subscription dialup, dial up without subscription and the superfast barQ ADSL. Rates continue to drop in order to attract more customers, with offers of free installation and a modem tied into yearly contracts. Internet cafe rates vary from QR 5 to QR 7 per hour. To access a Qtel HotSpot you will need a Wi-Fi enabled laptop or mobile device. Prepaid cards can be bought from the venue, in denominations of QR 30, 50, and 70.

Websites

A quick search on the internet will reveal a host of sites giving information and advice on Qatar. The government ministries have sites, most of them in English as well as Arabic, and many of the hotels have websites giving information on the country. The official site of the Qatar Tourism Authority is www.experienceqatar.com.

Websites

http://english.aljazeera.net	Qatar and world news in English
http://english.mofa.gov.qa	Info on country, government, economy & tourism
www.aiwagulf.com	Business directory
www.albandarrestaurant.com	Group of restaurants
www.ameinfo.com	Middle East business resource
www.arabinfoseek.com	Arab worldwide web directory
www.cia.gov	Country profile
www.cbq.com.qa	The Commercial Bank of Qatar
www.doha-online.com	Tourist information
www.doha-2006.com	The 15th Asian Games Doha 2006
www.english.education.gov.qa	Supreme Education Council
www.experienceqatar.com	Qatar Tourism Authority official website
www.gulf-times.com	Weather, daily news, economic development
www.gulfbusiness.com	Economic information
www.hmc.org.qa	Qatar health care provider
www.mannaicorp.com	Mannai Corporation QSC
www.nccah.com	National Council for Culture,Arts and Heritage
www.qatar-info.com	Background information, culture, religion
www.qatar-links.com	Links to Qatar info sites
www.qatar.net.qa	Qatar internet service provider
www.qatarbusinesscouncil.org	U.S. - Qatar Business Council
www.qatardutyfree.net	Qatar Duty Free
www.qatarembassy.net	A complete information resource
www.qatarglobe.com	Qatar and Middle East news
www.qatarolympics.org	Qatar National Olympic Committee (QNOC)
www.qbbf.com	Qatar British Business Forum
www.qed.com.qa	Qatar e-directory
www.qf.edu.qa	Qatar Foundation
www.qnb.com.qa	Qatar National Bank
www.qp.com.qa	Qatar Petroleum, with general info about Qatar
www.qtel.com.qa	Qatar Telecommunications (Qtel)
www.thepeninsulaqatar.com	Daily English language newspaper in Qatar
www.tradearabia.com	Middle East news and information
www.world-newspapers.com	Links to worldwide newspaper websites

connect

WITH

FLAVOUR

Qtelhotspot

At these locations:

GRAND JOUD
CAFÉ & RESTAURANT

EFC
Elle France Café

CREPAWAY

mint
LIVING CAFÉ

La maison
du
Café
NAJJAR

LENÔTRE
PARIS

AL SADD
Merweb
HOTEL

INTERCONTINENTAL.
DOHA

15TH ASIAN GAMES
DOHA 2006

PRESTIGE PARTNER

www.qtel.com.qa

Eid al Adha

Eid al Adha (the Feast of Sacrifice) marks the end of the Haj (the pilgrimage to Mecca). During this festival people dress in new clothes and visit friends and family, and a sheep will often be slaughtered to commemorate the time when Ibrahim was prepared to sacrifice his son to Allah.

Eid al Fitr

Eid al Fitr (the festival of the breaking of the fast) takes place at the end of the holy month of Ramadan. This occasion is often characterised by big family get-togethers and celebrations with feasts and gifts.

Independence Day

This national holiday celebrates Qatar's declaration of independence on September 3rd 1971 following the departure of the British from the Gulf region. The occasion is marked by the decoration of streets and public buildings.

Islamic New Year

Islamic New Year marks the start of the Islamic Hijri calendar, which is based on the lunar cycles. It should fall on January 31st 2006, but can sometimes be announced a day or two earlier or later depending on the sighting of the moon.

Motorbike Racing

The brand new Losail motor racing circuit outside Doha is the venue for the Qatar Grand Prix, a leg of the MotoGP World Championship. The circuit also hosts Superbike events and the Losail National Cup, and sometimes allows wannabe boy (and girl) racers to burn rubber on 'track days'. Visit the website for more info.

www.qatargp.net

Power Boat Racing

Class 1 offshore power boat racing is the fastest and most exhilarating of all water sports, and each year Qatar hosts two rounds of the world championship. Spectators can enjoy the spectacle along Doha's corniche and cheer on the local Qatar team, who

Qatari customs (Image courtesy Qatar Tourism Authority)

Power boat racing (Image courtesy Qatar Tourism Authority)

despite being a relatively new entrant to the sport have already posted some impressive results.

www.qmsf.org

Qatar International Tennis Tournaments

Attracting top names every year, the ExxonMobil Open is the men's event and the Total Open is for women. Both are held at the home of the Qatar Tennis Federation. The winners of the 2005 singles titles were Roger Federer and Maria Sharapova.

www.qatartennis.org

Qatar Masters Golf Tournament

The Qatar Masters is an annual event on the PGA European tour that attracts some of the world's best players to the Doha Golf Club. The 2005 event was won by Ernie Els (a week after winning the Dubai Desert Classic). The 2006 Masters is scheduled for March 9th – 12th.

www.qatarmasters.com

Qatar Summer Wonders

The Tarmac-melting temperatures often see expat families returning home for the summer, but for those who do stay, the Qatar Summer Wonders festival is an annual programme of family-friendly activities and events. These usually take place in shopping malls, and the Qatar International Exhibition Centre often stages entertainment shows and performances.

Qatar Annual Events – 2006

	January		
29 - 3	H.H. The Emir Volleyball Cup - Final	8 - 11	The Communications & Information Technology 'Comit Qatar 06'
26 - 29	Doha Int'l Food & Beverage	12 - 15	Marine Environment Conference
	February	21 - 24	10th International Energy Forum
10 - 13	Qatar Fencing Grand Prix	17 - 19	Getaway Exhibition
13 - 18	Doha Jewellery & Watches Exhibition	24 - 26	Charity Diplomatic Bazar
14 - 17	Qatar 10th International Table Tennis Tournament for Women		**May**
		2 - 5	Project Qatar
20 - 25	Qatar Total Open Tennis Tournament for Women	15 - 17	5th Int'l Exhibition of Internal State Security – Milipol Qatar
24 - 26	World Motorcycle Championship - Superbikes	24 - 27	Doha International Furniture Exhibition
25	Dhow Sailing - The Prime Minister Cup		**June**
25 - 28	Qatar Agriculture Exhibition	4 - 6	Education, Training & Development Exhibition
	March		
1 - 8	Qatar Junior Squash International Championship	12 - 15	Al Diyafa
		18 - 21	International Franchising & Branding Exhibition
5 - 9	International Trade Fair		
7 - 15	World Telecom Development Forum - WTDC 2006	27	Accession Day
			July
9 - 12	Qatar Masters Golf Tournament	1 - 31	Qatar Summer Wonders
11	Dhow Sailing - The Ahigr Cup		**September**
13 - 17	Arab Rowing Championship - Argo Meter	3	Independence Day
19 - 23	Qatar Int'l Tourism & Travel Exhibition 06		**October**
31 - 2	Flowers & Vegetables	1 - 4	Food & Beverage, Processing Requirement 'Foodexo6'
	April		
1	Class 1 World Power Boat Championship Grand Prix	23	Eid Al Fitr (moon)
			December
5 - 9	Egyptian Products Exhibition	1 - 15	The 15th Asian Games Doha 2006
8	Dhow Sailing - The Amiri Cup	31	Eid Al Adha (moon)

Moving couldn't be easier...

At Qatar Logistics we know the stress that comes with moving, whether it's an office move across town, or a family relocation to the other side of the world. Our team is there to take the stress out of your move, because we will care for your belongings as if they were our own.

Contact us anytime for a free assessment of your needs, and experience the unique Qatar Logistics sevice

QATAR LOGISTICS
قطر لوجستكس

P.O. Box 22770
Doha, Qatar
Tel: +974 455 0991
Fax: +974 455 0992
E-mail: sales@qatarlogistics.com

QATAR LOGISTIC
طر لوجستكس

Residents

EXPLORER

Residents

Highlights...

Health, Health, Health! *p.68*

Being away from the familiarity of home can be tough enough, but if you have health concerns it makes things even worse. The Health section provides helpful advice on Qatar's health system and useful numbers of doctors, dentists, and all manner of professionals who should have you feeling better in no time.

Easy as GCC *p.57*

*If you're new to Qatar and want to become familiar with your GCC neighbours, or if you've done your time in Doha and are heading off across the water, then the Explorer GCC **Complete Residents' Guide** series is a valuable source of information. As well as the **Qatar Explorer**, you will find information-packed guides to Dubai, Abu Dhabi, Oman, Bahrain and Kuwait.*

Overview

Arriving in Doha can be very daunting, especially if it is your first experience of a Middle Eastern country. Driving from the airport to your house or hotel can be a scary experience and may leave you wondering what you are doing in this crazy country. The standard of driving is atrocious; there is no lane discipline, especially at roundabouts where drivers haven't quite grasped the concept of staying in the correct lane all the way around and they cut across any number of lanes and exit from any lane, leaving the less-experienced driver feeling as if he is about to be squashed. The best advice is to start driving as soon as you feel courageous enough, as it doesn't seem so bad when you have control of the vehicle yourself.

You may be permitted to drive on your existing valid driving licence for one week, after that you have to obtain a temporary licence from the police department (see Driving Licence on p.43). Luckily, Doha isn't that big, so you can get from A to B in a relatively short time. Although the volume of traffic isn't too bad at the moment, the closure of a number of roundabouts in the future may change that (for the worse!)

The process of getting your residence visa will be the next hurdle you need to face. It is generally quite straightforward to get a work permit as the employer usually sorts out all the paperwork. However, rules change on a daily basis, so don't be surprised if the company asks for different documents than what they requested originally. A family residence visa can take more than a little time and patience, in fact a number of people have had to wait for as long as six months before their permits were granted. If you consider that one has to exit the country after 28 days, most families are forced to do a 'visa run', which involves travelling to a neighbouring country and then re-entering Qatar with an updated visa. However, this becomes expensive and tedious, especially for families with young children (more information in Residence Visa section on p.42).

Setting up home will be a considerable, but enjoyable, challenge. Finding a house can be time consuming, although some of the larger companies have a number of houses allocated for their employees, making it much easier for them. There are many real estate companies that can help you find a place you will be able to call home. Most families prefer to live on one of the numerous compounds as it makes socialising with people a little bit easier. However, getting a compound house isn't as easy as it sounds – most of the more popular compounds in Doha have extensive waiting lists even though, at first glance, there seem to be more than enough to go around.

Once you have your residence visa, your company will probably help you apply for your home telephone lines. It is a good idea to ask them to apply for an internet connection at the same time. Phone lines can take a little while to get, especially if you live in an individual villa or a new compound. Qtel is the exclusive telecommunications provider in Qatar so anything 'telephonic' has to be done by them. If you want ADSL you may have to wait an extra week after your lines are connected. It is worth noting that the technicians may not make an appointment to come to your house but just show up, so if you need to go out remember to make alternative arrangements so they can still access your property.

It is good to be aware that what you might perceive as unfriendliness on the part of the locals may just be a language barrier, and that friendliness and courtesy on your part will help overcome this. Speaking of friendly, most expats are more than willing to help newcomers sort out problems – after all, they know only too well how you feel, so don't feel shy to ask for help.

So, although the first few weeks can be very challenging, if you keep your sense of humour and have lots of patience, you will sail over the obstacles and never look back!

Another sunny day in Qatar

In The Beginning ...

In the beginning of your stay in Qatar, and probably all throughout your stay as well, you will be required to present various personal documents. Whether you are applying for a visa, driving licence, liquor licence, telephone, or even school applications, you will need to prove who you are. It is a good idea to have at least three or four copies of your passport and blood group, marriage certificate, valid driving licence and birth certificate on hand at all times. Keep a number of copies of your ID card that will be supplied to you once your residence visa is issued.

The original copies of all personal documents should be kept in a safe place, together with any no-objection letters from your sponsor and a salary certificate.

Along with the documents, you will require countless passport photos, so keeping a stash of them will save you time and trouble. There are a number of photo shops scattered all over Doha and most shopping centres have at least one photo shop with facilities for taking and processing photos and photocopying. Prices are reasonable, but remember that photographs with white backgrounds are not accepted.

There is a lot of information online that will help you get your bearings when you first arrive. For a detailed list, refer to the Websites table on p.32. You could also pick up a copy of *Qatar Happening*, a monthly magazine that contains an update of what's happening in Qatar. Copies can be found at Mega Mart in Landmark Mall.

Essential Documents

You will require various documents when first setting up in Qatar. You will need different paperwork for different procedures such as getting your residence visa, driving licence, liquor licence, telephone and even school applications. The best thing is to have all the essential documents ready as it will save you a lot of time.

You will need plenty of photocopies of your passport, marriage certificate, valid driving licence, blood group certificate and birth certificate. Also keep some copies of your ID card, which will be issued once your residence visa is completed. The originals may also need to be checked so keep them with you. You will also require, at various times, a no objection letter from your sponsor and a salary certificate.

All immigration forms must be signed in black ink. Passports must be valid for at least three months. You will require lots of passport photos, but those with white back grounds are not accepted. Most shopping centres have photo shops where you can get passport photos taken and have photocopies of documents made, at reasonable prices.

Documents

Entry Visa

Other options → Visas **p.16**

Rules regarding passports and visas are complicated and baffling to the inexperienced expat. The main points to remember are:

Passports must be valid for at least three months after the date of entry.

All immigration forms must be signed in black ink.

It is up to you as an individual whether to register with your home country's embassy or not. Bear in mind that, in a foreign country, embassies are a good source of up-to-date information and will be of assistance if you need it.

There are different types of visas, each with different requirements and validity.

Nationals of Gulf Cooperation Council (GCC) countries may enter Qatar without a visa, but all other nationalities require a visit visa. Residents of certain non-GCC countries are able to get a visit visa upon arrival, but others need to obtain the visa before travelling.

The following countries can get a visa on arrival: Andorra; Australia; Austria; Belgium; Brunei; Canada; Denmark; Finland; France; Germany; Greece; Hong Kong; Iceland; Ireland; Italy; Japan; Liechtenstein; Luxembourg; Malaysia; Monaco; Netherlands; New Zealand; Norway; Portugal; San Marino; Singapore; South Korea; Spain; Sweden; Switzerland; United Kingdom; U.S.A and Vatican City. This information may change, so check before you fly either with the nearest Qatar Embassy or at www.moi.gov.qa (the website for the Qatar Ministry of Interior).

If you are one of the lucky ones who can get a visa on arrival, your quest will be fairly effortless – go straight to a passport control desk where an immigration officer will stamp a 21 day visa into your passport. The visa will cost QR 55, but only credit or debit cards are accepted. You can purchase a card to the value of QR 250 and you will

They Mean the World to You

We understand the importance of making your relocation experience as smooth as possible. After all, we're not just relocating your possessions, we are helping to relocate the most precious things in your life. Crown Relocations is a leading provider of domestic and international moving and settling-in services with over 100 locations in more than 45 countries.

Well Connected. Worldwide.™

Dubai
Tel: (971) 4 289 5152
Fax: (971)4 289 6263
Email: dubai@crownrelo.com

Abu Dhabi
Tel: (971)2 674 5155
Fax: (971)2 674 2293
Email: abudhabi@crownrelo.com

Bahrain
Tel: (973)17 227 598
Fax: (973)17 224 803
Email: bahrain@crownrelo.com

Egypt
Tel: (202) 580 6628
Fax: (202) 580 6601
Email: cairo@crownrelo.com

Kuwait
Tel: (965) 299 7850
Fax: (965) 299 7800
Email: kuwait@crownrelo.com

Qatar
Tel: (974) 462 1115/1170/1439
Fax: (974) 462 1119
Email: doha@crownrelo.com

Turkey
Tel: (90) 212 347 4410
Fax: (90) 212 347 4413
Email: istanbul@crownrelo.com

Please Visit **www.crownrelo.com**
for details.

CROWN
RELOCATIONS

...pend the remainder of the money ...ree shops, once you have cleared ...ntrol. This visa may later be extended ...days for a fee of QR 50.

...als who cannot get a visa on arrival have ...eral different options: Visas are issued at the ...migration Department (airport section), or hotels can arrange tourist visas (sometimes at quite short notice) at a cost of QR 250 and a variable service charge. These visas are for a period of two weeks and can be extended by two weeks for QR 200.

Business visas are obtained by a company or recognised establishment, are valid for 14 days and can be extended for three months. Hotels can also arrange Business Visas, which are valid for three months at a cost of approximately QR 1,200.

Family visit visas can be obtained for family members if the husband/father earns over QR 5,000.

Multiple entry business visas are issued to UK or US passport holders and are valid for three years, with each individual stay not to exceed six months. The most desirable and most complicated visa is the residence visa, which is dealt with below in its own section.

Health Card

You must apply for a health card once your residence visa is processed; even if you have private medical insurance, as you will need this card should you need to be treated at any of the government facilities. Your employer should arrange for this card, but if not, it is quite easy. You can apply on line at www.e.gov.qa, simply follow the instructions, pay using a credit card and the card will be delivered to you, within one or two days.

Alternatively, you could go to the Health Card Office at the Rumeila Hospital or the nearest government health facility and complete the necessary forms. They will need to be accompanied by two photos, a copy of your Qatar ID card and a fee of QR 100. The card should be ready in two to three weeks and the receipt for the fee may be used at health care facilities until the card is issued. The health card will only be valid for the same length of time as your residence visa.

The Post Office has a great service for renewing health cards. For a fee of QR 100, you may submit your old health card, one photo and a copy of your Qatar ID card, and they will let you know when to collect your card by putting a notice in your post box.

Residence Visa

Other options → Visas p.16

All expats require a residence visa if they wish to reside in Qatar either for work or to accompany their working spouse. You will need a Qatari sponsor in order to obtain a residence visa. To start the process of obtaining this visa your employer (or sponsor) will apply for a no objection certificate (NOC), which should be done before you even arrive in the country, and which is stamped in your passport at passport control at Doha airport. You will not have to pay as your sponsor will have paid already. If it is to be done after you have entered the country, you will have to leave the country and re-enter (this tiresome chore has become known as a 'visa run'). Once the NOC is stamped into your passport, the residence process must be started within one month. If you leave the country before your residence visa application is complete, you will have to start 'at the very beginning'!

There are two main types of residence visas: work and family. If you have a work residence visa, you can sponsor your family provided you earn over QR 5,000 each month. If you arrive on a family residence visa and decide to start work, you will have to restart the entire process, including being fingerprinted again, on the off-chance that they have changed!

A residence visa is normally valid for two years, although in certain cases some are only issued for six months. The visa must be renewed before it expires and if you need to be out of the country for over six months, you will need a visa extension or you could lose your visa.

Renewing a residence visa is fairly easy (compared to obtaining it in the first place) and most companies will do this for you. Alternatively, you can get the relevant application form from the post office. This needs to be typed in Arabic, signed by you and submitted to the post office or immigration department, together with your original passport, ID card, photograph and QR 1,000 for men, QR 500 for women and QR 300 for children. The post office does offer a home delivery service, but although this is tempting, it is more advisable to collect it yourself after 72 hours.

Medical Test

The first thing you will be asked for is a blood-type certificate. This can be done at any clinic and costs QR 15. It is a relatively simple needle prick in the finger. All persons applying for residency must have this done, no matter what age – needless to say, young children really don't like this part very much! Your company will arrange for the application form to be typed in Arabic and then you are ready for the next hurdle – your medical test. Most companies will send someone who knows the procedures to show you the ropes, but if they don't, these steps should help you through the maze. You will need the following: an application form, a copy of your passport, two passport photos and QR 100.

The Medical Commission carries out these medicals and is situated towards the industrial area. It is an easy building to find as it stands alone. This facility has opened fairly recently and is a vast improvement on the previous location. Unfortunately, areas are not very well signposted, so follow these steps:

Firstly, try to remember that standards of hygiene may differ from your home country. Accept their methods as far as possible, but if you find you have strong objections, make your request known and it will probably be granted, although not always with good grace and a smiling face!

Men's and women's sections are in separate areas of the building – men's to the back and women's to the right. Go to the counter number one where they will check your documents, enter them into the computer system and relieve you of QR 100. Women who are pregnant do not have to have the x-ray done. You will then need to go to room number three, where they will again check your paperwork and where you will have your blood drawn for the test.

Room number four is the x-ray room and may be the most distressing, especially for women. You will be asked to undress and put on a gown, although if you wear a plain white T-shirt you will only need to take off your bra. You will be lined up, waiting for the x-ray machine. If you have long hair, remember to tie it up or they will do it for you with someone else's hair clip!

Before you rush out, take time to check in the office on the side of counter one that you have had all the necessary tests done – you do not want to have to come back a second time.

About a week after surviving your medical, you will be asked to go for compulsory fingerprinting. This is done on Suhaim Bin Hamad Street, opposite Blue Salon, beside the Law Offices and is a relatively easy process. The building is not well signposted, but is well known, especially to police officers.

Your company will supply you with the relevant paperwork to hand in. Individual fingers and full hands will be inked and printed, so it is advisable to take Wet Wipes to clean your hands with afterwards. Once your prints are taken, a form will be typed in Arabic (for a fee of QR 10), and then all that is left for you to do is to go to the Immigration Department a week later and collect your visa.

Children are not required to have either a medical or fingerprints.

No labour cards are issued in Qatar. If you have a work permit, it is noted on your ID card. Your ID card will be renewed with your residence visa. If you have entered the country on a family visa and you then decide to work, you will have to go through the process of fingerprinting again in order to apply for a work visa. You will then be issued with a new ID card, which states that you have a work visa.

Certificates & Licences

Driving Licence

Other options → Transportation p.78

If you have a valid driving licence from your country of origin, you can drive a rental car for a period of seven days. However, if you have an international driving licence, there is no time limit. Before the seven-day period is up, you will need to get a temporary driving licence that is valid for the period of your visa. All nationalities may exchange their country of origin's licence for a temporary Qatar licence, however you may not do so if you have already started the residence visa process. If this has been started, you will have to wait for the visa before applying for a permanent licence.

To obtain the temporary licence, you will need to apply in person at the Madinat Khalifa Traffic Department, where you will be required to complete an application form. This will have to be completed in Arabic (there are a number of typing shops within the confines of the traffic department who will assist, for a small fee). If you have entered the country on a business visa, your sponsor will need to sign the form.

The documents required for a temporary licence are:

• Application form as above

• Original licence from country of origin

- Original passport or your Qatar ID card
- Passport copy
- Three passport photographs (remember, if you normally wear glasses, you should be wearing them in the photo)

Upon presentation of the above documents you will undergo an eye test, which is performed there and then on the premises. You will need to find (not an easy task), and then pay, the cashier. The fee is QR 150 and you will need a credit card as no cash payments are accepted. You should be able to collect the licence the following day.

A temporary licence allows you to drive rental cars, however you may not be insured to drive a privately owned car – this is purely at the discretion of the individual insurance company and they should be contacted to ensure coverage.

Upon receipt of your residence visa, you will be able to apply for a permanent licence, which is valid for five years. If you are caught driving without a licence, the penalty is QR 100.

Holders of GCC driving licences can obtain a permanent Qatar driving licence automatically, regardless of their country of origin. The majority of European and western licences can also be automatically exchanged; however, due to the constantly changing regulations, it is prudent to check with the traffic department at the time of applying.

If you do have an exchangeable licence, you will need to apply in person at the Madinat Khalifa Traffic Department (489 0666) and complete an application form that then needs to be typed in Arabic and signed by your sponsor.

The documents required for a permanent licence are :

- Application form (as above)
- Original licence from country of origin
- No objection letter from your sponsor (in Arabic)
- Copy of trade licence (if you are sponsored by a company)
- Copy of your sponsor's ID
- Original passport or your Qatar ID card
- Passport copy
- Three passport photographs

Upon presentation of the above documents, you will undergo an eye test, which is performed immediately on the premises. Pay the cashier a fee of QR 155 (no cash payments are accepted so take your credit card!). You should be able to collect the licence the following day.

You'll soon learn to read the signs

If you are unfortunate enough to come from a country that is not allowed to automatically exchange licences, you will have to undergo a driving test. This involves both an oral test and a road test. The tests are conducted in manual transmission cars and there may be up to four people in the car, each one taking turns to drive. During the holy month of Ramadan ladies are not permitted to take a road test.

The operating hours for the traffic department are strictly 07:00 to 11:00 and 16:00 to 19:00, however, the ladies section is only open in the morning. At closing time, you will be asked to return either in the evening or the next day, regardless of how far you are in the queue! If you are prepared to wake up early and be there at 07:00, you will find it quite quiet.

Driving Schools	
Al Rayah Driving School	487 7700
Gulf Driving School	465 2822
Qatar Modern Driving School	480 3717
United Driving Company	468 1003

Liquor Licence

Other options → Alcohol p.152

Bars and restaurants inside hotels and some sports or leisure clubs are licenced to sell alcohol, although an extra charge of 17.5% tax can make it a rather expensive night out! The Qatar Distribution Company (469 9412 or 469 9413) is the exclusive importers of alcohol in Qatar, and because the brewing of alcohol is prohibited, are the only source of anything alcoholic. They are situated in the Industrial District in the Qatari capital and are the sole location where those with a special permit can buy alcohol. In order to obtain such a permit, you need a letter from your sponsor stating your basic salary (excluding your housing allowance or other benefits) and a copy of your ID. You will also need to pay a returnable deposit of QR 1,000.

The QDC calculates your monthly quota of alcohol based on your salary. This will not exceed 10% of your basic salary. They offer a good selection of wine from all over the world, as well as a number of brand-name spirits and a moderate selection of beers with 10 to 15 different brands available. QDC pays 100% landing tax on the import of all alcoholic beverages and no additional sales tax is added, making the prices reasonable, but not what could be described as cheap!

Points to remember are that no children are allowed in the shop and that QDC is closed during the holy month of Ramadan (so remember to stock up). You are allowed to purchase alcohol at the airport when leaving the country, but you may not bring it into Qatar.

Birth Certificate & Registration

Women must be married to have a baby in Qatar. An unmarried woman trying to deliver in any of the hospitals would run into serious trouble with the authorities. But do not panic, it is possible to get married in Qatar – contact your embassy or consulate for details.

Newborn babies must have their Residence Visas processed within two months; failure to do so will result in a QR 10 per day fine until the visa is issued. The hospital will issue you with the paperwork necessary to obtain a birth certificate, but it is the parents' responsibility to register the birth with their country's embassy or consulate.

Documents required for birth certificates:

- Child's local birth certificate from the Preventative Health Department
- Both parents' birth certificates
- Both parents' passports
- Parents' marriage certificate
- Payment of QR 308

To register the birth at the British Embassy costs QR 484.

Marriage Certificate & Registration

It is not that common for expats to get married in Qatar. Most either get hitched in their own country of origin or travel abroad. Christian churches are not officially sanctioned in Qatar, although there is a resident Chaplain and a resident Roman Catholic priest. Certain embassies are able to perform marriage ceremonies.

Death Certificate & Registration

The death of a family member or friend is difficult at any time, but the procedures in a foreign country may add to your stress and pain. Your national embassy will certainly assist wherever they can and will provide you with clear instructions of what needs to be done.

The police must be notified in the event of a death, so that they can issue a report stating that there was no foul play involved. Once this report has been issued, you need to go to the mortuary (439 2594) to collect the Notification of Death certificate (which is a yellow form).

Once you have the police report and the death certificate, you must go to the Preventative Health Department (located on Al Rayyan Road, near Lulu's) to obtain further paperwork.

In order to obtain all the relevant paperwork, you will need the following:

- 10 copies of the deceased person's passport
- 10 copies of the deceased person's spouse's passport
- 10 copies of the passport of the person handling the arrangements
- Copies of each person's ID card may also be required
- The cost will be approximately QR 100

Post mortems are not usually performed in Qatar, or any of the other Gulf countries, unless there is reason to believe that the death was not due to natural causes or accidental. If a post mortem is necessary, a relative must sign a form, which is written in Arabic, and which states that you have no objection to any organs being removed and destroyed in non-criminal cases.

You will then need to go to the CID with all the paperwork obtained from the Preventative Health Department in order to obtain a Transfer of Dead Body certificate. The CID is located in the same place where you normally go to have your fingerprints taken. You will need to purchase a QR 6 stamp and take it to the fifth floor.

Thereafter, you will need to return to the Preventative Health Department with all the paperwork and they will issue you with six sets of death certificates.

You must also register the death with the deceased person's embassy. They will require a death certificate and a completed Registration of Death form; available at the embassy. As an indication of cost, at the British Embassy, registration of a death costs QR 484 and a death certificate costs QR 308.

The embassy will cancel the deceased person's passport, which is necessary if the body is to be repatriated. The residence visa must also be cancelled, and the deceased person's sponsor should arrange this for you.

You will then need to make arrangements with an airline for shipment of the body, as well as with an undertaker in the country to which the body is being flown. Remember to advise the mortuary which flight has been booked. The mortuary will then make arrangements to transport the body to the airport.

The next step is to contact Qatar National Travel (462 6900), which is located at the cargo section of the airport. They will require copies of the deceased's passport and that of the accompanying person. They also need contact details of the undertaker in the home country. They will issue an airway bill for the body and will expect cash payment in advance.

There are no undertakers in Qatar. Eugene the embalmer will help with the preparation of the body. Eugene and a team of volunteers do not charge for their services, but will happily accept donations, which she then gives to local charities. Eugene will come and prepare the body 24 hours before it is due to leave the country. Eugene can be contacted on 442 7427.

You will need to order a coffin and this can be done through Gulf Timber (460 0822); alternatively you can call Mr Cesar (541 4768) or Mr Jaffer (551 0962/553 3145). It takes a maximum of two days to make a coffin once they have the measurements of the deceased. The approximate charge is QR 3,000, paid in advance, and they will deliver the coffin to the mortuary on the day the body is being flown home.

On the day of departure, you will have to take the paperwork, together with the deceased's original cancelled passport and the airway bill, to the airport. At Arrivals, go to the Customs counter, where they will stamp one set of papers. Then go to Immigration who will stamp the deceased's passport with an exit stamp. You will then have to return to QNT with all the stamped documents.

Work

Working in Qatar

Considering the small size of the country, Qatar has a large number of expat workers, and that number is growing rapidly with the vast number of new developments. Expats can enjoy a good standard of living in Qatar. Most international companies recruit employees from abroad and offer good packages.

Not having to pay taxes means more opportunity to save money (or spend it!). However, you will have to work hard to earn your money as people tend to work longer hours than they would at home, especially in certain industries that employ a large number of foreign workers (such as oil and construction).

As a rule, there is no need to speak Arabic, but it can be an advantage to be able to speak a few words. Greetings and pleasantries are worth learning as a mark of respect.

Generally the working week is Sunday to Thursday and the normal number of hours worked per day is eight. However, many companies only give their employees one day off, which is usually Friday, although most international companies will have a two-day weekend.

By law, workers must be given one month of paid annual leave once they have worked for a company for a full year. They are also entitled to an air ticket to their country of origin after two years of employment. International companies usually provide their employees and families with a ticket

14:30. Commercial offices sometimes work from 08:00 to 12:30 and then from 16:00 to 19:00; or a straight shift through to 17:00. Office timings vary from company to company.

Shopping centres are generally open from 09:00 or 10:00 to 22:00, but individual shops tend to follow the split shift, usually 08:00 to 12:30 and 16:30 to 21:00.

June 27 is Accession Day and September 3 is Independence Day, so these dates are always public holidays. There are also two Eid holidays – Eid Al Fitr and Eid Al Adha. Eid Al Fitr marks the end of the holy month of Ramadan and is determined by the sighting of the new moon. Ramadan dates are not always guaranteed, although a rule of thumb is that it begins about 11 days earlier than the previous year. Eid Al Adha falls around 70 days after Eid Al Fitr. Due to the uncertainty in pinpointing actual dates, public holidays are often announced at the last minute in the daily newspapers.

Finding Work

The majority of expats coming to Doha are transferred internally within their companies. Others may have applied for vacancies advertised in their home country, but not many people arrive looking for work as the visa process makes that very difficult. Finding work in Doha should not be a problem, as long as you have the right qualifications and experience – there is generally a shortage of professionals, particularly within the construction, oil and gas industries.

If you are already in Doha, a good way of job hunting is to present your CV personally to the companies and word of mouth will help put you in touch with the right contacts.

There are not many recruitment agencies in Doha at the moment, but that is bound to change as business needs increase. Key Resources, which is located in the Home Centre Building after the Jaidah Flyover, has a good reputation. You may be asked to take a test of some description when you register, but there is no registration charge.

Job vacancies are also advertised daily in the Gulf Times and the Peninsula newspaper.

Doha's striking skyline

home once a year, or the equivalent monetary value. They may also pay housing, medical insurance, schooling and often utility bills. Some international companies might even offer share option schemes, depending on company policy.

In general, working for an international company usually means that you will get better benefits than if you were to work for a local company. However, to compensate, local companies may offer a better salary package.

It is therefore wise to do your homework on all the expenses that you are likely to incur during your stay and find out who pays for what.

Working Hours

Working hours vary, depending very much on what type of industry you are in; but on the whole, people tend to work about eight hours a day. Some companies give their employees a two-day weekend, usually Friday and Saturday, but some only give one and a half days off, usually Thursday afternoon and Friday. Many offices work split shifts, but most work straight through. Government offices tend to work from 07:00 to

Recruitment Agencies	
Al Noof Recruitment Services	442 2076
A-One Placements	438 3820
Key Resources	435 3360

Voluntary & Charity Work

If you are accompanying your spouse to Qatar, you may find that due to higher salaries and not having to pay income tax means that you have the choice to work or not. If you opt not to work full time you can always offer your services as a volunteer. There are a number of charity organizations in Doha. However, it may be difficult if you do not speak Arabic. The Qatar Centre for Voluntary Activities (467 4888) may be a good place to start your search. The Cats and Dogs Rescue Home is always grateful for volunteers, as is the Qatar Animal Welfare Society (www.qaws.org).

Some other charity organizations in Doha are: Qatar Charity (466 7711), Qatar Red Crescent (443 5111), Sheikh Jasim bin Jaber Al Thani Charity Association (441 1011) and Sheikh Eid bin Muhammad Al Thani Charity Association (487 8061).

Business Groups & Contacts

The Qatar British Business Forum was set up in 1992 as a means for business people to meet up and share their knowledge with one another. They meet on a regular basis to discuss business developments and opportunities in Qatar. For more information call 487 4548 or visit www.qbbf.com.

The American Business Council of Qatar is a similar operation, with the aim of improving relations between the two countries and maximising business opportunities. For details call 483 6389 or visit www.abcgc.org/regmem/qatar for a list of contacts.

Other groups around Qatar are more social and you can find out about them through word of mouth. These types of organisations are a good way of making contacts, especially if you are in the market for a new job.

Employment Contracts

The employment contract (service contract) must be in writing and attested by the Labour Department. There will be three copies of the contract: one for the Labour Department and one each for the employee and employer.

The contract should include the following details:

- Name of employer and place of work
- Name, qualification, nationality, profession, address and ID of employee
- Expiry date of contact

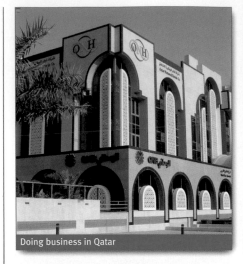
Doing business in Qatar

- Work duties and place of employment
- Commencement date of contract
- Duration of contract
- Salary and date and method of payment
- Probation period, if applicable

All benefits should be included in your contract (flights, leave, medical insurance, etc). If a woman has worked with the company for a full year, she will be entitled to maternity leave. This leave is for a period of 50 days (for expat women) with full pay. Nursing mothers are entitled to an hour a day for the first year, to go home and feed their babies.

Labour Law

The Ministry of Civil Service Affairs and Housing has a Labour Department that can give you invaluable advice on labour laws. You can also get a copy of the labour law book from this Ministry. Because of the complexity of the labour laws, if you are involved in a labour dispute, it would be advisable to seek the advice of a lawyer.

In Qatar employers may dismiss an employee without warning in certain circumstances. If the offence is not a serious one, the employer has to give the employee one written warning before the employee may be dismissed. The employee has the right to appeal to his employer within seven days and if his appeal is rejected, the Ministry will decide upon the appeal within a further seven days. Their ruling is final. Committees may be formed within companies, but only for Qatari nationals.

An employee has the right to the following public holidays: three days for Eid Al Fitr, three days for Eid Al Adha, and one day on Independence Day. A further three additional days may be given if announced by the government. A Muslim employee is entitled to 20 extra days, without pay, to go on the Haj (a religious pilgrimage to Mecca in Saudi Arabia).

Employees are entitled to three weeks of annual leave if they have been with the company for less than five years, and four weeks if they have been there for more than five years. Most international companies allow four weeks of annual leave after one year of service.

Sick leave is granted after three months of employment and consists of the first two weeks on full pay and a further four weeks on half pay.

Male employees are entitled to two days paternity leave for the birth of each child.

'Banning'

An employer is allowed to 'ban' an employee for a period of two years. This means that they can prevent an employee from working for any other company or getting their sponsorship to work in Qatar until your ban period is over. There isn't really much you can do if your employer does not give you a release letter, which is a compelling reason to stay on good terms with your employer. If you leave the company on amicable terms, it should not be much of a problem for you to transfer onto the new company's sponsorship, providing you have the release letter from your previous employer. This rule is currently under review.

Meeting

Local business, like in most Arab countries, is done at a more leisurely pace than you may be used to, which may be frustrating at first. Local businessmen like to do business in person, not over the telephone or via e-mail. You will need to check that appointment dates and times are still valid, but even so, be prepared for meetings to be cancelled at the last moment, sometimes without any notification to you.

Try to make sure that you remember the names of contacts, which may be difficult as many local men will be dressed the same, with similar sounding names! Eye contact is very important in the Arab world, much can be read in a person's eyes. Learning a few words in Arabic would be an excellent ice-breaker.

When conducting business in Qatar, you will require lots of business cards as they are a popular way of introducing yourself and you will find yourself handing them out continuously. If you are given someone's card, make sure to look at it and take time to read it as they make take offense if you just casually shove it into your pocket.

When making small talk, try to avoid inquiring about family matters as this is not a subject to discuss with strangers. Rather concentrate on sport, such as football or the upcoming Asian Games which Qatar is proudly hosting.

Before business commences, you may be offered something to drink. Make sure you accept something, even if it is a glass of water, as a sign of respect.

It is important not to promise anything that you might not be able to deliver. The spoken word is very significant and can be just as binding as a

Some new buildings reflect the past

written contract. Try to keep contracts simple and clear and keep all business dealings to yourself as confidentiality is invaluable.

Try to remember that, at the end of the day you are in a foreign country and any relationship in such a small, close-knit community, either pleasant or unpleasant, is bound to have an effect on your future dealings.

Company Closure

Be very careful when accepting a job with a recently launched company, especially if it is a small establishment. If the company closes down and doesn't pay you, you could end up with a major problem. If you are unfortunate enough to land in such a situation, the best advice is to contact a lawyer who will be able to advise you on the best solution to the predicament.

Financial & Legal Affairs

Bank Accounts

Qatar has a number of banks, operating mainly in Doha. There are seven Qatari owned banks (Al Ahli Bank, Commercial Bank of Qatar, Doha Bank, Grindlays Qatar Bank, Qatar National Bank, Qatar Islamic Bank and Qatar International Islamic Bank) and seven foreign banks (Arab Bank, Bank Sederat Iran, HSBC, Mashreq Bank, BNP Paribas, Standard Chartered and United Bank).

Standard banking facilities are available at most banks, including current and savings accounts, loans, credit cards, transfers (with reasonable fees), credit and debit cards, and exchange facilities. If you are paid in foreign currency, such as US dollars, you may be able to open an account in that currency.

Most banks are open from 07:00 to 13:00 Sunday to Thursday, although some also open in the afternoons. Certain banks have branches in shopping centres that tend to open a bit later in the morning and close later in the afternoon. Qatar National Bank has branches in the City Center and The Mall, which are also open on Fridays and Saturdays. There are a large number of ATMs scattered around Doha, representing all the major banks.

For contact details of the main banks see the table on p.29.

Financial Planning

The majority of expats living in Qatar will have some sort of saving scheme, usually offshore. Your stay in Qatar is the perfect opportunity to save, as most people don't pay for their accommodation and there is no personal income tax. Most international banks and some of the local banks have financial planners who will be happy to meet with you and discuss your options. Alternatively you can contact either Lloyds TSB or Barclays Bank in Dubai, who offer offshore financial schemes in the Isle of Man, Jersey and Guernsey. Qatar Financial Centre has recently opened and it is sure to have a wide range of facilities for financial planning. International companies may offer a pension scheme, but alternatively, QFC is sure to endorse companies that will be able to advise you.

Many expats look after their finances via the internet, and most large banks (both local and international) now offer internet banking. If you're considering buying a property in one of Qatar's new developments, The Commercial Bank of Qatar and Qatar National Bank both offer mortgages to expat buyers.

Cost of Living	
Beer (pint)	QR 20
Camera film (36 exp)	QR 8
Camera film processing (36 exp, colour)	QR 35
Cappuccino	QR 13
Car rental (daily)	QR 80
Chocolate bar	QR 2
Cigarettes (pack of 20)	QR 5.50
Cinema ticket	QR 30
Eggs (6) imported	QR 15
Eggs (6) local	QR 3
Fresh fruit cocktail	QR 10
Golf (18 holes, non-member)	QR 450
House wine (bottle)	QR 100
House wine (glass)	QR 25
Loaf of bread	QR 5
Milk (2 litres)	QR 8.50
Postcard	QR 2
Salon haircut (female)	QR 80
Salon haircut (male)	QR 70
Shawarma	QR 3
Takeaway burger	QR 10
Taxi (airport to city)	QR 15
Tin of tuna	QR 3.50
Water 1.5 litres (restaurant)	QR 12
Water 1.5 litres (supermarket)	QR
Whole roast chicken	QR 10

Choose your financial goals

we'll go the extra mile

www.standardchartered.com/qa

At Standard Chartered, we believe human endeavour knows no bounds. The spirit of achievement drives us towards success. We see problems as challenges, and challenges as opportunities. The highest goals are those we set for ourselves. And our ultimate goal is your financial success.

Call 465 8555

Standard
Chartered

Taxation

A huge benefit to living and working in this part of the world is the fact that there is no income tax. However, you are taxed on the purchase of alcohol – a whopping 17.5% when drinking in bars and restaurants.

Legal Issues

The legal system in Qatar is based on civil law. A new constitution came into effect on June 7 2005, and it allows for three divisions in the judiciary system. The divisions are the Al Shour Council, the legislative authority (where 30 members are appointed by votes and 15 are appointed by the Emir – the Emir himself is to take up the executive authority with advice from the Council of Ministers and the courts, which will be the judicial authority.

Qatar's legal system used to be based on Sharia law, which has its roots firmly in Islam. The court system was recently restructured and has brought together Sharia and civil courts to form a court called the Court of Cassation, which is the highest court in the country. There are two other levels of court, namely Courts of the First Instance and Courts of Appeal.

> **Under the Influence**
>
> *The penalty for drinking and driving is between one and six months in prison and a fine of between QR 1,000 and QR 6,000. There is no excuse for driving under the influence of alcohol in Qatar because taxis are cheap, plentiful and will get you home to bed in no time at all!*

All court proceedings are generally in Arabic. Laws in Qatar are strictly applied and there are certain crimes for which there is zero tolerance, such as possession of drugs. Few crimes are reported in the media, which leads one to mistakenly believe that no crime exists in Qatar. The best advice is to obey the laws and stay out of trouble as far as possible!

Law Firms

Al Kabbi Law Firm	443 6222
Arab Law Bureau	483 0202
Behzad Law Office	466 0333
Intl. Office for Advocacy &Legal Consul	435 7779
Law Offices of Abdulla Fakhrook	444 6749
Law Offices of Dr Najeeb Al Nauimi	431 1124
Law Offices of Mohsin Makki	442 0017
Patton Boggs Llp	447 8300
Rouhani & Partners	442 5815
Simmons & Simmons	483 9466

Housing

Doha offers a couple of housing options; there are individual villas, compounds and apartments available to rent. The majority of properties can be rented fully furnished. Most apartment blocks have security and maintenance. However, there are not that many good apartment blocks and those that are available tend to be expensive. Many do not have facilities such as a pool or gym. There are plenty of compounds all over Doha, but the good ones tend to have long waiting lists. Certain companies rent a number of houses in various compounds, so you may be lucky enough to get into a reasonable compound. Most compounds are equipped with facilities such as a swimming pool and gym, and the larger ones may have tennis courts, children's play areas, clubhouses and even small supermarkets. Individual houses are also available in different areas around Doha and some are stunning, with lovely finishes. There are many newly built villas and plenty still under construction. Various property developments, that will be available for purchase by expats, are already being built.

Renting in Qatar

Most internationally recruited staff have their accommodation paid for by their employers. Some companies give employees an allowance to find their own house and others will have a number of villas already rented for you to choose from, which means you can bypass the long waiting lists on popular compounds. Most people stay in Doha, although there are a few large compounds in Al Khor, which is about a one-hour drive from Doha. Low-rental, government-owned properties are not available for rental to expats.

Most newcomers tend to use real estate agents to help find a place to live. Going it alone might mean driving around in circles for ages, and when you do find somewhere suitable you may not be able to find out who to contact, or find yourself negotiating with someone with very little English. Agents will know which houses are available and whether or not the price is right. The landlord usually pays the agent a commission of one month's rent.

Renting directly from a landlord can reduce the rent, but it may be more of a hassle than it is worth in the long run. Getting any maintenance work done may be very difficult, so make sure you have a contact number for someone to do

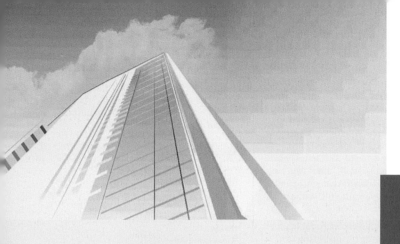

The Wall
REAL ESTATE

Property Investment And Management

Hard To Search?

Our goal is to make things a easy on our customers a possible. We have a superio property management servic which is able to do everythin required to keep you property leased, maintained and up to proper state an local safety codes. If you property needs to b maintained, cleaned, need new carpet, paint or mino and major repairs, we have th resources needed to get the jo done. There is no job too bi or too small. Let us impres you with our professiona services and courteou attitude.

Also we specializes in helpin property owners lease thei property. We take the stres out of leasing. We will show the property for you and mak sure the person leasing th property is qualified. We als have access to full servic maintenance and cleaning fo your maintenance needs to ge the property ready to leas You will be free to go abou your daily life, while we tak care of getting your propert leased.

ephone. +974 4553241 - 4553240 - 4665002
. +974 4665001   P.O.Box 22559   Doha - State Of Qatar

the maintenance in case you cannot contact your landlord.

Rent is paid for the period of your contract, usually in the form of postdated cheques. Most rental contracts are for one year, but you can request a longer lease, which will prevent your rent from increasing after one year. It is possible to negotiate the rental price with the landlord, especially if you pay for the entire year's rental with one cheque. However, don't be surprised if, after you have negotiated a price, the landlord changes his mind and increases it again; even after the contract has been signed!

If you are looking for shared accommodation, look out for ads on noticeboards in supermarkets or in the classified section of the local newspapers.

No Rent Control

Rents in Doha have recently gone through the roof. There is no official control over the rents, so landlords can basically do as they please. Some rents have increased by over half the price in only six months. Many landlords will quote one price when you meet them to look at the property and then, a couple of hours later, will increase the rent by a couple of thousand riyals. Finding a house can be very frustrating and tedious - be warned!

Neither electricity nor water is included in any of the contracts, and you will receive a monthly bill.

Always check that air conditioning units are included in the rent when looking for a villa, as some landlords do not install them and it can be an expensive item for you to buy.

Some apartment blocks have a no-pet rule and it is best to check with your landlord beforehand if you wish to have animals in the apartment. Landlords of individual villas may stipulate that dogs are not allowed, but this is not common.

Villa living

Real Estate Agents

You can rent accommodation through any of the estate agents in Doha. Word of mouth is a good way of finding out which ones are best for helping you find what you are looking for.

Real Estate Agents	
Adam Real Estate	441 5144
Ahmed Hassan Bilal	442 8877
Al Mana Real Estate	462 1222
Al Muftah Services	432 8100
Appollo	468 9522
Homes 2 Rent	438 3807
Jumbo Real Estate	435 7200
Manazil Real Estate	435 5154
Moon Real Estate	436 2719
The Specialists P.55	436 3990
The Wall Real Estate P.53	466 5002
XPO Real Estate	442 6977

The Lease

The lease should be in English, so insist on an English translation if one is not provided. Don't sign anything which is in Arabic, always have it translated. Most lease agreements will be signed by the company, unless you pay for your own rent. If your company signs the lease, they will attach a copy of the company's commercial registration and a copy of the sponsor's ID. If you sign your own contract, then you will need to attach a copy of your ID and your sponsor's ID.

The normal notice period is two months prior to expiry date on the contract.

To renew your lease, the landlord will issue a new contract to be signed and then payment will be made as agreed between both parties.

Main Accommodation Options

The most popular form of accomodation in Doha is a villa in a compound, but unfortunately the most popular compounds have long waiting lists. As a new resident you do have an advantage as you will be able to offer immediate occupancy, where as others on the waiting list may have an existing lease that requires a notice period. Larger compounds offer swimming pools, tennis and squash courts, childrens play areas and small supermarkets. The majority of the larger compounds do not rent through real estate agents

the specialists
complete home solutions

Tel: 3312662

Relocating to Dubai?

It's time to talk to **the specialists**

Our dedicated team of Specialists provide a complete range of services ready to assist companies, employees and families moving to Dubai. Established since 1998 we offer a personalised and unique service focusing on the successful transition and integration of relocatees into their new environment. With over 29 years of first hand experience of living in the Gulf we will ensure your move to Dubai is a welcoming experience. The Specialists will turn your house into a home, introduce to you the local culture and provide an after care service that is unrivalled.

Real Estate
Sales, leasing, management, development

Relocation Services
Orientation programmes, school and home search, cultural training

Home Furnishings
Upholstery, soft furnishings, curtains

Property Management
Facility Care

Property Maintenance
Plumbing, electrical, handy-man services

Suite 102, White Crown Building, Sheikh Zayed Road, PO Box 44644, Dubai, UAE
T +971 4 331 2662 **F** +971 4 331 2004 **E** info@thespecialistsdubai.com

UAE · Qatar · Kuwait · Oman · Bahrain

www.thespecialistsdubai.com

as they have waiting lists, so word of mouth is the best way of finding out about any villas that may be available. However, they won't be available for long! There are new compounds coming onto the market regularly but most do not offer the same ammenities as the large, older compounds. Many of the new compounds are much smaller and only offer a small communal swimming pool and little in the way of private gardens.

The alternative is an individual villa, and in general you will be able to get more house for your money. Some villas have a private swimming pool; check the lease to see who is responsible for the upkeep of the pool as this can get expensive.

Many expats are finding the rent increases to villas are taking them out of their price range, leaving apartments as the alternative. Again though, rental prices for apartments are increasing at the same rate if not faster than villas.

With the spiralling rents, don't be surprised if you find a property only to be told that the asking price has been increased. Accomodation is not exclusive to each real estate agency and it is not uncommon for someone to offer more than the original asking price.

When scouring the accommodation advertisements, these are some of the common abbreviations you may come across:

D/S - Double storey, F/F - Fully Furnished, S/F - Semi Furnished (with a/c and perhaps kitchen appliances), S/P - Swimming pool, Split A/C - airconditioning units on wall, U/F - Unfurnished

Residential Areas

Other options → Exploring p.86

As with other cities around the world, the price of accommodation depends as much on the location as on the age or state of the property.

This section gives brief details of some of the main residential areas in Doha. In addition to the areas listed, apartments are available in the Najma, Mumtaza and Al Mansour areas, with Najma probably being the cheapest.

Airport Area / Al Hilal

Probably the least popular area as it is the most densely populated. It is also the least convenient for those commuting into town, and access to the majority of schools is not as easy as from other areas.

The monthly rent for an unfurnished apartment with two bedrooms would be around QR 4,000, with three bedrooms costing QR 4,500. A

furnished apartment with two bedrooms would be QR 5,000 and three bedrooms QR 6,000. Unfurnished villas with three bedrooms go for around QR 9,000, and four bedrooms for QR 11,000. Furnished villas cost QR 12,000 for three bedrooms and QR 13,000 for four.

Dafna / West Bay

This area is considered to be the most desirable in Doha, with some virtual palaces available and QR 35,000 a month price tags to go with them! Access to DESS and downtown Doha is convenient but the trip to Doha College and the American School could be 30 minutes.

Unfurnished apartments with two bedrooms go for QR 5,000, and three bedrooms QR 5,600. For furnished apartments you could add up to QR 2,000 per month to that figure. Unfurnished villas with three bedrooms are in the region of QR 11,500, four bedrooms QR 16,000; and furnished villas with three bedrooms QR 15,000 and four bedrooms QR 19,000.

Salwa Road

Doha continues to expand and the natural direction is along Salwa Road. Both individual and compound villas are under construction, some of the most desirable large compounds are also located in this area. Local ammenities are good and access to Doha College and the American School is convenient. Access to DESS and downtown Doha is less convinient during rush hour with commutes of up to 30 minutes – a long commute for a Doha resident! Rents are just a little less than those in West Bay, but obviously depend a great deal on the individual property.

The above prices are approximate and of course depend on a variety of factors including available facilities. Also, as rents seem to be constantly increasing you may find them to be significantly more expensive when you go house hunting.

Other Rental Costs

Most companies pay for accommodation, which means they usually pay the deposits required for various utilities. The deposit for electricity and water is QR 2,000. Security deposits for rented accommodation are one month's rent. Qtel charges a monthly line rental of QR 100, which they charge three months in advance.

Commissions for real estate agents are paid by the landlord; usually one month's rent.

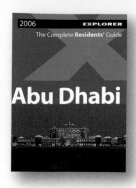

Life is for the Living, and the Living is Easy.
Complete Residents' Guides

Phone (971 4) 335 3520 · **Fax** (971 4) 335 3529
Info@Explorer-Publishing.com · www.Explorer-Publishing.com
Residents' Guides · Visitors' Guides · Photography Books · Activity Guidebooks · Maps

EXPLORER
Passionately Publishing...

Maintenance is usually taken care of by the landlord. If you live in an apartment or on a compound it is easier to get maintenance work done. If you live in an individual villa, it may be more difficult. If you rent directly from the landlord, you can expect to wait a considerable time for maintenance work to be carried out, if it ever gets done! Try to get the landlord to commit to a company that can carry out routine maintenance work. This way, if he is unavailable, you have a contact number for someone to help.

The garden, if you have one, is the tenant's responsibility. The water charges are not that expensive in Qatar, so it doesn't cost a fortune for the upkeep of a garden. Qataris don't seem that keen on gardens, so the majority of the properties have either interlocking bricks or tiles instead of grass. Most landlords will allow you to lift the tiles and plant greenery if you wish, but this can work out to be rather pricey, especially if you have a large outside area.

Purchasing a Home

Buying a property in a foreign country always carries an element of risk. If you are serious about buying a property in Qatar, it is important to do your research. It is also advisable to consult a lawyer with regard to the contract before signing anything.

Remember that only Qatari nationals may buy undeveloped land to build on.

The Pearl is the largest real estate project in Qatar that offers freehold properties to non-nationals and it should be ready for the first investors to take up residency by early 2007. More development projects are currently in the planning stages.

Constructing the future

If you are interested in purchasing a property on the Pearl, you should contact United Development Company (446 3444). Their office is on the second floor of Al Fardan Centre on Grand Hamad Street. The sales team will be happy to give you a presentation on the project and answer any queries that you may have. With the purchase of a property on the Pearl, the buyer will be given a residence visa for himself and his dependants until the resale of the property. For resale, UDC have first refusal, and if they opt not to buy it back from you you can sell the property yourself or advertise through a real estate company. There is a 2.5% management fee if you choose to resell the property.

Once you have purchased the property, you may rent it out if you wish.

Mortgages

When buying a house on the Pearl (currently the only project in Qatar where non-nationals may purchase property), Qatar National Bank (440 7407) and the Commercial Bank of Qatar (449 0000) can arrange mortgages for you. Either bank will assist you in getting a mortgage suitable to your needs and will be able to assist you with any queries once you have chosen your property. It's likely that other banks will also offer mortgages in the future. For contact details see the table on p.29

Other Purchasing Costs

Be sure to check for other (hidden) costs when purchasing a property in Qatar. There is a maintenance fee, which is QR65 per square metre and is paid on an annual basis.

Real Estate Law

Buying property for expats is a new venture for both the developer and the investor. United Development Company is planning to open a division to deal with all queries regarding legal proceedings when buying a property. More advice is available on their website – www.thepearlqatar.com.

It would be advisable to have a will written, if you haven't already got one, when you purchase a house. The houses on the Pearl are freehold leases, so a valid will would ensure that, should anything happen to you, your property is allocated according to your wishes.

Housing options in Qatar

Moving Services

There are numerous moving companies available in Doha. The prices vary, with some being quite reasonable while others seem a bit pricier. However, this is one area where the old saying is true: you get what you pay for! Your best bet would be to get a couple of quotes from various companies. Many international employers will pay for your relocation and may have a particular moving company that they prefer to deal with.

For local moves you could pack your belongings yourself and hire a truck, which can be found in the Najma Souk area. However, with this option you are taking a risk, because if something is broken en route, your items won't be insured.

Removal and Relocation Companies

Allied Pickfords **P.61**	466 7100
Crown Relocations **P.41**	462 1115
Gulf Agency Company (GAC) **P.63**	431 5222
Inchcape Shipping Services	432 9810
International Freight Services (IFS) **P.61**	466 7100
Overseas Cargo	435 8469
Qatar Logistics **P.36**	455 0991
Royal Cargo Services	431 5515

Furnishing Accommodation

Other options → Home Furnishings & Accessories **p.162** Second-Hand Items **p.168**

Many rented houses in Doha come furnished with all main items. Some houses come semi-furnished, which usually means with kitchen appliances (cooker, fridge, washing machine). It could also mean with air conditioners although some houses are rented without any air conditioners and it is wise to check this before you sign any contracts.

Doha has lots of furniture shops if you need to furnish your house yourself (refer to the Shopping section on p.162 for the best places to shop for furniture). Unfortunately, Doha doesn't have an IKEA (yet!), but it does have ID Design, which is very similar.

The majority of international companies will give employees an allowance to buy their own furniture, which then becomes their own after two years' service. Other companies will give employees a relocation allowance to spend on whatever they wish. A few companies will allow employees to choose from a selection of furniture that they already have in storage.

People in Doha seem to arrive and leave all the time, so there are a number of second-hand furniture sales. Some people put up lists on noticeboards in supermarkets and schools, and others have garage sales. Both are an excellent way of picking up furniture at bargain prices.

There are places where you can get furniture manufactured to your specifications, but the furniture does not always turn out exactly as you would want, so be careful. It is a good idea to ask around and go somewhere that has been recommended.

Lulus and Carrefour have a wide range of household appliances and most items are reasonably priced. You may find second-hand appliances from people who are leaving the country, but just be sure to check that they work before you hand over your money. Do some research into current market prices, so that you can be sure that you are actually getting a bargain.

Household Insurance

Although cases of theft from private properties is still rare in Qatar, isolated incidents do occur. It is advisable to buy insurance cover if you have costly household goods and valuables. If you would like your home and contents insured, contact an insurance company and they will guide you through the relevant types of cover and procedures. Qatar Insurance Company is highly recommended.

Al fresco dining area in a compound

moving?

relax.
we carry
the
load. SM

Door to door moving with Allied Pickfords

Allied Pickfords are one of the largest and most respected providers of moving services in the world, handling over 50,000 international moves every year.

We believe that nothing reduces stress more than trust, and each year thousands of families trust Allied Pickfords to move them. With over 800 offices in more than 40 countries, we are the specialists in international moving and have the ability to relocate you anywhere anytime. Move with Allied to Allied worldwide.

In Qatar Allied Pickfords are represented under an exclusive agreement by our Authorised Representatives - International Freight Services.

IFS

www.alliedpickfords.com

Call us now in **Doha** on **466 7100**
or email us at **alliedpickfords.doha@intfrtsvcs.com**

Laundry Services

Although there are no launderettes available to do your own washing, Doha has many laundry shops that offer numerous services. For a very reasonable amount they will do dry cleaning, washing, drying, ironing, and even rug cleaning. You can actually get your shirts ironed for QR 1 each! Some shops offer a home pick-up and delivery service.

Laundries and Dry Cleaners

Al Ahmadi Laundry	Al Sadd	444 1840
Al Rayes Laundry	Al Messila	480 5965
Dawn Laundry	Musheirib	442 5535
Nasco	Al Matar Al Qadeem	466 1924
Oasis Laundry	Al Hitmi Al Jadeed	486 0983

Domestic Help

Other options → Entry Visa p.40

One of the advantages of living in the Middle East is the ease with which you can hire someone to help you with your household chores. The majority of expat families in Doha have domestic help.

There are a few agencies that can assist you to find a live-in housemaid. The advantage of using an agency is that, if for some reason your maid does not work out, they will send her back to her home country and provide you with a replacement at no extra cost, as long as it is within six weeks. Agencies also sort out all of the visa procedures, which can be daunting if you try to do it on your own.

If you would like to hire a housemaid, you have to get a no objection letter from your sponsor. Single men may not have a live-in maid and a no objection letter will only be given once the spouse has her Residence Visa. Once the no objection letter has been issued, you can start the residence visa procedure, medical testing and fingerprinting of the maid. Once the visa has been issued you are responsible for your maid's welfare and behaviour.

Alternatively, you could find a maid through word of mouth. Some expat families advertise a vacancy for a maid in the local newspaper. When expats are leaving, they often advertise their maid's qualities in order to help her find a new job. This is a useful way of finding someone with good references.

Domestic Help Agencies

Al Baidha Cleaning Co.	469 2696
Jassim Decoration & Services	447 7305
Rose Services & General Cleaning Company	469 7711

A maid's salary often depends on her nationality. Filipinos are usually paid between QR 1,500 and QR 1,800 per month, while Sri Lankan and Indian ladies tend to be paid between QR 800 and QR 1,200 per month. Most expats will subsidise the housemaid's pay by buying food and clothing.

Babysitting & Childcare

If you live on a compound, finding someone to look after your children will be easy. There may be several live-in maids who want to earn extra money, or teenagers who may be interested in babysitting. Most expats don't mind their maid helping out if they don't need her themselves. Some of the domestic help agencies also offer a babysitting service.

There are mother and baby groups that may be able to help you with childcare options. Some of the nurseries accept young babies. Most expats have maids who look after their children if the need arises. Most maids do not have formal qualifications, but may have experience with children from a previous job. Many housemaids have children of their own, but have left them in their own country while they earn money in Qatar. It may be possible to get a professional child carer who has come to Doha with her husband, but generally there isn't a demand for them as people can get the services of a maid for a lot less than they would have to pay a nanny. If you insist on having a professional nanny, an option would be to bring one over from your home country. Hotels offer babysitting if you fancy a night away at one of the many hotels in Qatar.

Shopping centres and gyms do not have crèche facilities, as there is not a huge demand for such services.

Doha has a number of nursery schools; see the nursery school section on p.76 for more details.

Domestic Services

There are a few options you can try when looking for plumbers, electricians or carpenters. The streets around the Najma area have a number of carpenters who will be able to assist you. There are quite a few small businesses on Al Arabiya Street where you can locate electricians and plumbers. If you live on a compound, they will either provide someone to do the maintenance work for you, or give you a number to contact. Alternatively, ask around for recommendations.

GAC Qatar International Moving
Quality, Reliability, Flexibility

Relocation in itself is a challenge. And we believe that you already have enough to do without worrying about your forthcoming move. That's why when it comes to moving your home or office, GAC treats each item with care and every move with pride.

With more than 30 years of experience in moving household goods in and out of the Middle East, GAC provides comprehensive, high quality door-to-door services for any relocation need. Moves are professionally planned, starting with a free initial survey and recommendations on the most efficient shipment mode. All necessary services, including professional export packing, custom built crating, forwarding and secure storage facilities, are also provided.

 www.gacworld.com

GAC Qatar P.O.B 6534. Doha, State of Qatar
Tel +974 431 5222   Fax +974 431 4222   Email moving.qatar@gacworld.com

Pets

It is possible to bring your pets with you to Qatar. However, the Government has a list of forbidden dog breeds that are not allowed into the country. You can ensure that your dog is not one of the forbidden breeds by obtaining a list from the Ministry of Agriculture (443 4040) or the Government Veterinary Clinic (465 3083). Cats and dogs must have all vaccinations up to date and must be vaccinated against rabies.

In order to bring your animals into the country, you will have to obtain an import permit, which you can get at the Ministry of Agriculture (office near Parachute Roundabout, on Airport Road). You will require a health certificate issued by a reputable vet in your home country and the animal's vaccination record. You need to get the health certificate no earlier than two weeks before the animal is going to be imported into Qatar.

Shipping agencies can arrange the documents for the import of animals in two weeks. It may be easier to use their services than doing it yourself. The shipping agency will ask you to supply the following documents: health certificate, vaccination record, photos (if it is a dog), passport copies of the owners and flight details or airway bill.

Some airlines allow animals to travel as cargo or on the same flight as their owners as an accompanied pet. You will have to check with the airline office in your country of origin. Your pet will be released after customs clearance; there is no quarantine requirement in Qatar.

Purchasing a dog or cat in Qatar is not recommended as the standards of pet shops are not very high and many of the animals may be sick or undernourished when you buy them.

There are many stray animals which have been dumped by their owners when they leave Qatar and there are a few rescue organizations for cats and dogs, such as the Animal Rescue Kennels (551 1769), Qatar Animal Welfare Society (528 6335), and Pampered Pets Kennels & Cattery (588 4132).

The above organisations will also be able to assist you with boarding kennels for your pets when you go on holiday.

Veterinary Clinics	
Animal Care Center	487 7144
Bustan Veterinary Care	436 0052
Government Veterinary Clinic	465 3083
The Veterinary Surgery	468 4391

You are allowed to walk your pets on empty land around buildings and villas, but animals are not allowed into parks or on beaches.

To take your pets back home with you, they need to be vaccinated against rabies and have all their vaccinations up to date. EU countries require a blood test to show that the vaccinations have been effective. Some countries will require the animals to be de-wormed and have tick and tapeworm treatments before they arrive. Check the regulations of the country to which you are taking your pet.

You need to get a health certificate seven days before the animal is due to travel. This can be done at the government veterinary clinic, free of charge. Remember to take your pet's updated vaccination record.

Pet Boarding/Sitting	
Animal Care Center	487 7144
Animal Rescue Kennels	551 1769
Pampered Pets	588 4132

Once you have the health certificate, you will have to take it to the Qatar National Travel office (QNT), which is located at the airport cargo section (462 6900). You will have to book flights and pay the amount in full, including handling fees, before they issue the airway bill. This needs to be done five days before you want the animal to travel.

Make sure you have a suitable travel kennel that is approved by the airline.

Remember that the health certificate needed for exporting an animal is only valid for one week and the travel arrangements have to be made five days prior to departure.

Man's best friend

Utilities & Services

Electricity & Water

The Qatar Electricity and Water Department is the sole distributor of water and electricity. When you rent accommodation make sure the electricity and water are connected before you move in. This is easily done if your company or the real estate agency doesn't arrange it for you.

Top Tap Tip

In the summer months it is impossible to get cold water out of the taps. Fill the bath with water in the morning and by the evening it will have cooled down, then all you have to do is top it up with hot water to get just the right temperature.

You will find the reference number on the outside wall of your villa. For apartments, ask the building management where to locate it. This number, together with a no objection letter from your sponsor and a copy of his ID; an application form signed by the same person who signed the lease, a copy of the lease and a security deposit of QR 2,000 (QR 1,200 for electricity and QR 800 for water) must be taken to one of the Kahramaa (Electricity and Water) offices.

Bills are sent out every month. For the first five months the bills are estimates and from the sixth month an actual meter reading will be taken. This is known as a reconciliation bill and is generally higher than the estimates. Apartment bills tend to be between QR 200 and QR 400 and villas tend to be between QR 800 and QR 1,000.

You can pay your bill online at www.kahramaa.com, by telephone on 465 1100, at any of the banks in Doha, or at the Customer Service Centre. Customer Service Centre contact numbers are: Doha Centre: 462 8373, Salwa Centre: 469 3764, Post Office: 483 1876.

The voltage in Qatar is 240 volt and the sockets are three-pin, although most appliances you buy will have two-pin plugs! So, stock up on adaptors.

Tap water is safe to drink, but most expats drink mineral water, which you can either buy from the supermarket in boxes or have delivered to your residence in five-gallon bottles. The five-gallon bottles can either be used with a water cooler or a pump.

Water Suppliers	
Al Manhal	460 3332
Rayyan Mineral Water Co.	487 7664
Safa International	460 6699

Sewerage

Most houses are connected to the main sewerage system. Many of the new houses have been built in areas which are not yet connected to the main sewerage system; these houses will have septic tanks wich will be emptied on a regular basis.

Gas

There is no mainline gas in Qatar, so if you have a gas cooker, you will have to use gas cylinders that will be delivered to your residence. The gas cylinders cost QR 140 for the first time and thereafter QR 35 for a refilled cylinder. Initial payment is more expensive as you have to pay for the cylinder. It can be fairly difficult to get the gas from the trucks delivering the cylinders as they do not carry mobiles. This means you must listen carefully for them and catch their attention as they drive past.

Gas Suppliers	
Ahmed Al Rayes for Gas	465 1555
Mashahdi Gas Co.	442 3016
Qatar Gas Import and Distributing Co.	442 1892

Rubbish Disposal and Recycling

Usually villas have a green bin outside their gates, applied for by the landlord. Garbage trucks come round and collect the rubbish a number of times a week, depending on which area you live. If you live in an apartment, they will have garbage chutes which are emptied by the municipality garbage trucks. All rubbish is taken to a landfill, which is located about an hour's drive outside the city.

There are no recycling systems in place in Qatar yet.

Telephone

Qatar Public Telecommunications Corporation (Qtel) is the exclusive telephone company in Qatar. Your sponsor can apply for your telephone line once you have your residence visa, or you can visit a Qtel service centre yourself to fill in the application. You'll need a copy of your ID card. Make sure you apply for an ADSL internet connection at the same time, if you require one.

Local phone calls (landline to landline) are free, while calls made to or from mobiles are charged at reasonable rates. International calls can be made at reduced rates between 19:00 and 07:00 Saturday to Thursday, and all day Friday and on public holidays. For international directory assistance, call 190.

The rental charge for a standard landline is QR 100 per quarter. For bill enquiries call 146, and to pay your bill by credit card over the phone dial 149. Landline customers can opt for additional services including call barring, call waiting, call forwarding, conference calling and caller ID.

Qtel is also the only mobile phone network provider in Qatar. To apply for a postpaid account you can take a letter from your sponsor, or you can pay a deposit instead. There is a one time connection fee of QR 250 plus a monthly rental of QR 50, and customers get access to a number of services including fax, data, and the 'Freedom' package that includes news, entertainment and ringtones. An alternative to postpaid is the 'pay as you go' option called Hala. Hala SIM cards are available at Qtel offices, and the scratch-off recharge cards, with values of QR 30, QR 50 and QR 100, are widely available in shops, supermarkets, and Qtel offices. (These 'Q-Cards' can also be used to make local and international calls from landline phones.) There are two types of Hala SIM cards - Hala Plus and Hala Talk. A Hala Plus SIM card costs QR 300, contains QR 50 of credit, and is initially valid for 360 days (but this can be extended). The Hala Talk SIM card is cheaper at QR 200, and comes with QR 100 of credit, but is valid for only 60 days so is more suited to tourists and short term visitors. Again though, the validity of this card can be extended.

For information on these services and more, visit the Qtel website at www.qtel.com.qa.

Qtel Customer Service Centres	
Airport Post Office	483 9111
Al Khor	472 1122
Al Najada	431 2999
Al Rayyan	480 7111
Al Sadd	440 0123
Al Shamal	472 1170
Al Wakra	464 7711
City Center	483 9111
Hamad Hospital	435 8847
Hyatt Plaza	469 3536
Landmark Mall	486 3923
LuLu Center	465 5073
Mesaieed	477 0269
Musheireb	440 0404
Salwa Road	469 9702
West Bay Post Office	472 1122

Internet

Other options → Websites p.32
Internet Cafes p.202

You can get connected to the internet by applying to Qtel once you have your residence visa. Qtel offers a range of packages and services for internet access, the cheapest of which is the 'Eshtirak' dial-up connection for residential use that costs QR 2 per hour plus a QR 20 monthly fee. You will need a letter from your sponsor and it is a good idea to apply for the internet connection at the same time as you apply for your landline telephone. Qtel will provide you with a password and a user name, and will also install the necessary software onto your computer, so make sure you have your computer available when they come to install the internet. ISDN and ADSL are also available. There is a new high speed ADSL service (called barQ ADSL) with the following package options: 256 Kbps (five times faster than normal dial-up), which costs QR 200 per month; 512 Kbps (10 times faster) which costs QR 300; and 1 Mbps (20 times faster!) which costs QR 400.

If you subscribe to the new barQ ADSL for a year, you will receive a free modem and free installation, which will save you about QR 500. If you want to upgrade your current ADSL speed, you can submit an ADSL application form to any of the Qtel customer service centres.

It is possible to access the internet without subscribing to any of the above packages, as prepaid dial-up cards (known as Ebhar) can be bought from any of the Qtel customer service centres and a number of shops and supermarkets. These allow users to access the net by plugging a computer into any telephone line – time online is deducted from the prepaid card and not charged to the phone line.

A further option is 161 Instant Internet. Without the need for a subscription, usernames, passwords or special equipment, users simply plug into any phone line and dial 161 from their computer. Surfing on 161 is charged at QR 6 per hour and will appear on the phone bill at the end of the month.

Qtel Wi-Fi HotSpots are cropping up all over the place, mainly in hotels and cafes. Customers with a wireless-enabled laptop, PDA or mobile can buy prepaid HotSpot cards in denominations of QR 30, 50, and 70, allowing them to get online without any wires.

There are several internet cafes scattered around Doha too. They charge around QR 6 per hour. You

can also get 10 minutes free internet access at the main post office.

For details of Qtel's internet packages and up to date charges, and for a current list of HotSpot Wi-Fi locations, visit www.qtel.com.qa.

Bill Payment

Phone bills are paid on a monthly basis in Qatar. You can pay your bills at certain banks (some offer facilities such as telephone banking and direct debit), the Post Office, and Qtel customer service centres. If you miss a bill payment, you will be barred from making any calls until your bill has been settled. Call 146 for bill enquiries.

Postal Services

Other options → Post & Courier Services p.30

You will be able to find the Post Office without too much effort. On Doha's corniche, it is a large building with lots of small arches all around the outside. It has a four-level car park that you have to drive through to get to the main entrance. When you enter the car park, drive straight up the ramps until you reach the top and you will find the entrance into the building on the left-hand side.

Post Office

There are no postmen in Qatar like there are in European countries, but they have recently launched a new delivery service (QPP) for the delivery and collection of important documents. The documents are tracked through all stages of handling and confirmation of delivery is done on the internet.

Post office boxes can be obtained from any post office branch. You need to complete an application form, attach a copy of your ID card and pay the subscription fee. Once this is processed, a box number will be allocated to you. If you apply to the head office you will be given an electronic card to

access your box, other branches use keys. The rental costs for the electronic boxes are :

Small box	QR 205 and QR 145 for renewal
Medium box	QR 235 and QR 175 for renewal
Large box	QR 315 and QR 255 for renewal

Electronic cards will cost QR 60 extra, which you pay when you first get your post box.

For other branches (non-electronic) you are given three keys at a cost of QR 60. The rental costs for these boxes are:

Medium box	QR 165 and QR 105 for renewal
Large box	QR 180 and QR 120 for renewal

Post seems to arrive fairly speedily, although during Ramadan it may take a little longer and during Eid the Post Office will be closed completely.

Television

There are two television channels operated by Qatar Television – Channel One, which is in Arabic and Channel Two, which is mostly in English.

Qtel offers cable television (Qatar Cablevision) which supplies all available networks with one decoder. The MVDS system has a range of programs suitable for both English and Arabic viewers. This system has many channels, including Star, Orbit, ART and Showtime. The other package from Qatar Cablevision is the Combo, which means you can watch all the free satellite channels, together with the MVDS channels, on one decoder. Most expats subscribe to one of these networks. You can subscribe to any of the networks through a number of companies.

Satellite TV & Radio

Orbit offers a wide range of channels, including BBC Prime, America Plus, movie channels, news channels, ESPN, children's channels and many more. They often have promotions which include a free dish, decoder and installation, so check the local press for the latest offers, or visit the Orbit website (www.orbitnet.com). Packages start at QR 129 per month.

Showtime offers a huge selection of channels to suit the whole family. There's sport, news, current programmes, movies and children's channels. Packages start from QR 126 per month. You can subscribe to all the channels for only QR 220 – definitely an option worth looking at.

ART is great for sports and also has a number of English channels. Star has a few English channels, but caters mostly to the Asian community. Channels from all four satellite networks are available on cable vision. There are a number of packages to choose from, starting at QR 60 per month, with the most expensive being QR 110. You can subscribe to as many packages as you want. If you were to subscribe to all the channels, it would cost you about QR 495 per month.

The renowned South African satellite TV option, DSTV, is available, but is not strictly legal. It will cost you about QR 5,000 for the first year and then QR 1,500 every year for a new card. Many expats use this option as it has an amazing selection of sports channels. Hot Bird is also available for a one-time payment of QR 650. However, it does not have many English channels.

Satellite/Cable Providers	
Gulf Security	467 3845
National	441 7575
Orbit	447 7177
Qatar Communications	432 0075
Qatar Multitech	435 3513
Showtime	www.showtimearabia.com
Tradtech	441 0060

Downtown Doha

Health

General Medical Care

Qatar has a wide range of medical facilities, with some of the best specialist doctors in the world practising at one of the medical departments in the Hamad Medical Corporation (Qatar's government hospital). Both government and private sectors have the latest equipment and medical technology available.

There are a number of government health facilities that expats may use if they have a health card. Visitors may also use the clinics and hospitals, but will be charged for the consultations, tests and prescriptions. The government primary health centres are situated in various areas in Qatar (identifiable by what look like lampposts with green hexagons on top). You are supposed to use the clinic closest to your residence. The HMC has four hospitals: Hamad General Hospital, Women's Hospital, Rumailah Hospital and Al Amal Oncology Hospital.

Hamad General Hospital has facilities for surgery, paediatrics, internal diseases, anaesthetics and laboratory work. It also has an A & E department which has a good reputation.

The Women's Hospital is mainly for maternity patients, but they also have an IVF unit and a neonatal intensive care unit, which is the best option for delivery if your baby is born prematurely.

Rumailah Hospital has facilities for plastic surgery, ENT surgery and ophthalmology. It also has a stroke unit and a rehabilitation centre for disabled persons and handicapped children.

Al Amal Hospital is new and is mainly used for tumour diagnosis and cancer treatments. This hospital comes highly recommended and has all the latest equipment needed for early detection and treatment of cancer.

Doha has a number of private clinics and hospitals. The private hospitals are: Al Ahli Hospital, Al Emadi Hospital, the American Hospital and Doha Clinic Hospital.

Al Ahli Hospital was due to open fully by the end of 2005, and is expected to become one of the best private hospitals in Doha. At present they only accept outpatients during clinic hours. The hospital is closed on Fridays, and at the time of writing didn't have an emergency room in operation.

المركز الاستشاري لطب الاسنان
CONSULTANT DENTAL CENTER

طب الأسنان فن نتفوق به ...
Dentistry Is An Art..We Excel In It!

Smile Like A Star

شارع النجمة – الهلال

هاتف : ٩٧٤٤٦٧٧١٦٦،٤٦٧٧١٩٩+ – فاكس : ٩٧٤٤٦٦٥٠٠١+ – صندوق بريد : ٢٢٥٥٩ – الدوحة – ق

Al Emadi Hospital has facilities for eating disorders, general, plastic and reconstructive surgery, dermatology, dental care and maternity.

The American hospital has an emergency room and was the first private hospital to open in 1999.

Doha Clinic Hospital was originally opened as a clinic and, after numerous renovations, has become one of the most popular hospitals among expats in Qatar. They have outpatient as well as inpatient facilities, with a well-equipped x-ray department, maternity ward and emergency room.

Emergency care

Government Hospitals

Al Amal Oncology Hospital	Al Rumaila West	439 7830
Hamad General Hospital	Al Rumaila West	439 4444
Rumailah Hospital	Al Rumaila West	439 2222
Women's Hospital	Al Rumaila West	439 6666

Private Hospitals

Al Ahli Hospital	Bin Omran	489 8888
Al-Emadi Hospital	Al Hilal West	466 6009
American Hospital	Al Hilal West	442 1999
Doha Clinic Hospital	Al Mirqab Al Jadeed	438 4333

The medical facilities are generally of a high standard, although some patients (especially children) may find the staff lack the same kind of 'bedside manner' that they are used to back home.

One of the main reasons people use private clinics rather than government facilities, is that you may have a long wait at the government ones due to the volume of patients. It is not unusual for a patient to wait up to two hours before being able to consult a doctor.

Government Health Centres/Clinics

Abu Baker Clinic	468 1797
Abu Hamour Health Centre	469 1261
Airport Health Care Centre	467 5633
Al Gharrafa Health Centre	486 9969
Al Montaza Health Centre	443 5784
Al Shahaniya Clinic	471 8995
Madinat Khalifa Madinat Health Centre	486 2655
Umm Bab Health Centre	471 1704
West Bay Health Care Centre	483 7788

Private Health Centres/Clinics

Al Ahli Hospital	Bin Omran	489 8888
Al-Emadi Hospital	Al Hilal West	466 6009
American Hospital	Al Hilal West	442 1999
Doha Clinic Hospital	Al Mirqab Al Jadeed	438 4333
Family Medical Centre	Al Mirqab Al Jadeed	431 0707

Dermatologists

Al-Emadi Hospital	466 6009
American Hospital	442 1999
Doha Clinic Hospital	438 4333
Dr Nawal Chaarani - Skin Clinic	4880887

Most international companies have private health insurance cover for employees and their dependants. Nevertheless, you should still get your health card as soon as you have your residence visa.

Pharmacies can help with minor ailments, but it is wise to consult a doctor for more serious complaints. You can buy a surprising range of medicines over the counter, but will need a prescription for antibiotics and stronger medications.

Ambulances may have a difficult time trying to locate an injured person, but have been known to meet victims at well-known landmarks, such as roundabouts. If you are able to transport an injured person yourself, it may be the quicker option, but only do so if the injured person is a friend or family member and you are sure that you will not be causing any further damage by moving them.

Maternity

Other options → Maternity Clothes p.164

Some expats return to their home countries to give birth, but many opt to stay in Doha and deliver. Maternity facilities are good and are improving all the time, so it is no longer necessary for women to travel back home. If you decide to have your baby in Doha, you must first decide in which hospital you want to deliver. The Women's Hospital has a large maternity unit, but because it is a Government Hospital, men are not allowed into the delivery room, a fact that puts most expats off. Doha Clinic is a popular place for expats to deliver. Al Emadi has a maternity unit that is relatively new and is also becoming very popular as the nurses and staff have developed a good reputation. Al Ahli hospital maternity unit was due to open in November 2005.

Typical prices for a normal delivery are QR 4,500 at Al Emadi and QR 4,000 at Doha Clinic. The average cost for a Caesarean delivery is QR 7,500 at Al Emadi and QR 9,000 at Doha Clinic. Doha Clinic charges extra for antenatal check ups, and together with three ultrasounds this amounts to QR 800. Private hospitals charge for many extras, so your bill may end up considerably higher than you anticipated!

At the Women's Hospital, you only have to pay for your room. Costs vary depending on whether you take a private or shared room, but neither option costs more than QR 1,000.

Most health insurers will only cover pregnancy costs if you have subscribed at least nine months prior to falling pregnant. Epidurals are common for pain relief and for elective caesareans (spinal blocks are also available). Qatar law requires that women are married before bearing children, if a woman delivers and is unmarried, she could face serious charges.

Maternity Hospitals & Clinics

Al Ahli Hospital	489 8888
Out patient facilities	
Al-Emadi Hospital	466 6009
Ante natal and post natal care, delivery	
American Hospital	442 1999
Ante natal and post natal care, delivery	
Doha Clinic Hospital	438 4333
Ante natal and post natal care, delivery	
Dr.Amal Badi's clinic	432 4349
Ante and post natal, can deliver at pvt hosp	
Family Medical Centre	431 0909
Ante natal and post natal care, no delivery	
Women's Hospital	439 6666
Ante natal and post natal care, delivery	

Gynaecology & Obstetrics

Al Ahli Hospital	489 8888
Al-Emadi Hospital	466 6009
American Hospital	442 1999
Doha Clinic Hospital	438 4333
Dr.Amal Badi's Clinic	432 4349
Family Medical Centre	431 0909
Women's Hospital	439 6666

Paediatrics

The paediatric department at Hamad Hospital has a very good reputation. The Paediatric Emergency Centre located on the corner of Al Sadd Street (Map Ref 12-E1) is also excellent and has an outpatient section. The nurses are friendly and are very good with children. However, they do not handle trauma cases such as broken bones or deep cuts, so go to either Hamad General Hospital or Doha Clinic for these treatments. The Family Medical Centre located on Al Mirqab Street (Map Ref 12-E2) also has two very good attending paediatricians.

Paediatrics

Al Ahli Hospital	Bin Omran	489 8888
American Hospital	Al Hilal West	442 1999
Doha Clinic Hospital	Al Mirqab Al Jadeed	438 4333
Family Medical Centre	Al Mirqab Al Jadeed	431 0909
Paediatric Emergency Ctr	Al Sadd	431 0909

Dentists/Orthodontists

There are numerous dental clinics in Doha offering various treatments. The dental facilities are of a high standard, with state-of-the-art equipment. As with many services in Doha, the best way to find a good dentist is through word of mouth. Cosmetic dentistry is available at some of the dental clinics, however the prices may be higher than what expats are used to.

Dentists/Orthodontists

American Dental Center	467 5995
Consultant Dental Center p.69	467 7166
Doha Clinic Hospital	438 4333
Dr.Tamim Dental Polyclinic	443 5959
Family Medical Centre	431 0909
German Orthodontics	441 1711
The International Specialist Dental Centre	444 1050

Opticians

Opticians can be found in shopping centres as well as in various other areas. Opticians have a wide range of products available, including an extensive selection of contact lenses, both prescription and fashion. They will also be able to provide you with prescription reading glasses, as well as sunglasses. Doha Clinic has an Ophthalmology Department.

Everyone has to have an eye test when applying for a driving licence, but this test is performed on the premises when you request a licence at the police station.

Opticians		
Al Jabor Vision Technology	Al Muntazah	442 7152
Bahrain Optician	Diplomatic District	483 8848
Magrabi Eye & Ear Center	Wadi El-Sil	486 6148
Optic Gallery	Al Matar Al Qadeem	467 8100
Qatar Optics	Madinat Khalifa	486 6649
Royal Optician	Al Sadd	413 1300
Yateem Optician	Al Sadd	413 1363

Hairdressers

Hairdressers are plentiful and many work at hotels or private clubs. There are also a number of stylists who will come to your home, which is convenient if you have small children or if you want the whole family done at the same time. Ask around as their numbers are usually passed from one satisfied customer to another.

Many expat women use Marie Claire, a beauty salon on Salwa Road which will provide manicures or pedicures at the same time. Their prices are reasonable and most customers seem to be pleased with the results.

Perhaps the most popular beauty salon with expats is the Diplomatic Club Beauty Salon where the general prices range from QR 100 for a cut and blow dry to QR 600 for a cut, colour and blow dry.

There are men's barbers at most hotels, where you will pay between QR 60 and QR 100. However, you can get a cheap and cheerful cut at one of the barbershops in the Najma area, near the second-hand furniture souk, for QR 20.

Children can have their hair cut at salons designed especially for kids. Try the one in City Center (on the third floor near the children's play area), Landmark (in Circus Land) or the Hyatt Plaza (near Jungle Zone). There is no need to make an appointment – they work on a first come, first served basis.

Hairdressers		
Coiffure Francaise	Salwa Road South	468 9211
Diplomatic Club	West Bay	483 9000
Intercontinental Hotel	West Bay	484 4444
Maria	Doha	547 0050
Sheraton Hotel	Diplomatic District	485 4444
Special Touch Beauty Center	Al Mirqab Al Jadeed	441 3801
Studio 1	Al Mirqab Al Jadeed	444 7494

Cosmetic Treatment & Surgery

Cosmetic surgery is not that common in Doha and it might be preferable to travel to a country that has more facilities. Clinics that do have reasonable reputations include Plastic Surgicentre (466 2260) and Euro Clinic (444 0156). With any private clinics not affiliated to a hospital, be sure to check their credentials before you go ahead with any treatments. The Ministry of Health is clamping down on non-qualified practices.

Alternative Therapies

Alternative therapies are available in Doha, although most are not recognised by the Ministry of Health. All homeopathic remedies and treatments have recently been banned in Qatar, but there are a number of expat therapists who work from their homes. Acupuncture (a Chinese healing treatment using needles), reflexology (pressure point treatment) and reiki (a healing form of meditation) are also available. Heather (591 5925) and Karen (574 5799) are both qualified reiki practitioners.

There are various massage parlours scattered around Doha. Hotel spas usually have qualified masseurs.

Acupressure/Acupuncture

The options for acupressure and acupuncture treatment in Doha are limited, with Euro Clinic (444 0156) being one of the few practices to offer it.

Reflexology/Massage Therapy

Other options → Massage p.136

Reflexology/Massage Therapy	
Doha Club	432 9273
Intercontinental Hotel Spa	484 4444
Karen	574 5799
Marriot Hotel Spa	429 8520
Sheraton Hotel Spa	485 4600
The Spa	484 8173

Back Treatment

The Doha Chiropractic Center has qualified chiropractors with good reputations who can assist you with all types of back ailments, such as sciatica, slipped discs and general back pain.

Back Treatment	
Doha Chiropractic Center	465 0012
Dr. Cyrus Nassery	466 3661
Dr.Yasser El Bardini	432 3985

Rehabilitation & Physiotherapy

Anyone with a sports injury can usually be treated at one of the hospitals – they have well-trained therapists and the equipment to deal with most problems.

Rehabilitation & Physiotherapy	
Al Ahli Hospital	489 8888
Al-Emadi Hospital	466 6009
American Hospital	442 1999
Doha Clinic Hospital	438 4333
Hamad General Hospital	439 4444
Pauline	547 8343

Counselling & Therapy

People suffering from any form of mental illness, whether minor or severe, should seek professional help from a psychiatrist or counsellor. Doha has a few counsellors and psychiatrists who work from home. Al Rumaillah Hospital houses Qatar's main psychiatry unit. Many private hospitals also have psychiatrists on their staff. Penny Richardson is a counsellor, therapist and psychotherapist who specialises in marital and family counselling.

Counsellors/Psychologists	
Al Rumaillah Hospital	439 2222
Kimberly Sheedy	571 6816
Penny Richardson	571 4645

Support Groups

New people arriving in Qatar often have difficulty settling down, especially if they have never lived in an Arabic country before. Many people suffer from culture shock and the homesickness can sometimes become too much to handle. One of the best ways of dealing with it is to talk to other people, as most of them will have had similar feelings and the expat community in Doha is very friendly. People will usually be happy to lend you a shoulder to cry on.

If you feel you can't handle things on your own, give one of the following ladies a call. They are both qualified therapists. Kimberley Sheedy, Child and Clinical Psychologist (571 6816) or Penny Richardson, Counselor, Therapist and Psychotherapist (571 4645).

You will find details of support groups on compound noticeboards and through chatting with other people. A particularly good source of community support is the Qatar section of www.expatwoman.com.

Support Groups	
Alcoholics Anonymous	560 5901
Qatar Diabetes Association	487 4310
Qatar National Cancer Society	447 8128
Social Development Center	432 4666

Education

Qatar has numerous schools offering various curriculums to suit many nationalities, including British, American, French, Indian, Filipino, Egyptian and many more. Education is of a high standard in both government and privately owned schools.

The Supreme Education Council is committed to creating a world-class public school system in Qatar. At the heart of its education reform initiative is a network of government-funded Independent Schools that are granted a certain amount of autonomy yet still held accountable to ensure the quality of schooling being offered. These Independent Schools are predominantly for citizens of Qatar, but non-citizens can attend if their parents work in the public sector. There are also numerous private schools catering for other nationalities. Some of these schools are non-profit organizations and are sponsored by their embassies.

If you are moving to Qatar, contact the schools as soon as possible to find out if there are any places available. Some schools have waiting lists, but because Doha's population is a transient one, chances are good that a place will become available sometime during the school year.

When submitting an application form (which can be done by e-mail at some schools), the following documents are required: copy of passport, copy of recent school report, two passport photos and an up-to-date immunisation record. Schools accept students any time through the school year, if a place is available.

Because
their future
is **bright**...

EDUCATION FOR A NEW ERA

Education reform is creating a modern, world-class public school system for Qatar

Every nation wants its children to become engaged citizens, innovative thinkers, and productive members of the workforce.

For the state of Qatar, these aspirations are now rooted in an unprecedented initiative: comprehensive education reform.

At the heart of education reform are autonomous, government-funded schools - known in Qatar as Independent Schools. Today, more than 30 Independent Schools offer new models for curriculum design, teaching methods, and collaboration. They're changing the lives of thousands of Qatari children and families every day.

Education reform means the brightest future for every child - and a strong, competitive future for our entire nation. Reform is still a work in progress. But reform is here to stay.

The Supreme Education Council and its three institutes - the Education Institute, the Evaluation Institute, and the Higher Education Institute - oversee education reform, help it grow, and objectively monitor its progress. Membership in the Council and the Institutes is drawn from Qatar's top leaders in government, business, and academia.

The Supreme Education Council is responsible for education policy in Qatar.

The Education Institute directly oversees the Independent Schools and supports them with professional development for teachers and a wide range of other resources.

The Evaluation Institute develops and conducts periodic assessments of student learning and evaluates school performance.

The Higher Education Institute advises individuals on opportunities for higher education and careers and administers a scholarship program.

...Qatar's future is **bright**

المجلس الأعلى للتعليم

SUPREME
EDUCATION
COUNCIL

تعليم لمرحلة جديدة
Education for a New Era

WHAT MAKES REFORM WORK

Reform is realizing the full potential of Qatar's most precious resource: its children. Working together, Qataris are developing intellectual resources that will rival their nation's natural resources - and create a critical mass of future leaders.

Reform is committed to making Qatari children - and Qatar itself - globally competitive. New rigorous curriculum standards in Arabic, English, mathematics, and science are based on international benchmarks. Children aren't merely memorizing information. They're learning how to be the kind of critical, creative thinkers that the 21st century demands.

Reform is defined by accountability and transparency. All public and private Arabic schools in Qatar are held accountable through regular, objective assessments. These assessments, along with report cards on each school, will be shared with the entire nation.

Reform offers parents a choice and a voice. Over time, parents will be able to choose the best school for their children from a growing number of alternatives. In Independent Schools, parents' input is sought on important school decisions through school meetings and weekly reports.

Reform is ensuring every student has the best post-secondary opportunities. Students will be able to take advantage of career and college counseling, post-secondary education training, and scholarship support—whether they decide to pursue a college education at home or abroad.

Reform classrooms are student-centered. Lively discussions, hands-on learning, and projects that nurture leadership, team-building, and research skills are hallmarks of the classroom experience.

Reform is transforming teachers into true classroom leaders. Independent Schools grant teachers the autonomy to pursue best practices, share ideas, and develop creative approaches to meeting the internationally benchmarked curriculum standards. The Education Institute supports teachers at every phase of their careers with a wide range of professional development programs.

Children start school at four years and finish when they are 17 or 18.

The curriculums at the more popular schools are International, British, French, American and Indian.

Schools are open Sunday to Thursday and timings are generally 07:30 to 13:00. However, in summer, schools may start and finish earlier due to the heat. The school year is split into three terms: Autumn (September to December), Spring (January to March/April) and Summer (April to June/July).

When your stay in Qatar is due to end, and the children need to transfer to another school, their current school will be able to advise you of the necessary procedures.

Ministry of Education

Mum's the Word is a newsletter sent out via e-mail which has information on activities and facilities available in Doha, specifically aimed at parents with young children. If you would like to be added to the mailing list, then all you have to do is e-mail Katie at erasmus@qatar.net.qa.

Nurseries & Pre-Schools

Not many of the various nursery schools in Doha are registered with the Ministry of Education.

Different nurseries accept children from different ages, such as from birth, three months, six months, 12 months or two years. There are usually no waiting lists at the nurseries, so you should have no trouble getting a place at one that is suitable for your child. However, not all nursery teachers are qualified, so take the time to check. If you are looking for a more structured nursery, try Sunbeam, Elder Tree and Central English Speaking School's kindergarten.

School time

Most nurseries are open from 07:00 to 13:00, although some are open from 06:00 until 15:30 or later. They tend to offer two, three or five days per week, but this depends on the nursery.

There is one Montessori nursery in Doha, part of the Doha Montessori School, accepting children from two years of age as long as they are toilet trained.

Pre-schools are attached to schools and will take children from three years old. Here all the teachers are qualified, but they may have waiting lists, so confirm in advance that they can accept your child. Schools which have pre-schools are: Doha English Speaking School, Doha College and Park House (see primary and secondary school table for contact numbers).

Nurseries & Pre-Schools	
Central English Speaking School	467 2570
Doha College	468 4495
Doha English Speaking School Kulaib	487 0170
Doha Montessori British School	469 1635
Doha Nursery & Creche	469 1045
Elder Tree Nursery	455 1020
Park House English School	442 3343
Sunbeam Kindergarten	444 0108
Tinkerbell Nursery	468 4729

Primary & Secondary Schools

Admittance into certain years may require the child to pass an entrance exam; this usually applies to applicants for year six and above. Schools usually like to meet the family prior to admittance. As schools may have a waiting list, it is best to apply as soon as you know you are moving to Qatar.

The schools follow national curriculums from various countries (British, French or American, for example). The exams sat by the children are in accordance with the curriculum which the school follows – GCSEs and A Levels (or equivalent exams for the various curriculums). The standard of teaching is high, with many extra curricular activities and facilities available.

Most schools are open Sunday to Thursday from 07:30 to 13:00 or 15:00. Primary school fees range from QR 2,500 to QR 7,500 per term. Secondary school fees range from QR 6,000 to QR 9,500 per term.

Other fees may include enrolment fee (usually QR 1,500); tuition fee of QR 500 (for books, etc) and field trips which are paid for separately.

Primary & Secondary Schools	
Al Khor School	473 4666
American School of Doha	442 1377
Doha College (Primary)	486 4495
Doha College (Secondary)	486 7379
Doha English Speaking School Kulaib	487 0170
Doha Montessori British School	469 1635
Dukhan English School	471 6147
French School	483 5800
International School of Choueifat	493 3110
Modern Indian School	466 0366
Park House English School	442 3343
QAFCO Norwegian School	477 1323

University & Higher Education

Education City, the flagship project of Qatar Foundation, has campuses from some of the best universities in the world, including Virginia Commonwealth University, Weill Cornell Medical College, Texas A&M University, Carnegie Mellon University, and Georgetown University. These offer a wide range of diploma and degree courses over one, two, three or four years. There are numerous courses available for students to choose from, including Design Art (VCU), Business and Computer Science (CMU), Medical Degrees (WCMC-Q), and Engineering (TAMUQ).

Education City

Universities	
Carnegie Mellon University Qatar	492 8260
CHN	488 8116
College of The North Atlantic Qatar	482 5555
Georgetown University	492 7655
Qatar Aeronautical College	437 5805
Qatar Foundation	492 7000
Texas A & M	492 7369
University of Qatar	485 2222
Virginia Commonwealth University - Qatar	492 7369
Weill Cornel Medical College	492 8650

The universities provide great opportunities, especially for Qatari women, to obtain degrees without having to leave Qatar.

The entrance requirements vary, depending on which course you wish to follow. Boys will need to get a visa through the relevant university, but girls don't have to worry as they can stay on their father's sponsorship, or their husband's (if married).

Special Needs Education

Schools in Doha will not always accept children with major learning difficulties because they may not have the facilities to accommodate special needs. However, there are some institutes with good facilities for children with learning problems. The Learning Centre (492 7888, www.qf.org.qa) offers education, and speech therapy, for children with specific learning difficulties and disorders. Sunbeam Centre of Excellence (444 0108) is for children aged 12 and under who have learning difficulties. The curriculum is based on the British Special Educational Needs programme and the centre has qualified staff, teachers, therapists and psychologists. Cedars Tutoring Centre (468 8192) is a licenced British curriculum tutoring centre helping primary and secondary school children with special needs. Doha Montessori British

School (469 1635) has been known to accept children with special needs. Al Noor Institute for the Blind can be contacted on 593 8292. The Qatar Society for Rehabilitation of Special Needs (466 3232) may be able to assist you if none of the above options are exactly what you are looking for. Finally, Kimberley Sheedy (571 6816) is a Child and Clinical Psychologist who works with children with behavioural and learning challenges including ADD and ADHD.

Learning Arabic

Other options → Language Schools p.142

Knowing the local language can be a great advantage. Arabic is difficult to master, but the basics will come in very handy. There are a few places which offer Arabic language courses, such as the British Council (442 6193) and ELS Language Centre (469 9223). Courses are offered at various times throughout the week, catering to all abilities. Arabic is not taught at all private schools.

Transportation

Other options → Getting Around p.24
Car p.26

Most people get around in Qatar by car. If they don't have their own car, they catch one of the local taxis, which are very cheap. The road system in Qatar isn't great, but plans are underway to improve the roads. At the moment there are innumerable roundabouts, which are slowly being changed into junctions. This is a great relief for residents as negotiating the roundabouts is a frightening experience and most car accidents happen on roundabouts! Parking in most areas isn't that difficult. However, parking in the souk area can be challenging. Paid parking meters are

Taxi

being installed, which is sure to make a lot more space available.

Vehicle Leasing

Until your residence visa process is complete, your only option is to lease a vehicle. Bank loans and car finance cannot be finalised until your visa is stamped in your passport anyway, you won't be able to buy a car. In order to lease a car, you will need a credit card, copy of your passport and a valid driving licence. You may only drive on a foreign licence for one week, after which time you must have a temporary Qatar licence. People holding GCC licences can drive leased cars for three months.

There are a number of reputable leasing companies in Doha, many of which are internationally recognized. Some companies have branches at the airport, making it convenient if you frequently fly in and out of Doha and require a car.

You can lease by the day, week, month or year. The longer the leasing period, the better the discount you will be given on the price. The monthly rate for leasing a car starts at QR 1,600 and QR 3,500 for a 4 WD.

With leasing, you don't have to worry about the car breaking down or being without a car if you have an accident, as the leasing company will provide you with a replacement car. You also don't have to pay for insurance or maintenance. Some expats feel that it is cheaper to lease long term than it is to buy their own car, but this obviously depends on how long you intend to stay.

Vehicle Leasing Agents		
AAB Rent-A-Car Company P.iv		443 7000
Al Muftah Rent a Car P.ix		432 8100
Al Rayah Transport P.81		444 2111
Al Saad Rent a car Co		444 9300
Budget Rent-A-Car		468 5515
Europcar		466 0677
Mannai Autorent P.79		455 8640
National Car Company		487 1995
Oasis Rent a Car		431 1505
Payless Car Rental		437 3267
Prestige Rent a Car		483 8500
Thrifty Car Rental		466 6655

Buying a Vehicle

If you decide to buy a car, you will have to wait until your residence visa is issued. Many expats are pleasantly surprised to find that the cost of running a vehicle is less than in their home

The road to satisfaction
leads to Mannai Autorent

Small Cars-Luxury Cars
Special Weekend Rates
Leasing & long Term Hire Facilities

MANNAI
aut⊕rent
MEMBER OF MANNAI CORPORATION
Tel: 455 8640/36/37, Fax 455 8638,

country This allows people to purchase cars that they wouldn't be able to afford at home, so you see quite a few sports cars! Also, there is generally no age limit on insurance of certain cars, as there are in many other countries, so people find that they can have the car of their dreams before they reach 40. If you want to buy a new car you should have no trouble finding something suitable, as there are a number of new vehicle dealers in Doha. The only problem you may face is that many dealers only import a few of each model, and you may have to wait for the next shipment if they don't have the model you want in stock. Big 4WD vehicles are very popular and recommended if you have children – not only for more space, but for safety as well. Most western families have at least one 4WD, usually driven by the wife! Toyota, Mitsubishi, BMW, Mercedes and Nissan are among some of the more popular makes.

Good quality used vehicles can be a little bit more difficult to find. There are lots of second-hand car shops, but the quality isn't always very good. It is best to go to a reputable dealer so you don't regret your purchase. Expats come and go from Doha continually throughout the year, so you may be able to pick up a bargain second-hand car from someone who is leaving for home. People wanting to sell cars will advertise on noticeboards in supermarkets, schools and compounds. You may also find adverts in the local newspapers. If you

are unsure of the state of the car, you can always ask to have it checked over by a professional.

If you buy a used vehicle, it is relatively easy to transfer ownership. You will need to go to the police station traffic department with the current owner of the car and complete the necessary paperwork. You must then get insurance and take a letter from the bank if you are buying it with a bank loan. This will involve stopping at a number of different counters – nothing unusual for Doha!

Used Car Dealers	
AAB Trade-In Division P.iv	443 7538
Al Fardan Automobiles	447 7577
Doha Marketing Services Co.	601 1117
Jaidah Advantage Used Car	446 6878
Mannai Trading Company W.L.L. P.79	455 8888
New Cars Centre	431 4685

Vehicle Insurance

You must have insurance valid for a period of 12 months before you can register a car. Insurance is based on the value of the car. Insurance rates are generally about 6% of the value of the car for saloon cars. If you buy a high performance vehicle, then the rates will be much higher. The insurance is valid for 12 months and you have a one-month grace period to renew your policy.

Qatar Insurance Company has a network of offices throughout the Gulf, and is highly regarded by many expats. Other companies that will be able to assist you include Alico Qatar, Arabia Insurance Company, and Doha Insurance Company.

Most policies will cover you for driving on rough terrain, but if you wish to go out dune driving, check with your insurance company first. If you want to cross the border of the country, you can obtain an orange card to show you have insurance cover for the vehicle in GCC countries, with the exception of Saudi Arabia and Oman. Insurance cover that is valid in these two countries can be bought at the border.

New Car Dealers	
Abdulla Abdulghani & Bros Co. P.iv	462 9222
Toyota	462 9320
Lexus	462 9259
Al Fardan Automobiles	447 7577
BMW, Mini	
Doha Marketing Services Co.	447 7800
Honda, Volvo	
El Naael Co	443 2111
SangYong, Citroen	
Gulf Automobiles & Trading Co.	465 4777
Audi, Porsche, Volkswagen	
Mannai Trading Company W.L.L. P.79	455 8888
Hummer, GMC, Cadillac, Opel, Subaru	
Nasser Bin Khaled & Sons Automobiles	444 3838
Mercedes-Benz	
New Cars Centre	431 4685
Saab, Jaguar	
Qatar Automobiles Company WLL	4699665
Mitsubishi	
Rolls-Royce Motor Cars Doha	447 7577
Rolls-Royce	
Saleh Al Hamad Al Mana Co.	4441334
Nissan	

Vehicle Insurance	
Al Khaleej	441 4151
Alico Qatar	465 5057
Arabia Insurance Co	442 2151
Doha Insurance Company	433 5000
Libano - Suisse Sal	466 4406
National Insurance Co of Egypt	442 3422
Qatar Insurance Company	449 0490

AL- Rayah Transport W.L.L.

الراية للمواصلات ذ.م.م

اتصل - ٤٤٤٢١١١

Call - 444 2111

خدمة ليموزين ٢٤ ساعة

24 Hours
Limousine Service

ص.ب: ٣٩١٠٠، الدوحة – قطر
بريد الكتروني: alraya@qatar.net.qa

P.O. Box : 39100, Doha - Qatar
e-mail : alraya@qatar.net.qa

Registering a Vehicle

When you buy a new car, the dealer will arrange registration for you. Cars only need to go through the road test if they are more than three years old. Note that your car will not pass the road test if it doesn't have a fire extinguisher. Qatar Technical Inspection Company (460 4029 or 460 4604) is where you need to take the car for its road test. The test costs QR 75 and you will be instructed on the procedures once you are there. QTIC are located on Street 24 in the industrial area and they will fax you a map if you request it. You will need to take your old road permit with you. They are open from 07:00 to 17:50 Saturday to Wednesday and 07:00 to 12:00 on a Thursday. Saturdays can be really busy and you may have quite a wait before being attended to. QTIC have some mobile units that offer the same service. Details can be obtained by calling one of the numbers above.

Once you have the road test report, you will need to go to the traffic department, which is located on Al Khalifa Street before the flyover (if you are driving west). Here you will have to complete an application form, which you can then get typed in one of the rooms on the grounds. Typing will cost between QR 10 and QR 15. You will then have to take the completed form, valid insurance and the road test report to the registration counter where they will give you the new road permit and two coloured squares (which are to be stuck onto your registration plates). Your car will have to be re-registered every year.

Traffic Fines & Offences

The current penalties are :

Speeding QR 300 – QR 500

Driving without a licence QR 1000

Parking fine QR 200 to QR 300

Blocking emergency vehicles from passing QR 500

Driving through a red light QR 1,000

Driving with expired temporary licence QR 300

Driving without carrying licence QR 150

Driving under the influence of alcohol QR 1,000 to QR 6,000 + jail sentence of one to six months

You can pay your fines at the nearest police station, although the fine won't be logged into their system for three days.

You can find out more about police fines and methods of payment at www.moi.gov.qa.

Breakdowns

If you breakdown on a busy road, you should try to move your vehicle out of the way of the traffic. If you cannot move it yourself, then call a towing service. The police may assist you if the car is blocking a main road or causing congestion. If you are planning a trip into the desert, it is always best to go with at least one other 4WD vehicle. In this way, if you breakdown, you won't be stranded for hours waiting for someone to help you.

Recovery Services/Towing (24 hour)

In the event of a breakdown in Doha, Al Maqased Transport (460 0229) are able to provide a round-the-clock towing and recovery service.

Traffic Accidents

Other options → Car p.26

There are a number of traffic accidents on the roads of Qatar every day. Over 100 people are killed every year. If you are involved in an accident, you must call the police and wait for them to come and assess the damage before you move your car. If someone has been injured, call an ambulance, but don't try to move the victim unless you are medically trained.

Always carry your driving licence, registration card and car insurance papers in your car. Failure to produce any of these papers could result in a fine. At the scene of the accident, the police will issue you with a police report which you must produce in order to have any repair work done or to make an insurance claim.

Repairs (Vehicle)

When you take a vehicle to a garage for repairs you will need to provide the original police report. No garage will fix your car without this police report. If you car is less than one year old, it will generally be repaired by the dealer. Insurance companies have approved repairers for cars over two years old. You can pay an additional premium on new vehicles if you want it to go to the dealer for repairs. This can be arranged for three years if the car is new (depending on your insurance company). There may be a deductible for claims, depending on each individual policy, and it could be approximately QR 500.

Snip snip snip!

Red tape – it's that boring bureaucratic stuff that makes you want to cry, with queues, forms, documents, dead-ends, and a whole lot of wasted time. From visas and licences to housing and driving, this vital guide cuts through the paperwork.

Supported by

HADEF
AL DHAHIRI
& ASSOCIATES
ADVOCATES AND LEGAL CONSULTANTS

betterhomes

Phone (971 4) 335 3520 · **Fax** (971 4) 335 3529
Info@Explorer-Publishing.com · www.Explorer-Publishing.com
Residents' Guides · Photography Books · Activity Guidebooks · Practical Guides · Maps

EXPLORER
Passionately Publishing...

WOMAN'S BEST FRIEND?

...NOT ANY MORE

woman today

INTELLIGENT
INDEPENDENT
INSPIRING

Qatar's only working woman's magazine

If you want to reach an exclusive segment of successful women professionals and entrepreneurs of Qatar, **Woman Today** is your best choice.

Carrying a mix of articles, tips, and interviews, all presented in a style that is appealing to women on the go, **Woman Today** is the working woman's guide to living better, working smarter and looking greater.

As an advertising medium it delivers an upmarket, affluent readership unmatched by any other womans magazine in the country.

Reach today's modern women with **Woman Today** – a brand that is more than just a magazine, it is their best friend.

To know more about **Woman Today** call us at +974 4550983 or mail us at wtoday@omsqatar.com

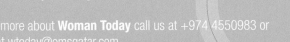

Oryx Publishing & Advertising Co.
Suite #4, Al Khalejia Bldg, No 18, 930 Al Wafa St, Al Hilal, Area No 41, PO Box 405, Doha - Qatar
Tel: (+974) 4672139, 4550983, Fax: (+974) 4550982, 4672511

Exploring
EXPLORER

Exploring

Highlights...

Walk the Corniche [p.90]

The corniche is quite literally the heart of Doha's attractions. Not only is it the most photo worthy spot in the city but also it attracts all ages and nationalities, visitors and residents who come for a relaxed stroll, to picnic in the huge park or to soak up the local heritage. Whatever the reason for stopping by the Corniche everyone leaves with the same smile!

Get out of Town [p.108]

It may be true that the majority of Qatar's attractions are located in and around Doha, but if you get the chance to escape from the capital you'll find more than a few places worthy of a day-trip. Whether you're into old forts or deserted unspoilt beaches, there's a whole country out there just waiting to be discovered.

Explore the GCC [p.114]

While Qatar is relatively small at about 11,437 square kilometres, it is also located smack bang in the middle of the GCC, opening up a whole host of places to explore. So if you want to go a little further afield, whether it is Kuwait, Bahrain, Oman, Dubai or Abu Dhabi, then pick up a copy of the respective Explorer guide and let the journey begin!

Exploring

In terms of visitor attractions, heritage sites, and areas of interest, it has been said in the past that Qatar doesn't have a great deal to offer. However, that is beginning to change. To attract and accommodate more tourists and visitors, Qatar has embarked on an ambitious programme to develop residential, commercial, leisure and entertainment projects, and to completely overhaul the country's infrastructure. Qatar already hosts a number of prestigious international events, but the 15th Asian Games to be held in Doha in December 2006 will present Qatar to a world audience. Athletes, officials and spectators from over 40 countries will converge on the capital, bringing with them masses of media attention that tourism officials here will be keen to exploit. To coincide with the new sporting and accommodation facilities being built for the games, the government is constructing a number of exciting cultural projects that will make Qatar even more attractive to visitors and residents. These include the Museum of Islamic Art, the Photography Museum, and the National Library all coming up along the Doha Corniche. In addition to these brand new projects, many of the existing attractions in the country (and in Doha especially) are undergoing comprehensive redevelopment. While it may seem that Qatar will only be worth exploring once all this development work is finished, the country does already have a variety of attractions that are well worth a visit. Being a peninsula, Qatar is blessed with kilometres of beaches and coastline, much of which is accessible to the public, and Doha is famed for its corniche where walkers can enjoy views of the Arabian Gulf. The interior of the country is characterised by barren desert plains and impressive sand dunes. A trip to Khor Al Udaid in the south-east provides an opportunity to drive a 4WD through the mountainous dunes and witness the impressive 'Inland Sea' as it meanders like a river through the desert. Closer to home, a dedicated army of municipality workers and regular irrigation ensures that visitors and residents have a good selection of pleasant green parks and open grassy areas to choose from. Many have facilities such as cafes and restrooms and are especially popular in the late afternoon and evening. To keep the younger generation occupied, Qatar, and Doha especially, has some exciting amusement and entertainment centres. For those in search of heritage and culture, Qatar does boast several forts, museums, and sites of archaeological interest. Some of these historical sites are outside the main populated areas and may be difficult to find, but there are various tour companies that organise trips. Within Doha, the sprawling souks offer a fascinating glimpse of an age-old Arabian shopping experience, while shoppers who prefer their creature comforts won't be disappointed with the selection of stores in Doha's modern malls.

Museum roundabout

The following is a list of the 'must sees' and 'must dos' in and around Qatar. There's plenty to keep you amused in the capital Doha, such as shopping, eating and sightseeing, but anyone who wants to escape the city should also find something that takes their fancy. For those that love the great outdoors, a thrilling trip to the 'Inland Sea' or a night beneath the stars in the desert is the perfect antidote to the hustle and bustle of modern life.

Shopping [p.149]

Modern malls such as City Center and Landmark give shoppers plenty of opportunities to part with their hard-earned cash. And when you've shopped till you're ready to drop, there's no end of cafes, restaurants, and even cinemas to help revive the weary.

Fish Market [p.176]

A visit to the fish market is a great experience, especially if you can drag yourself out of bed before sunrise to watch the auctioning take place before the actual market opens to the public. Beware though, it is a bit of a smelly way to spend a morning!

Doha Corniche [p.90]

Perhaps the most picturesque part of the capital, the corniche extends seven kilometres in a horseshoe around Doha Bay. It's a popular destination for walkers and joggers, and there are ample places to sit back and enjoy the skyline or the night lights.

Qatar National Museum [p.104]

The country's main museum features a comprehensive history of Qatar, with displays of Islamic relics, Bedouin artifacts, and sections on oil, gas and minerals. (The museum is currently closed for renovation but should reopen soon).

Relax at the Ritz [p.204]

With rich mahogany tables and chairs, lush sofas, and a chilled atmosphere, the Habanos Cigar Bar at the Ritz Carlton makes for a great escape - perfect for pre-dinner drinks, late-night cocktails, or a spot of luxury loafing any time of the day.

Shisha [p.201]

Smoking a shisha is a favourite pastime of locals, and there are many cafes where you can sit back, relax, and sample the different flavours of tobacco on offer. Apple and grape are popular, but for a change why not try a cappuccino shisha?

Palm Island [p.109]

Located in Doha Bay, Palm Island is an ideal destination for families, with children's play areas, sports facilities, a cafe and a licenced restaurant. To reach the island, visitors take a ten-minute boat trip from the jetty near the Sheraton Hotel.

Doha Zoo [p.113]

Doha Zoo houses a good collection of familiar animals from around the world, plus desert creatures indigenous to the region. You can expect to see oryxs, giraffes, elephants, baboons and zebras among the lush and spacious landscape.

Umm Salal Mohammed [p.102]

For a fascinating journey back in time, escape from the city and travel north from Doha to this historic village. You'll marvel at the ancient buildings and architecture, including the impressive fort and Barzan Tower.

Dhow Trip [p.90]

This is a fabulous way to see Doha from the water. The best time to take the cruise is in the evening, so you can enjoy the sunset and witness the city's skyline by night. Evening cruises will often include dinner and drinks too.

Courtesy Qatar Tourism Authority

Khor Al Udaid [p.112]

This area, also known as the 'Inland Sea', is at the south-eastern end of the country and requires a four wheel drive and an experienced driver to reach. The towering dunes and calm waters make it a great spot to go for a swim or even try your hand at sand skiing or boarding.

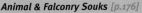

Souk Waqif [p.92]

Souk Waqif is the oldest Arabian-style market in Qatar. You can quite literally lose yourself in the fascinating maze of alleyways, with their small shops selling anything and everything imaginable from pots and pans to clothing, spices, baskets, and perfumes.

Al Khor Corniche [p.96]

40km north of Doha, Al Khor is a small coastal village with a beautiful waterfront. It's a great location for a picnic lunch or dinner, especially during the cooler months. There is a quaint little museum on the waterfront that is free of charge.

Animal & Falconry Souks [p.176]

Near the fruit and vegetable markets off Salwa Road, these souks trade in sheep, chickens, ducks, camels, geese, rabbits, birds, domestic pets, and of course falcons. The souks are always full of colour, activity and interesting characters.

Arabic Dining [p.186]

Restaurants such as Al Majlis on Al Sadd Street and Balhambar on the corniche provide visitors with an unforgettable local dining experience. Enjoy some of the finest dishes this region has to offer while soaking up the unique atmosphere.

Al Rumeilah Park [p.107]

Still sometimes known by its old name of Al Bidda, this public park opposite the corniche is especially popular in the evening and at weekends. It has lots of green spaces, cafes and facilities, and a heritage village built in the traditional style.

Wakra [p.96]

 Wakra is a pleasant little town just down the coast from Doha, with a museum, dhow harbour and beaches. It's also a haven for heritage lovers, with no end of historic architecture in the form of old houses and mosques.

Al Shaqab Stud [p.109]

Owned by His Highness the Emir, Al Shaqab Stud occupies a large site alongside Education City. The aim is to breed thoroughbred horses and to maintain the breeding of the Qatari horse. There is a riding school too, offering lessons to all ages and abilities.

Overnight Desert Trip [p.108]

An overnight desert trip is a great experience and a must for amateur star gazers. You will be far from all the city lights thus allowing you to fully enjoy the entire solar system, and you may even be lucky enough to see one or two shooting stars!

Courtesy Qatar Tourism Authority

Oryx Farm [p.113]

The oryx is the national animal of Qatar and can be visually described as a mix between a goat and a ram. The largest oryx farm in the world is located in Shahaniya, west of Doha, and it is open to visitors by prior arrangement or through a tour company.

Sheikh Faisal's Museum [p.105]

 Housing a private collection to match the best public museums in the region, access to the Sheikh's Shahaniya farm can be arranged by appointment. Inside you'll find weapons, ceramics, jewels, currency, classic cars, and much more.

Camel Races [p.112]

For the locals, a trip to the camel races is one of the highlights of the Qatar social calendar. You'll be entranced by the sights and sounds of the whole spectacle and you should even get to witness the new robot jockeys.

Doha - Main Areas

The city of Doha is quite compact and the modern road network – including the ring roads – makes it fairly easy to get from one side of town to the other. One thing you will quickly get used to is the number of roundabouts across the city. These roundabouts often have names, based on the sculptures that adorn them or on their location, and will commonly be used when giving directions. Also worth noting is the fact that there doesn't seem to be any single residential area in the city that is seen as more desirable among the expat community (except perhaps the new West Bay development). This is because smart apartment buildings and self-contained complexes of luxury villas can be found almost anywhere around town. Also, when it comes to area names, residents tend to use the names of nearby buildings or landmarks to describe a location, rather than the actual name of the area. The following is a description of some of Doha's main areas, to give you an idea of what you're likely to find and help you get your bearings.

Doha Corniche

The corniche is arguably the most picturesque area of Doha and a great place to explore whether you've got just half an hour or a whole day. Just east of the 'proper' start to the corniche, on Ras Abu Aboud Street, are a number of hotels and clubs including the Doha Marriott Gulf Hotel, the Oasis Hotel and Beach Club, the Doha Sailing Club and the Doha Club. Near the Museum Roundabout is the Al Nasaa restaurant complex with its notable architecture featuring traditional windtowers. Beyond this same roundabout (with its large urns,

Doha Corniche

or perfume bottles) is the Qatar National Museum. Based around the restored palace and former home of the ruling family, the museum is currently closed for renovation but is rumoured to be opening up again later in the year. Beside the museum is a small grassy park area which, while short of facilities, does provide some welcome shade. Across the main road (Al Corniche Street) is the port area, which is undergoing development also. The construction work is in aid of the new Museum of Islamic Arts, which is being built on its own jetty of reclaimed land. When it opens in 2006 the museum will be home to the world's largest collection of Islamic art and artefacts; see p.8. On from the 'water pot' roundabout is the start of the attractive pedestrian stretch of the corniche that loops in a semi-circle all the way round to the unmistakable Aztec pyramid-shaped Sheraton Hotel. With its views across Doha Bay this is always a popular destination for walkers and joggers. Another jetty leads to the the largest wooden dhow in the world, and the popular dhow restaurants. At the entrance to this jetty, on the corniche, is the familiar pearl sculpture that features in many visitors' photo albums. Continuing westward you'll see the imposing building of the Ministry of Foreign Affairs across the road and the impressive Emiri Diwan building just beyond. With its lush landscaped gardens and cascading water feature, the massive Diwan building is the official home of Qatar's government.

> **Snap Happy**
>
> You should be careful with your camera when in the vicinity of the Diwan, as the authorities tend to get a little sensitive if you take pictures of official buildings or royal palaces.

Worth keeping an eye on is the plot of land next to the Ministry of Interior, as this is the proposed site of the new Photography Museum. The design for this museum features a futuristic wing-like roof that will open and close to control the amount of light that can enter.

If you keep heading in a north-west direction past the Ministry of Interior you'll reach Rumeilah Park (sometimes known as Al Biddah Park) which features a variety of attractions and facilities making it very popular with families, especially in the evenings and at weekends. The park has restaurants, toilets, children's play areas, and the impressive Heritage Village which was built to resemble a traditional Qatari hamlet. The village often hosts workshops of local arts and crafts, and local musicians sometimes perform here. Looking out to sea from here gives a good view of Palm

Island, which can be reached by dhow from near the Sheraton. The island is a favourite spot for families, as it has a beach, watersports, a children's play areas, plenty of shade and a (licenced) restaurant.

The Qatar National Theatre and the National Council for Culture, Arts & Heritage are next to Rumeilah Park, and next door is the site for the Qatar National Library. Once completed, the bold and futuristic library building will be an unmissable landmark on the corniche. Just over the main road, on a small area of land jutting into the sea, is the Balhambar restaurant famous for its traditional Qatari cuisine. Balhambar has been undergoing renovation but should be open again soon, and at the moment the restaurant is almost obscured by the giant 'Orry the Oryx' mascot counting down the days until the start of the 2006 Asian Games. Carrying on around the corniche you'll pass some striking examples of Doha's architectural achievements, with commercial and residential towers enjoying commanding positions overlooking the sea.

The other end of the corniche is marked by the landmark Sheraton Hotel. There is a pleasant grassy park beside the water just before you reach the Sheraton, with a shop and cafe, children's playground, bathrooms, and plenty of space to sit and relax and enjoy a picnic. This is also the place to catch a dhow over to Palm Island – they leave every ten minutes and the journey also takes about ten minutes.

The many sights and attractions along the corniche make it a very popular destination, and the parks and roads around them can get very busy and congested in the evenings and at weekends (although they do have lots of car parking). At most times though, the traffic moves smoothly along the dual-carriageway Al Corniche Road.

Musheirib & Souk Area

Musheirib and the area that extends inland from the port is known for being the traditional shopping district. There is a mix of old and modern buildings and at the moment a fair bit of construction and development going on. This is not a residential district as such, although there are some old villas and many of the shops have low-rent apartments above them. With such a variety and quantity of shops this is a popular area, where expats and locals alike can enjoy rooting around for bargains if they have the time to spare. Single women should

be warned though that this is a very 'male' area, and they may feel uncomfortable and find themselves on the receiving end of unwanted stares and attention. On Fridays this area can be heavily congested as it is the main day off for most workers, and evenings can be busy too, with parking sometimes proving problematic. The recent introduction of parking meters on some of the main streets may or may not alleviate matters. As with many stores and businesses in Qatar the opening hours are usually 09:00 or 10:00 – 13:00 and then again from 16:00 – 22:00. Friday opening is often in the afternoon only.

Heading east along Wadi Musheirib Street, from the junction with Al Diwan Street, there is a big selection of electronics shops and plenty of stores selling lamps and light fittings (their electricity bills must be huge). This street comes out at the busy roundabout with a wooden dhow in the middle. Not surprisingly this is often called Dhow Roundabout, but you may also hear it referred to as Arab Bank Roundabout. Just off the roundabout, behind a large mosque, is the Najada Shopping centre, and within its courtyard is where you'll find the famed Windtower House. One of the last surviving original examples of such a building in the capital, this is also often referred to as the Ethnographical Museum, although its days as a museum seem to be over. The house is definitely worth a photo though.

On Qasim bin Mohammed Street, towards the corniche, stands the Doha (or Al Koot) Fort. The fort is open to the public (mornings only) and displays locally produced handicrafts. It's possible to climb the stairs and walk around the fortifications. Yet another heritage site that has been closed for renovation (including the repositioning of the main door) the fort will hopefully be open for business again soon.

Behind the fort are the traditional shopping areas of central Doha, known in the Middle East as souks.

Souks are bazaars or markets that sell virtually everything. Qatar's first souk, Souk Waqif, still exists today. It is full of old-world character and makes for an interesting shopping experience, and you can rest assured that shopping in the souk is safe and most of the retailers will be quite friendly. It is also a great place to practise your bargaining skills. You should never accept the first price you are quoted unless there is a sign in the shop that says they have fixed prices. Take a leisurely stroll through the souk before you come to any conclusive purchases.

Souk Waqif

This is the original souk in Doha. It used to be the weekend market where the Bedouins would come to town to trade their meat, wool, milk and other goods. This is an interesting souk as it can be seen as a bit of a maze with various alleys that sell everything from perfume, national clothing, luggage, tents, spices, incense, oils, sweets, rice, nuts, dried fruits, and herbs. One can find beautifully embroidered 'bukhnoqs', the head coverings worn by Qatari girls that are adorned with gold and silver thread. The 'thobe al nashl', also embroidered in gold is worn by women and girls on special occasions. Head scarves and 'abayas' or black cloaks that the ladies wear can also be found here. One can also purchase the heavyweight camelhair cloaks that are worn by men in the winter. As you pass by the shops you can actually watch the embroiderers at work.

The perfume shops sell everything from essential oils to imitation French fragrances. Several shops actually spill over into the alleys forcing you to walk through their tight spaces. Along with the perfumes, make sure you smell the various types of Arabian oil called 'oud' which is a sweet smelling agarwood. Frankincense from Oman as well as 'bokhur', or the fibrous balls of white musk, sandalwood oil, and rose oils can also be purchased here. Make sure to pick up a typical Arab incense burner for all these purchases!

The spice traders give the souk such an aromatic sense. There are several colourful whole and ground spices on display in boxes and sacks. Spices are usually sold by weight.

The Gold Souk

Behind Al Ahmed Street you'll come across several tiny jewellery shops. They sell imported and locally made gold. If there is something that you want and the store does not carry it, they will actually bring it to you from another shop to try on. It is a feast for the eyes walking through the gold souk with all the hanging gems in the windows. Most of the gold is 21 carat so it may be more yellow in tone than the gold you are used to in your home country, but it is certainly of a high quality. Rest assured that all the gold in Qatar is tested and marked, so you can be sure that you're buying the real thing. If you are looking for silver jewellery there are a couple of shops that sell it. You can also have jewellery repaired here as most of the shops have their own workshops and you can even get them to create a unique piece from your own design for a very reasonable cost.

Doha - Other Areas

Al Sadd & Al Rayyan Road

Al Rayyan Road heads west from Doha Fort and the souk area, all the way out of town and towards the district of Al Rayyan on the outskirts of Doha. Certainly worth knowing about is the location of the Hamad General Hospital and the neighbouring Women's Hospital. These can be found occupying a plot of land that is bordered by Al Rayyan Road, Mohammed bin Thani Street, and Ahmed bin Ali Street. The Al Amal Oncology Hospital is also nearby, just across Ahmed bin Ali Street. As elsewhere in Doha there is a good deal of construction work taking place in this area, including new apartment blocks at the junction of Al Rayyan Road and Jawaan Street (next to Sports Roundabout). One block further north is the site for the Athletes' Village, designed to house the competitors and officials for the 2006 Asian Games. Located right next to the existing hospitals, the plan is to convert the Athletes' Village into a state-of-the-art medical facility once the games are over.

Al Sadd Street runs parallel to Al Rayyan Road and this area is also seeing lots of development. Already home to the Royal Plaza shopping mall and the Merweb Hotel, these will soon be joined by new shopping centres and hotels including new premises for Millennium Hotels and La Cigale.

Diplomatic Area and West Bay

The Diplomatic Area is at the north end of the corniche, just after the Sheraton Hotel. So-called because it is home to the embassies and consulates of various foreign countries, the district is now undergoing a lot of development, with new construction projects constantly springing up. Just beyond the Sheraton, Doha has a new landmark in the shape of the West Bay Complex, with an imposing office tower, two apartment towers, 20 townhouse villas, a 110 berth marina, and the five-star Four Seasons Hotel which opened its doors in 2005. The area just inland is home to a number of ministry headquarters and the Qatar International Exhibition Centre. Opened in 1991, the QIEC hosts major trade fares and conferences throughout the year, and in 2005 it was the venue for a variety of shows and performances from around the world as part of the Qatar SummerWonders Festival. Next to the Exhibition Centre is one of the country's best-known shopping destinations – City Center Doha. With 350 shops, a water park, ice rinks, children's amusement centre and countless food outlets, City Center was for a long time the biggest shopping mall in the Middle East (that title was snatched by Dubai with the opening of the Mall of the Emirates). City Center really does have something to keep the whole family occupied, whether you love shopping or hate it. Salam Plaza department store is also nearby, on Al Wahda Street as you head back towards the corniche. In the opposite direction along Al Wahda Street you'll reach another useful landmark for Doha's motorists, the Rainbow Roundabout. Actually the sculpture in the middle of the roundabout is more reminiscent of an arch than a rainbow, especially as it's almost entirely blue in colour.

If you go straight at the roundabout and pick up Al Jamiaa Street you eventually reach the impressive and sprawling Qatar University campus, while a right turn onto Al Istiqlal Street takes you parallel to the coast in the direction of the West Bay Lagoon. Before the lagoon, on the right, the road leads to the Hotel InterContinental and Qatar's biggest amusement park Aladdin's Kingdom (aka Entertainment City). The huge construction site just north of Aladdin's Kingdom will eventually become the Cultural Village. This new attraction will portray the heritage of the region, with traditional architecture and handicrafts, and the complex promises to make a pristine stretch of beach available to the public.

Continuing north along the coast reveals even more construction, with palatial villas springing up within the West Bay Lagoon development, and villas, towers and a hotel planned for the area nearest the coast. This is also the point where the prestigious Pearl Qatar joins the mainland, its causeway connecting between the Diplomatic Club and the imposing Ritz Carlton.

To the north of the lagoon sits another Qatar institution, the Doha Golf Club. The club is home to the annual Qatar Masters tournament and, not to be left out, is currently undergoing some redevelopment that will see improved facilities both on the course and in the clubhouse.

At the moment this end of town is relatively quiet (save for the construction noise) and there's very little traffic on the roads (save for the construction trucks), but that will undoubtedly change once more and more villas are handed over and once the first residents move onto the Pearl.

Khalifa Street & Al Luqta Street

Khalifa Street runs from the Oryx Roundabout near the corniche to the three-level interchange near the Immigration Department, where it becomes Al Luqta Street and continues west. This road heads cross country, eventually reaching Dukhan on the west coast.

The Khalifa International Tennis and Squash Complex is located near the Oryx Roundabout, on Majlis Al Taawon Street. This is the venue for the annual ExxonMobil tennis tournament for men and the Total Open event for women, both of which attract some of the best players in the world. It will also be a venue for the Asian Games and is undergoing some redevelopment in preparation.

The Diplomatic Club

Further along Khalifa Street you'll pass the Al Jazeera and Qatar TV headquarters, just before the appropriately nicknamed TV Roundabout. Beyond this is Markhiya, one of the older areas of Doha and a mainly residential district with some old-style villas. There's a large selection of independent restaurants that are popular amongst the expat and local communities. Markhiya has not escaped the developers though, and many of the old homes are being demolished to make way for new retail and residential complexes, while new buildings are also appearing on every available plot of vacant land. To the south of Khalifa Street is the Doha Player's Theatre, the Doha English Speaking School (DESS), and the Qatar Centre for the Presentation of Islam (QCPI) which provides Arabic language courses and workshops on Islamic culture.

Continuing west, Khalifa Street then divides Madinat Khalifa, a built-up district of both old and new villas, apartments and compounds. This is also the location of the Traffic Department where you'll need to go to arrange driving licences and to register vehicles. Just after the Traffic Department is the big triple-decker flyover where Khalifa Street meets the D Ring Road. One block north from here (on the D Ring Road/Al Shamal Road) is the popular Landmark Mall, with a wide selection of local and international outlets. The mall has lots of free parking, but can get very busy especially in the evenings and at weekends. Back at the big interchange, a left at the roundabout followed by a quick right brings you into a neighbourhood of large old-style villas, where you'll find Doha's Weaponry Museum. The museum displays quite an impressive selection of ancient weapons and Islamic artefacts, but casual callers are not always welcome and it may be better to arrange a visit through one of the local tour companies.

The Immigration Department is located just by the interchange, and from here Al Luqta Street continues west towards the Qatar Foundation and Education City. A regional centre for teaching and research excellence, and home to a number of international university campuses, Education City is an impressive development that is set to grow further with the addition of the Science and Technology Park and a speciality teaching hospital. Behind Education City is Al Shaqab Stud and Stables, where visitors can view thoroughbred horses and take lessons at the riding school.

After Education City a left turn will take you to Wajbah Fort, the site of a famous battle where Qatari forces defeated the Ottomans.

The main road passes the unmissable Royal Palace on the left and carries on west to Al Samriyah and Al Shahaniya. Sheikh Faisal bin Qasim al Thani has a farm at Al Samriyah, and it is here that he has established a museum featuring an astounding collection of ancient weaponry, textiles, woodwork and metalwork, currency, vintage cars, and much more.

A few kilometres along the road brings you to the Oryx Farm on the left and the camel racetrack on the right. Both the museum and the Oryx Farm are open to the public, but visits must be arranged prior to arrival (the local tour companies will be able to do this).

Salwa Road

Not so much an area, but a main artery that heads in a straight line from the Ramada Interchange, out of the city and eventually towards Saudi Arabia and the highway to the UAE. The Ramada Interchange is another Doha mainstay. Where Salwa Road and Suhaim bin Hamad Street (C Ring Road) cross, each of the four corners has a variety of shops and outlets (including the big Jarir Bookstore on Salwa Road). But it is the abundance of fast food joints and American-style eateries (including McDonald's, Burger King, Pizza Hut and KFC) that has led many expats to rename this 'cholesterol corner.' It's not all burgers, pizza and chicken though, as there are some more upmarket restaurants here too, including the ever-so-hip Mint cafe.

Away from the city centre, Salwa Road heads south-west towards the triple-decker interchange with the D Ring Road (Al Amir Street). On the right hand side, just before the interchange, you'll find Bateel Cafe which is a good spot for lunch or just a coffee, and for picking up freshly baked bread and pastries. For those with an extra-sweet tooth they have a wide selection of icecream and confectionery, and you could even sample the wares of the chocolate shop next door. After the interchange, Salwa Road turns into a seemingly endless parade of shops and garages set back from the road. There isn't that much variety, but if you want car spares, tyres, or furniture, you'll be spoilt for choice. Sporty types would be advised to track down the Skate Shack, selling bikes, skateboard gear, and watersports equipment. (It's on the left as you drive away from Doha, just after the roundabout for the wholesale markets).

The markets are worth exploring for the experience alone, even if you have no intention of buying

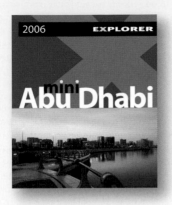

Made with hand luggage in mind

Don't be fooled by their diminutive size, these perfectly pocket proportioned visitor's guides are packed with insider info on travel essentials, shopping, sports and spas, exploring, dining and nightlife.

Phone (971 4) 335 3520 • **Fax** (971 4) 335 3529
Info@Explorer-Publishing.com • www.Explorer-Publishing.com
Residents' Guides • Photography Books • Activity Guidebooks • Practical Guides • Maps

EXPLORER
Passionately Publishing...

anything. Nearest Salwa Road are the fruit, vegetable, and fish markets, and then the huge bales of straw on trucks beside the road announce your arrival at the livestock market. The traders buying and selling sheep and goats here are a real friendly bunch, who always have time for a wave and even a chat (language barrier depending!).

North of Salwa Road, just off Al Waab Street that runs parallel, you'll see the redevelopment of Khalifa Sports City taking place in preparation for the Asian Games. The arched structure of the Khalifa Stadium's roof is quite a sight. The Aspire Academy for Sports Excellence is also based nearby. Offering unrivalled coaching and training facilities for various sports, Aspire aims to produce the sporting champions of tomorrow and will further help to promote Qatar as a top-class sporting destination.

For those that prefer flexing their plastic rather than their muscles, Hyatt Plaza mall is further along Al Waab Street (just look for the giant shopping trolley in the car park). It is soon to have a new neighbour in the form of Villagio, billed as a retail, leisure and sports destination.

After Hyatt Plaza, a left onto Al Furousiya Street takes you past Doha Zoo and back to Salwa Road at the Fort Roundabout.

Qatar - Other Areas

North of Doha

Al Shamal (meaning north) Road heads out of Doha city and leads all the way up to the northern tip of the peninsular at Madinat Al Shamal. About 15km out of town the road passes Umm Salal Mohammed, with its fort and the Barzan Tower. Another 20km or so and there's a right turn that takes you to the coastal town of Al Khor. Road '1A', which starts by the Doha Golf Club north of West Bay Lagoon, runs parallel to the Al Shamal Road and is actually a smoother drive and has less traffic. It passes the new Losail Moto GP circuit, the sleepy village of Simaismah (which has a deserted beach and a couple of shops), and then leads straight to Al Khor.

Al Khor is a pleasant coastal town, with a corniche, a dhow harbour, a museum (on the corniche near the fishmarket) and watchtowers dotted along the coast. Near the dhow harbour there's a public lending library that actually has a small selection of English language books, as well as the daily English language newspapers (open 07:00 – 13:00 and 16:00 – 18:00, except Friday mornings).

Further up the coast is Ras Laffan Industrial City (RLC), which is at the heart of Qatar's massive investment to exploit its substantial natural gas reserves. RLC is managed and administered by Qatar Petroleum. As the name suggests, this is something of an industrial area so there is not much for visitors to see or do, but the proposed growth will see more and more people moving to the area which means more leisure, retail, and entertainment facilities.

Continuing in a loop around the coast takes you by the Al Jassasiyeh carvings and numerous sandy beaches such as those at Fuwairat and Al Ghariyah. Madinat Al Shamal is a relatively new town that primarily acts as an administrative centre for the smaller towns and villages in this northern part of the country. The north-west coast has numerous fortifications and ancient buildings, including those at Al Jemail (also spelt Al Gamel) where you'll find an abandoned village with the ruins of houses and a small mosque. Further down the coast is Al Zubara with its striking fort and museum, and the nearby archaeological dig that is uncovering the remnants of a settlement buried in the sand.

South of Doha

Ten kilometres south on the road past Doha aiport brings you to the fishing town of Al Wakrah. There's an interesting dhow harbour, a museum, a beach (admittedly not that clean), and a park that's green and pleasant enough but with facilities that could do with a little TLC. Al Wakrah has lots of old traditional houses and mosques, some renovated but others crumbling, and is a real treat for ancient architecture fans. Messaieed (or Umm Said as it's sometimes written) is a further 20km south, but like Ras Laffan in the north and Dukhan to the west, this is chiefly an industrial area so has little to entice or amuse visitors. The coastline that stretches south though has kilometres of good beaches and at the Sealine Beach Resort you can hire quads and hit the dunes right beside the sea. From here it's a thrilling off-road trip through the desert to the 'inland sea', or Khor Al Udeid, where you'll marvel at the impressive dunes and the calm waters meandering through the sand like a river

West of Doha

The road west from Doha takes you through Al Rayyan and passes a number of sites of interest.

Al Wajbah Fort is on the left, just before the grandiose palace of the Emir. About ten kilometres further is the village of Al Samriyah where Sheikh Faisal bin Qasim Al Thani has his museum housing a comprehensive collection of rare antiques. The Oryx farm is located in the next village, Al Shahaniya, as is the camel racetrack which is a hive of activity on race days during the winter months.

On the west coast, Zekreet, just north of Dukhan, has fine sandy beaches but facilities are somewhat limited. The name of Dukhan holds an important place in Qatar's history, as it was here that the first oil discoveries were made in the 1930s, and the area is still home to the country's oil industry at Qatar Petroleum's Dukhan City. There are some further pleasant beaches, despite the unlikely location, along the west coast bordering the Dukhan oil field, especially the one near Umm Bab (known as 'Palm Tree Beach'). There are also beaches at Salwa near the Saudi border, but again there's little in the way of facilities.

Museums, Heritage & Culture

Qatar undoubtedly has an interesting culture and history, and a number of museums, forts, and heritage sites do exist around Doha and the rest of the country. However, it must be said that the region's rich heritage is not exploited to the best of its potential. Erratic opening hours and a general lack of information and/or facilities means that many venues are far from visitor-friendly. Until recently though, Qatar was never considered a tourist destination, and therefore such issues were not a priority. With the expected rise in tourist and visitor numbers (thanks especially to the 2006 Asian Games and the surrounding publicity),

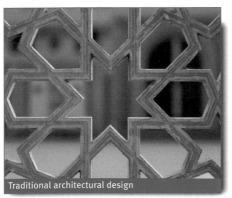
Traditional architectural design

enormous amounts are being spent creating world-class cultural centres (such as the Museum of Islamic Art and the Photography Museum) and rejuvenating existing ones. An unfortunate short-term effect of this regeneration is that visitors may find some attractions closed until the work is finished. In time though, Qatar will come to be known locally and internationally for its cultural and heritage sites and museums. For the time being, bear in mind that some venues may be hard to find and perhaps inaccessible, and that the displays and information may not be of a very high standard. For first-time visitors who are not sure of the exact locations of some attractions, it may be best to arrange a trip through a tour operator in Doha.

> ### Heritage Hotline
> *Some of the listed forts and museums do have individual phone numbers, but you may be able to get additional information by calling the National Council for Culture, Arts and Heritage on 466 8777, or the Department of Museums and Antiquities on 443 8123.*

Archaeological Sites

Very few archaeological sites exist in Qatar, despite the country's history dating back thousands of years. Around 20 years ago archaeologists began excavations of the buried city of Al Zubara on the north-west coast, and some of the finds are now displayed in the museum at the neighbouring fort. Slowly but surely the outlines of old walls and buildings are emerging from the sand, and if you're lucky you may get to talk to someone on the dig. The only other archaeological site of interest to visitors is at Al Jassasiyeh (details below).

Al Jassasiyeh

Location → Al Huwailah | na
Hours → See below
Web/email → na   Map Ref → 1-B1

These rocky hills that overlook the north-eastern coast of Qatar between the two villages of Al Huwailah and Fuwairit contain various stone carvings and engravings believed to date back to prehistoric times. There are more than 900 carvings depicting different types of boats, seen from above and the side. The carvings also depict rows of cup-marks or depressions, believed by some to have been used for traditional games called al-Aailah and al-Haloosah which were played using stone counters. Others though believe that the depressions were designed simply to catch rain-water. The carvings were first photographed in 1962 by a Danish archaeological team and were later catalogued in 1974. Al Jassasiyeh is considered the most significant of several similar sites in the country as it is the only one to feature carvings of boats.

This is an open site and anyone can simply go and look around. There are no entrance fees. Jassasiyeh is around 60km north of Doha, on the road to Al Huwailah. As the area may be difficult to find, and the carvings could prove difficult to spot, you may want to take along someone who's been before, or arrange a trip through a tour company.

Forts

Qatar has several old forts dating back hundreds of years. Some have been restored and some are currently used as excavation sites for archaeologists, but visitors may be disappointed by a lack of information once they reach a particular site. Some forts have no proper gates or doors so can be visited anytime, while others may open from 08:00 – 13:00 and then 16:00 – 19:00. Entry is nearly always free of charge. Note that summer opening hours vary greatly and some may close their doors for the whole summer season. Many of these forts are outside of Doha city in unpopulated areas.

Doha Fort

Al Rakiyat Fort

Location → Al Rakiyat · NW Qatar | na
Hours → 08:00 - 13:00   Fri closed
Web/email → na   Map Ref → 1-B1

Al Rakiyat Fort was constructed between the 17th and 19th centuries, and restored in 1988. It is made of stone and mud and, similar to other forts in the country, is rectangular with a tower at each corner – three square and one round. The fort is located just off the coastal road between Al Zubara and Madinat Al Shamal, near a camel farm. You'll have to drive off-road for a few hundred metres but it is possible in a normal car. The site is open to the public, but apart from the building itself there's little else to see at the site.

Al Wajbah Fort

Location → Nr Emir's Palace · Al Rayyan | na
Hours → 08:00 - 13:00   Fri closed
Web/email → na   Map Ref → 2-B3

With its high towers and thick walls, this fort is considered one of the oldest in the country. It was the site of a famous battle in 1893, when the people of Qatar (under the leadership of Sheikh Qasim Bin Mohammed Al Thani) defeated the Ottoman forces. As a result, the name of Al Wajbah evokes a strong feeling of pride among local people. The fort has two large towers and inside there is a small display of weaponry and details of the fort's history. To reach the fort, turn off the roundabout before the Emir's palace (if driving from Doha), go over the speed bumps and turn right at the end of the gravel track. Entry is free.

Al Zubara Fort

Location → Al Zubara · NW Qatar | na
Hours → 08:00 - 13:00 16:00 - 19:00 Fri AM & Sat closed
Web/email → na   Map Ref → 1-B1

Located 110km from Doha, on Qatar's north-west coast, Zubara is an important archaeological site that is famous for its fort. This fort was built in 1938 during the reign of Sheikh Abdullah bin Jassim Al Thani, and erected beside the ruins of a neighboring, much older, fort. The impressive structure is square in shape, with high, thick walls, and has circular towers in three of its corners and a rectangular tower in the fourth. The fort once served as a coastguard station, and until the mid-1980s it was still being used by the

Al Zubara Fort

enter Qatar's IP hub

The First Global Data Center in Qatar

A single global network for faster and secure data transfer and hosting.

Qtel has partnered with NavLink to connect Doha to the AT&T Global Network and by using Qatar Data Center, your company can benefit from services such as Hosting and Co-Location, Internet and Network Connectivity, On Demand and Custom made Solutions and more.

Qatar Data Center

In Doha for the Region

 in partnership with: **NavLink** & **AT&T**

www.qatardatacenter.com

military. It now houses a small museum that contains one or two artefacts from the nearby archaeological dig of the old town. It's a long drive from Doha, along rather bumpy roads, so probably not worth a special trip but definitely worth checking out if you're in the area.

Doha Fort (Al Koot Fort)

Location → Beh Souq Waqif · Al Jasra | 443 8123
Hours → 07:00 - 12:00 16:00 - 21:00 Fri 16:00 - 18:30
Web/email → na   Map Ref → 10-D4

Located in the heart of Qatar's capital, this white Moorish-style fort now houses a museum featuring a small exhibition of local handicrafts, paintings, weavings, gypsum carvings and ornate wooden door pieces. Established in the 1880s, Al Koot Fort was originally used as a guard and police post for the nearby Souk Waqif. Located on the corner of Jasim bin Mohammed and Al Qalaa streets, it is one of the remaining military forts in Doha. There is a large open courtyard and it is possible to climb the steps and walk around the exterior wall. Entrance is free of charge.

Umm Salal Mohammed Fort

Location → Umm Salal Mohammed | na
Hours → 08:00 13:00 16:00 - 19:00
Web/email → na   Map Ref → 2-B2

Located in Umm Salal Mohammed, approximately 20km north of Doha, this fort was built during the late 19th and early 20th centuries. It is notable for its thick high walls and impressive facade. The fort is next to Barzan Tower, which is the western tower of two that were built as watchtowers. Its 'T' shape is considered a unique architectural style in the Gulf region. The fort is actually something of a ruin, but climbing around and exploring is great fun. There are no doors as such, so entrance is free of charge.

Heritage Sites - City

Other options → Museums - City [p.104]
Mosque Tours [p.108]

Other than the the museums mentioned later in this section, there are few other sites of historical interest in the city. Souk Waqif is a must though for a taste of traditional shopping (see p.92), and the nearby Windtower House is certainly worth a visit.

Windtower House

Location → Grand Hamad St · Al Najada | na
Hours → na
Web/email → na   Map Ref → 10-E4

This is one of the last traditional windtowers in Qatar. It is located off Grand Hamad Street and Ali bin Abdullah Street, and is actually enclosed within the Najada Shopping Plaza. Windtowers, known as 'barjeel' in Arabic, were used in the days before electricity as a primitive form of air conditioning. They function the opposite way to a chimney, by sucking fresh cool air into a house. This building was once the Ethnographical Museum and you may still see it described as such, but the museum is closed and sadly the house is no longer open to the public (although some people have reported being able to talk their way inside for a look around). Even if you do have to appreciate it from the outside only, this is a worthwhile stop and a good photo opportunity.

The Windtower House

Umm Salal Mohammed

Heritage Sites - Out of City

Other options → Tours & Sightseeing [p.107]
Museums - Out of City [p.105]

In addition to the forts, museums, and archaeological sites mentioned elsewhere in this section, there are one or two others dotted around the country that may be worth a visit if you're passing by. If you have a spare day, the coastal drive from Doha all the way round to Dukhan (or vice versa) and back to Doha will while away a few hours. At the top end of the peninsula you'll pass plenty of traditional old fishing villages, which, while not dedicated 'heritage sites' as such, can still give you an idea of how life may have been before the advent of the modern world. There's also a number of watchtowers and fortifications along the coast, a reminder of the relative instability in the region just a few generations ago.

Museums - City

Other options → Heritage Sites - City [p.102]
Mosque Tours [p.108]

Doha city has two main museums, the Qatar National Museum and the Weaponry Museum (details below). However, the ambitious (and expensive) building projects coming up on the corniche mean that in a couple of years Doha will also boast the world-class Museum of Islamic Art and the Photography Museum, providing a real treat for heritage and culture lovers. See p.6 for details of these museums.

Qatar National Museum

Location → Nr Doha Corniche | 444 2191
Hours → 08:00 - 13:00 16:00 - 19:00 Fri am closed
Web/email → na | Map Ref → 11-B4

The museum has been under renovation for a number of months and is scheduled to reopen to the public in the near future. The museum portrays a history of Qatar through the years, with various archaeological artifacts, coins, jewellery, traditional clothing, household items and tools. There are also areas that recreate Bedouin scenes, and the section on Qatar's geology takes an interesting look at the oil industry. A large aquarium contains marine creatures native to local shores. The museum is located just off the corniche, and is based around the restored Old Salata Palace of Sheikh Abdullah Bin Qasim. If you look in front of the museum there is a water lagoon

Qatar National Museum

that indicates where the original shore of Doha used to be located. For further information and updates on the reopening, call the National Council for Culture, Heritage and Arts on 466 8777.

Weaponry Museum

Location → Btn Al Luqta St & Makkah St · Al Luqta | 486 7473
Hours → Timings on request
Web/email → na | Map Ref → 7-A3

This museum is located in a complex of three villas in Al Luqta, near the Gharrafa Interchange, and is home to a superb collection of weapons and antiquities from Qatar, the Gulf, and around the world. There are countless gold and silver swords and 'khanjars', pistols and rifles in all shapes and sizes, plus armour and artwork portraying ancient weapons and battles. There are also many knives, and bows and arrows on display. Much of what is on show was once the private collection of Sheikh Hassan bin Mohammed bin Ali Al Thani – he donated it to the museum for others to enjoy. The third villa also contains a selection of gifts given to the Emir by visiting dignitaries or during state trips abroad. Visits to the museum must be arranged in advance, either by calling the above number, or through a Doha tour company.

Museums - Out of City

Other options → Tours & Sightseeing [p.107]
Heritage Sites - Out of City [p.104]

In addition to the museum at Al Zubara Fort (see p.98) there are three further museums outside of Doha that are worth a mention.

Al Khor Musuem

Location → Al Khor Corniche	472 1866
Hours → 09:00 - 13:00 16:00 - 19:00 Fri am closed	
Web/email → na	Map Ref → 1-C2

The museum at Al Khor is located in a former police station and customs house by the dhow harbour. The building was restored in 1987. Portraying the history of the region and its people, the rooms on the ground floor showcase the fishing and pearling industries and dhow building, and feature displays of traditional clothing and examples of natural history. There are also samples of incense burners, which traditionally are the speciality of Al Khor's craftsmen. The upper floor displays archaeological finds from the neolithic and bronze

Al Khor Museum

ages that were discovered nearby. There's a shaded area next to the museum with a children's playground and pleasant views of the harbour and out to sea – a good spot for a picnic (depending on the weather). After visiting the museum you could drive further along the corniche and visit the old watchtowers that still stand guard over the town.

Al Wakrah Museum

Location → Nr Dhow Harbour · Al Wakrah	464 3201
Hours → 09:00 - 13:00 16:00 - 21:00	
Web/email → na	Map Ref → 2-C4

Based in a restored traditional house, Al Wakrah Museum depicts the natural history of the area, as well as the region's distinctive architecture. There are displays of the fishing and pearling industries and reminders of the town's seafaring heritage. The museum also has some fine examples of traditional old Arabic wooden doors. You'll find the museum next to the 'Buoy' Roundabout by the coastguard station and fishing harbour. Nearby is one of the oldest mosques in the country, and it's well worth taking a drive around this old area for a fascinating glimpse of traditional Arabian buildings and mosques in varying states of repair.

Sheikh Faisal bin Qasim Al Thani Museum

Location → 1km before Al Samariyah RA · Shahaniyah	522 0530
Hours → By arrangement	
Web/email → www.fbqmuseum.com	Map Ref → 2-A2

Sheikh Faisal's personal collection at his farm near Al Shahaniya is considered by many to be one of the best museums in the country. Housed within a huge rectangular fort complex, the museum has thousands of fascinating and rare exhibits. Hall number one contains a large collection of Islamic art, including glass and ceramics, jewellery, and metalwork. There's an impressive range of ancient weaponry too, with guns, daggers, swords and armour, some of which dates back to the 15th century. Hall number two has more Islamic artefacts such as doors, furniture, and a selection of antique Mogul carts. This hall is also where you'll find the Sheikh's impressive collection of vintage cars, including Model T Fords and classic 50s motors complete with fins and lots of chrome. Hall three displays old currency, while hall four contains rare books and manuscripts with examples of Arabic calligraphy. Hall number five is home to various fossils and archaeological finds from around the region, and hall six has textiles, clothing and embroidery from the Ottoman era. One corner of the museum recreates a traditional Qatari house, and there is also a library with over 12,000 books covering history, religion and poetry. To visit the museum you have to ring in advance to make arrangements. The 'advisor', Dr. Talib Al Baghdadi, can be reached on 556 1498, while the 'administrator', Shadi A. Aall, is on 522 0530. Alternatively, you could ask one of Doha's tour companies to arrange the visit for you.

Parks & Beaches

Beach Parks

Currently, Qatar does not have any municipality, council, or government-run beach parks. Those who like to go to the beach tend to use hotel facilities. Some of the most popular hotel beach clubs frequented by visitors and local residents are the Intercontinental, the Sheraton, the Ritz Carlton, the Marriott and the Sealine Beach Resort. Most offer day rates for casual visitors, whilst others require full membership. For contact details see the Hotels table on p.23.

Beaches

Other options → Beach Clubs [p.132]
Swimming [p.138]

As Qatar is a narrow peninsular jutting into the Arabian Gulf, it's hardly surprising that it has numerous beaches with sandy shores. Popular spots south of Doha include Al Wakrah by the dhow harbour and the stretch of coastline extending from Messaieed down past the Sealine Beach Resort to Khor Al Udeid. On the west coast, there are beaches at Zekreet and along the coast by the Dukhan oil fields, including the 'palm-tree' beach near Umm Bab. North of Doha offers the most options for beach lovers. Al Simaismah on the road to Al Khor is worth a visit, as is Al Khor and the area to the immediate south-east. The northern tip of the country has many fine beaches with shallow waters, including those around Al Huwailah, Fuwairat, and Al Ghariyah.

More often than not these beaches have no signposts, directions, or dedicated parking areas, and to reach them it's usually a case of driving to the town or village and stopping when you reach the sea. Don't expect any facilities either, as sunshades, loungers, showers and toilets are not provided. You should also be extra careful when

swimming, as there are no lifeguards. Another factor to consider is that unlike the hotel beaches that are cleaned regularly, public beaches are at the mercy of the tides and may contain garbage that has washed ashore. During the summer months especially, jellyfish can be a problem in the waters around Qatar. Some people carry a bottle of white vinegar, which can help to neutralise a sting if applied to the affected area.

If conditions at these beaches sound a little primitive, you may prefer to use the facilities provided by some of the hotels – see p.138.

Parks

If you need to escape from the stresses and strains of city life, there are plenty of oases of green within Doha to help you unwind. In line with the rebuilding and redeveloping ethos currently sweeping the city, the municipality's 'beautification department' has been hard at work improving the facilities at all of Doha's parks, so don't be surprised to find some areas are off-limits for the coming months. In addition to the public parks listed below, many residential neighbourhoods have enclosed, sometimes gated, areas with lawns and trees, for the use of residents.

Al Muntazah Park	
Location → Al Muntazah	na
Hours → 09:00 - 22:00	
Web/email → na	Map Ref → 13-C3

This is one of the older parks in Doha, and has large grassy areas and mature trees. Located at the corner of the C-Ring Road and Al Muntazah Street, the park is only accessible to women and children (boys up to the age of nine), and tends to be busiest evenings and at the end of the week. Entrance is free of charge. Note that the park was recently closed for renovation; the date for reopening was given as 'late 2005.'

Dahal al Hamam Park	
Location → Madinat Khalifa North	na
Hours → 16:00 – 24:00, Fri & Sat 08:00 – 24:00	
Web/email → na	Map Ref → 7-B1

Work is still in progress on this new park at the corner of Arab League Street and Al Markiyah Street, but when finished it aims to be the Municipality's flagship park in Doha. The large plot will eventually feature cafes, toilets, playgrounds, football pitches, cycle tracks and even a showground with seating.

The park has plenty of greenery, with palm trees and open grassy areas, and at night the floodlights illuminate the whole area making quite an attractive sight. In line with other parks in the city, this is open to families only, so <u>no single men</u> will be allowed. Entry is free.

Museum Park

Location → Nr Qatar National Museum · Doha Corniche	na
Hours → 08:00 - 23:00	
Web/email → na	Map Ref → 11-B3

Next to the museum and overlooking the corniche and Doha Port, this large grassy area provides plenty of shade and places to sit and enjoy a picnic. Facilities are thin on the ground at the moment, as the park, along with the neighbouring museum, is undergoing renovation, but it still makes a pleasant stop-off if you're in the area.

Rumeilah Park (aka Al Bidda Park)

Location → Doha Corniche	na
Hours → 08:00 - 23:00	
Web/email → na	Map Ref → 10-B1

Located opposite the corniche, this is a beautifully landscaped park that tends to be busiest on Fridays and in the evenings. It has an open-air theatre that is used during the annual Cultural Festival, and the impressive Heritage Village that was constructed to resemble a traditional Qatari village. There are a few shops that are open sporadically depending on the time of day and season of the year, and well-maintained toilet facilities. A gallery, displaying artwork by local artists, is open 09:00 – 12:00 and 16:00 – 21:00. There is also a small kiosk where you can buy beverages and pre-packed snacks. The park is run by the Municipality and entry is free of charge, although single males or groups of men are not allowed as this is designated as a family park. The park stretches over two miles along the corniche, and can be accessed at most points along its length, although the main entrance (and the entrance to the Heritage Village) is on Majlis Al Taawon Street.

Sheraton Gardens

Location → Nr Sheraton Hotel · Doha Corniche	na
Hours → 08:00 - 23:00	
Web/email → na	Map Ref → 8-D3

At the north end of the corniche, just before the Sheraton Hotel, this is another pleasant park enjoying great views across Doha Bay. There's a car park, as well as plenty of parking on the road, and you'll find a little kiosk selling refreshments. This is also where the dhows leave from to take you over to Palm Island (see p.109).

Tours & Sightseeing

Other options → Weekend Breaks [p.114]

An organised tour is a great way to discover some of the attractions that Qatar has to offer, especially places that are a little off the beaten track or hard to get access to. Tours can range from a relaxed half-day shopping trip around Doha, to a full-on excursion into the desert with overnight camping. Tours of Qatar's historical sites are also popular. This section lists some of the available options and gives details of the various tour companies operating in the country. If you are staying at a hotel, they may recommend a company and should be able to help you book your trip.

Activity Tours

A number of tour companies arrange trips that involve some level of activity. A trip into the desert can often incorporate the novel experience of sand skiing or boarding – it's a little different from snow, but worth a try just so you can say you've done it! If you're on a tour that ends up near the coast there should always be some spare time for a refreshing swim in the sea. QIT offers diving trips for groups of six or more people, visiting one of the many coral reefs off the coast of Qatar. All equipment, plus a packed lunch, will be provided. QIT can also arrange PADI diving courses for beginners. QIT, and Alpha Tours also, organise deep-sea fishing trips with an experienced skipper and all equipment and bait provided.

Boat Tours

Tour companies such as QIT, Gulf Adventures, Arabian Adventures, and Alpha Tours offer evening dhow cruises that either sail around Doha Bay, affording spectacular views of the city skyline by night, or venture further afield to one of the many islands off the coast. Dinner and traditional music and entertainment are provided, and the trips usually last around three or four hours. Boats generally depart from the dhow harbour off the corniche.

City Tours - In Doha

If you are in Doha on a short visit, or you want a crash course in finding your way around, or you are travelling in a large group, then a city tour of Doha may be ideal for you. You will spend the day in an air-conditioned bus, with commentary provided by an experienced, English-speaking tour guide. Typical stops on the tour include some or all of the following: the camel market, the Weaponry Museum, the corniche, the dhow-building yard, the falcon market, the fish market, the gold souk and the fruit and vegetable market. Some tour companies (such as QIT and Alpha) offer shopping tours in the city, concentrating on the traditional souks and the modern malls. Both the city tour and the shopping tour can be taken as full-day or half-day trips.

City Tours - Out of Doha

QIT offers a tour that takes you north of the city to discover the history of Qatar, visiting Al Khor Museum and the fishing harbour, before stopping to explore the excavations in Al Zubara and the Al Raquiyat Fort. A visit to a traditional Qatari house in Al Ruwais and the Al Jassasiyeh rock carvings rounds off this seven-hour trip. A minimum of four people is required for this tour, which takes place in an air-conditioned bus and includes a packed lunch.

Mosque Tours

Other options → Museums - City [p.104]

Throughout the country there are plenty of small mosques, some of which are very old, that are still used for daily prayer by local Muslims. Unlike other, more relaxed Islamic countries where tourists are allowed to enter and explore certain mosques, Qatar is more conservative. Non-Muslims are not necessarily forbidden from entering some of the mosques (although some mosques, such as the Grand Mosque on the corner of Jasim bin Mohammed Street and Al Rayyan Road is totally off limits), but it is unusual and there are no organised tours. To respect the Islamic faith, it may be better to appreciate the beauty of Qatar's mosques from the outside only. If you do happen to gain access to the inside of a mosque you should remember to dress appropriately. That means shorts, sleeveless tops and low cut shirts are out, and ladies should cover their hair.

One of Qatar's many mosques

Safari Tours

Unlike in Africa where a safari involves spotting wildlife in game reserves, a safari in this part of the world means an excursion into the desert. You will be picked up in a powerful 4WD, driven by an experienced (and often charismatic) driver, to head off into the dunes for some thrilling off-road driving and spectacular scenery. For your own safety and enjoyment, it is probably better to stick to the more reputable tour companies when booking your desert safari (such as Arabian Adventures, Travco, Alpha and QIT).

Tours commonly head south out of Doha, stopping at Sealine Beach Resort to meet up with other cars in the convoy and deflate tyres, before heading across the sand to Khor Al Udeid (also known as the Inland Sea). Seatbelts are compulsory and as you barrel up and over gigantic sand dunes, you'll understand why! At times you might feel like the car is going to tip over, but put faith in your driver and just enjoy the ride. When you stop at Khor Al Udeid you can try

Off-Road in the UAE
If you enjoy off-roading in Qatar, then wait till you see what the **UAE Off-Road Explorer** has to offer. Detailed satellite maps and step-by-step instructions will lead you and your 4WD over stunning mountains, through lush green wadis, and across dramatic sand dunes. Be sure to grab a copy before your next trip to the Emirates.

your hand at sand boarding or have a quick dip in the calm, shallow water. Watching the sun set over the desert dunes is a serene, beautiful experience and a great photo opportunity. You can choose to stay in the desert overnight – the tour companies have their own permanent campsites set up among the dunes, and in the evening you can enjoy a delicious Arabic barbecue, accompanied by music, belly dancing and a puff or two on a traditional shisha pipe.

Tour Operators

As Qatar steps up its tourism efforts and opens the country up to more visitors, there are more and more tour operators being established. Most tour companies are locally owned, and locals who are familiar with the region are provided as guides. If you are staying in a hotel, they will be able to recommend reputable tour companies, provide contact information and even make bookings on your behalf.

Tour companies usually provide a pick-up and drop-off from your hotel or house. Prices are

Tour Operators

Tour Operators	
Alpha Tours	434 4499
Arabian Adventure	436 1461
Cleopatra	441 1010
Desert Adventure	436 2455
Destinations of the World	467 1200
Gulf Adventure	431 5555
Navigation Travel Tourism	462 2880
Net Tours	431 0902
Qatar Adventures Co.	467 1752
Qatar International Tours (QIT)	466 7782
Tourist Travel	442 1832
Travco Qatar	523 0891

fixed and there may be a stipulated minimum number of passengers on certain tours. If you do not have the minimum number of people you can still do the tour, but the price per person will probably increase.

Other Attractions

Al Shaqab Stud

Location ➜ Beh Education City · Al Rayyan
Hours ➜ 06:00 - 22:00   Fri closed
Web/email ➜ www.alshaqabstud.com

| 481 2061
Map Ref ➜ 2-B3

Owned by the Emir, HH Sheikh Hamad bin Khakifa al Thani, this farm provides the opportunity for viewing some of the best quality thoroughbred Arabian horses, many of which are world champions. Located in old Rayyan, behind Al Rayyan Football Club and next to Education City, the stud has world-class facilities to care for the horses, including a therapeutic pool. There's also a riding school providing classes for all ages and abilities. Visits can be arranged through one of the local tour operators, at least 24 hours in advance, or by contacting the stud directly on 4800348 or 4803353 (the above number is for the riding school).

Palm Island

Location ➜ Doha Bay
Hours ➜ 09:00 - 22:00   Open until 23:00 Thu, Fri & Sat
Web/email ➜ na

| 486 9151
Map Ref ➜ 10-D1

Located in the centre of Doha Bay, this palm-fringed island is an ideal open-air destination providing distractions and entertainment for both adults and children. Just a 10-minute dhow ride from the jetty

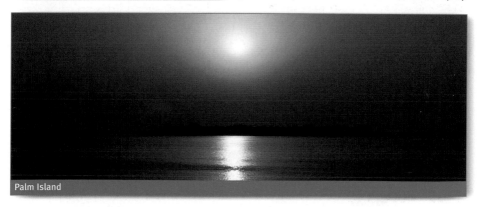

Palm Island

near the Sheraton Hotel, the resort has a cafeteria, a restaurant, children's playground and a sandy beach with shade, changing facilities and shallow water – ideal for novice swimmers. While leaving your children to enjoy the amusement rides and water sports, make sure you try the restaurant's tasty seafood selection. It is also worth mentioning that this is one of the few places where you can get alcoholic drinks outside the boundaries of hotels, which makes dining here even more unique. During the holidays the island offers entertainment activities such as live music and swimming galas. The entrance fee is QR 20 for adults and QR 15 for children. This includes a two-way dhow trip to the island in addition to soft drinks, but the rides, games and activities cost extra. Note - private boats are not allowed access to the island.

Amusement Centres

Jungle Zone

Location → Hyatt Plaza · Alwaab | 469 4848
Hours → 13:00 - 22:00 Sat 10:00 - 22:00
Web/email → na Map Ref → 12-A4

Jungle Zone is located at the Hyatt Plaza and is open daily. This children's area has nine attractions that all are themed around the jungle world. It is located in the foodcourt area so parents can let the children play and eat all in one spot. Prices are QR 45 on weekends (Thursday - Saturday) and QR 30 during the week.

Winter Wonderland

Location → City Center Doha · Diplomatic District | 483 1047
Hours → 13:00 - 22:00 Fri 13:00 - 23:00
Web/email → na Map Ref → 8-D2

Winter Wonderland is where you'll find the ice-skating rinks located in the middle of City Center, which can be seen from each floor. When the temperature outside gets unbearable, what better way to cool down than a quick skate on the ice? The rinks are open every day. The cost is QR 35 for an hour and a half of skating, and spectators can pay QR 10 to sit in the bleachers.

Amusement Parks

Other options → Water Parks [p.113]

Kingdom Of Aladdin

Location → Al Istiqlal · Diplomatic District | 483 1001
Hours → 16:00 - 23:00 Sun closed
Web/email → na Map Ref → 6-D2

The Kingdom of Aladdin provides 18 different activities for children of all ages. It houses a theatre, cafeteria and an artificial lagoon. Located

Kingdom of Aladdin

See you at the border

off-road Oman

Oman trekking

Whether you're visiting for the weekend or going for good, there's an Explorer product to help you make the most of Oman. With the Oman Explorer, Oman Off-Road Explorer and Oman Trekking Explorer, whatever you plan to do it's safe to say we've got the country covered.

Phone (971 4) 335 3520 · **Fax** (971 4) 335 3529
Info@Explorer-Publishing.com · www.Explorer-Publishing.com
Residents' Guides · Visitors' Guides · Photography Books · Activity Guidebooks · Maps

EXPLORER
Passionately Publishing...

near the West Bay area, across from the InterContinental Hotel, this park is also a major attraction during Muslim religious festivals (such as Eid), as international dance groups perform various shows at the park attracting huge crowds.

Entrance fee is QR 6 for adults and QR 4 for children (under 10 years old). Additional tickets for various activities can be bought inside the park. Mondays and Wednesdays are reserved for women and children only, and Tuesdays and Thursdays are dedicated to families. It is worth mentioning that the standards of upkeep at this park don't quite meet those of amusement parks in other parts of the world.

Camel Racing

Other options → Camel Rides [p.123]

Camel racing is a popular local sport throughout the GCC and is still widely practised in Qatar. A good racing camel is worth quite a lot of money and the owner of the camel who is first past the post stands to win a large cash prize and/or a luxury car. The camel race track is in Al Shahaniya and several trainers and owners live nearby. During the cooler months races are held in the afternoons, and in summer they are held in the

Robot Jockeys

For some time camel racing has been the subject of international outrage because of the use of child jockeys. Children as young as three have been 'bought' from their impoverished parents in countries like Pakistan or Bangladesh, and brought over to the GCC to be trained as camel jockeys. These young boys are often made to live in poor conditions and receive too little food in an effort to keep their weight down. During the races, there is a high risk that they could fall off the camel, facing serious injury and even being trampled to death. Even the vigorous bouncing around that they endure while on the camel can lead to internal injuries. Fortunately, along with some other Gulf countries, Qatar has imposed a ban on child jockeys and has made efforts to rehabilitate and repatriate young boys. They have introduced a robot jockey that can control a camel - it is even designed to look like a human with an electronic whip! The robots are controlled by hand held joysticks and computer technology. Future robots will have cameras in their 'eyes', so that owners can have a true view of what the robot 'sees' from atop the camel.

early morning. It is traditionally a male-dominated sport and you will rarely see local women at the track cheering on their favourite camel. Being a favourite sport of locals, you don't often see many expats attending races. However, you should try and get down there at least once, just to experience a true Arabian sport that you are extremely unlikely to see in your home country. It is free of charge to visit the camel races and times are never set for races. It is advisable to call the racing committee before heading out to the tracks to get exact times (487 2028).

Horse Racing

Other options → Horse Riding [p.126]

As in most GCC countries, equestrian activities are very popular and often given special attention by the rulers. Horse racing is organised mainly by the Qatar Racing and Equestrian Club (QREC) and the racing season is usually from October until May. Seven races are run every Thursday between 16:00 and 19:30. Entrance to the races is free. It's not quite Ascot, and there are no restaurants or food stands, no bars, and definitely no gambling! Apart from the race nights, you can have a tour around the QREC, which is open from 08:00 to 12:00 and 16:00 to 19:00. Local tour operators can organise this for you, or you can contact the QREC directly by phone (480 3098), fax (480 3016) or via their website (www.qrec.net).

Nature Reserves

Although they are not official nature reserves, Qatar does have two sites that are important for the indigenous fauna of the region.

Khor Al Udaid	
Location → South-east Qatar	na
Hours → na	
Web/email → na	Map Ref → 1-B4

Khor Al Udaid, also known as the 'Inland Sea', is an area of outstanding natural beauty located approximately 60km south of Doha. One must have a 4WD to get there and it is essential to drive in convoy with at least one experienced off-road driver. The Inland Sea is an important area for resident and migratory bird species, such as flamingoes, cormorants, waders, gulls and terns. Plans to make the Inland Sea a protected conservation area are under discussion.

Oryx Farm

Location ➜ Al Shahaniya	na
Hours ➜ See below	
Web/email ➜ na	Map Ref ➜ 2-A2

Located in the Al Shahaniya region in central Qatar, this protected farm houses a herd of oryxes, which once were on the brink of extinction. The oryx is the national animal of Qatar, and the mascot of both its national airline and the Asian Games. To visit this farm you need a special permit from the Ministry of Municipal Affairs and Agriculture, but visitors will probably find it easier to go through a tour operator.

Powerboat Racing

This is a popular and important sport in Qatar and is run under the umbrella of the Qatar Marine Sports Federation (QMSF), which organises world-class events in powerboat racing and equips local sportsmen to take part in international competitions. There are no membership fees but registration fees are required to take part in the events.

The leading powerboat sports here are Class 1 Offshore Powerboat Racing and Formula 2000 Powerboat Racing (Boat GP). Every year the QMSF organises two rounds of Class 1 Offshore Powerboat Racing, one round of Formula 2000 Powerboat Racing and one round of the Middle East Formula 2000 Powerboat Championships. For more information on the QMSF and the events they organised, visit their website (www.qmsf.org) or call them on 437 9744.

Water Parks

City Center Water Park

Location ➜ City Center Doha · Diplomatic District	483 9163
Hours ➜ 10:00 - 22:00 Fri 13:00 – 22:00	
Web/email ➜ na	Map Ref ➜ 8-D2

Open daily this water park is for younger kids (age one to nine) who must be accompanied by an adult. There are no instructors in the water but there are two lifeguards on duty. The water levels are quite low (below the knee of an adult) making it perfect for younger kids and there are small water boats and waterfalls in addition to basic water slides. While there are no food outlets, there is a supervision/spectator area where parents can sit, and you are allowed to bring your own snacks and drinks.

Zoos

Other than the Oryx farm mentioned on the left, the only other venue where you can visit animals in captivity is the Doha Zoo.

Doha Zoo

Doha Zoo

Location ➜ Al Furousiya St. · Salwa Road South	486 2610
Hours ➜ 08:00 - 12:00 15:30 - 20:30	
Web/email ➜ na	Map Ref ➜ 15-A2

The Doha Zoo is located 15km out of Doha city on Salwa Road, in the industrial area near the Equestrian Club. It houses over 1500 animals from around the world. The collection includes oryx, giraffes, elephants, baboons and zebras. Many of the animals (with the help of their trainers) give frequent live shows to enthusiastic audiences – the elephant performance should not be missed. The zoo has a cafeteria and children's playground located within its beautiful 42 hectare grounds. A trip to the zoo makes a great weekend excursion for children and adults. The entrance fee is QR 5 for adults and QR 2 for children under nine. Tuesday afternoons are for ladies and children only.

Weekend Breaks

Other options → Tours & Sightseeing [p.107]
Hotels [p.21]

A weekend break to recharge your batteries is essential now and again. Mini holidays can be as simple as checking into a local beach resort or popping into your travel agent to book a quick trip to a neighbouring GCC country. Doha International Airport is easily accessible and has daily flights to nearby destinations like Muscat, Dubai and Bahrain. Your travel agent will be able to advise you on packages that include flights, accommodation, car rental and perhaps even an organised tour.

For a weekend break within the country, many residents head south for a night or two at the Sealine Beach Resort. This small resort, run by Qatar National Hotels, is located right on the beach. You can relax on a sun lounger or try some adventurous watersports, depending on what kind of 'R & R' appeals to you!

Most residents choose not to travel beyond the borders of Qatar by car – women have to be accompanied by either a brother or husband to cross over into Saudi, and once they do they are not allowed to drive or show their hair. It is easier just to fly. For a list of suggested destinations, refer to the Weekend Breaks table.

Weekend Breaks Outside Qatar

If you fancy getting away from Qatar for a few days there are many interesting and varied opportunities just a short hop away in neighbouring GCC countries. The local operators, including Qatar Airways, Oman Air, Gulf Air, Emirates, and Air Arabia, offer regular flights throughout the region, plus you may find a flight with one of the international carriers who often make stopovers. Depending on your nationality you may be eligible for a visa on arrival in certain GCC countries. Just remember, if you are in Qatar on a visit visa and you leave, you will need another one to get back in. However, access is a little easier now the government allows 33 nationalities to obtain visas on arrival. See Entering Qatar on p.16.

Bahrain

Bahrain is a popular jaunt for residents of all the GCC countries. There should be a little something for everyone, from the wide selection of fine dining (and drinking!) to a spot of shopping and sightseeing. You could visit a fort or two, take in a museum, have a spin around the new grand prix circuit or hop on a boat to one of Bahrain's many islands. For more information and inspiration, check out the *Bahrain Explorer* from Explorer Publishing.

Beautiful Oman

Kuwait

While Bahrain, UAE and Oman may be quite popular spots for residents of Qatar, Kuwait is not always immediately considered as a weekend break destination (no alcohol don't forget), however, the colourful and somewhat tainted heritage of this small yet rich country means it is still worth a visit. Kuwait may be one of the world's smallest countries but its 500km coastline has endless golden beaches that remain refreshingly tranquil. From the Grand Mosque to the Kuwait Towers there are many architectural splendours to take snaps of while Al Qurain House, which still shows the scars of war with its immortal bullet holes, gives you a fascinating insight into the troubled times of the Iraqi invasion. There is also Green Island, an artificial island linked by a short bridge and home to restaurants, a children's play area, and providing a great alternative view of Kuwait's shoreline. For more information and inspiration, check out the *Kuwait Explorer* from Explorer Publishing.

Oman

There are countless reasons to visit Oman, and with frequent flights from Qatar there's really no excuse not to. The Gulf of Oman's rich sea life, the historic buildings, the wildlife, and the variety of unspoilt landscapes including vast dramatic deserts, rugged mountains and lush green wadis and valleys, are all things that you will remember fondly. The fascinating sights and sounds of the capital Muscat will provide more than enough to keep any weekend visitor busy, but Oman has much more. You should also consider exploring the Mussandam Peninsula with its amazing dive sites, the historic mountain towns and villages with stunning scenery, the turtle beaches in the east, and the blissful summer rain in the southern Dhofar region. For more information on all these areas and details of all there is to see and do, grab a copy of the *Oman Explorer* from Explorer Publishing.

UAE

Often described as the city of gold, a shopper's paradise, and one of the best nights out in the Middle East, Dubai is by far the favourite destination in the Emirates. There's so much to see and do you're unlikely to fit everything into one weekend, but some visitor 'musts' include exploring the creek and the historic souks, enjoying the thrill of a desert safari, doing some serious shopping, and then treating yourself to some hard-

Dubai

earned pampering at one of Dubai's luxury spas. The range of eating, drinking, and dancing options is also worth the airfare alone! Don't forget the other emirates though, including Abu Dhabi, Sharjah and Fujeirah. There's bags of culture and heritage to discover, no end of golden sandy beaches, and the east coast has some great snorkelling and diving sites. To help you make the most of any trip to the Emirates, don't miss the *Dubai Explorer*, the *Abu Dhabi Explorer*, the *UAE Off-Road Explorer*, and the *UAE Underwater Explorer* – all from Explorer Publishing.

Travel Agencies

Other options → Tour Operators [p.109]

Doha is home to a number of travel agencies that can help you decide where to go on holiday. For a comprehensive list of popular agencies in Doha, refer to the travel agencies table below. Some agencies stand out because of special service: Regency Travel is good because they are open seven days a week; while Mannai Air Travel are renowned for attention to detail and personal customer service.

Travel Agencies	
Ali Bin Ali Travel	444 1161
Arabian Adventures	436 1461
Around the World Travels	442 7992
Darwish Travel	441 8666
Mannai Air Travel P.19	444 2402
Qatar International Tours	466 7782
Rayan Travel & Tours	441 8587
Regency Travel	434 4444
Thamco Travel	442 4244
Time Travel & Tours	443 7575
Travco Qatar Holidays	436 6737
United Tours & Travel	486 6280

Activities

EXPLORER

Activities

Highlights...

The Games are Coming!

The 15th Asian Games Doha 2006 is poised to be the world's second biggest multi-sporting event, with the addition of several sports (including Chess and Triathlon) that are featured for the first time in the Games' history. The Doha 2006 Games will be the first to be held in the Arab World, the first to include 39 sports, the first to feature 423 events, and the first to welcome 10,000 athletes and team officials representing, for the first time, 45 countries and regions!

Be Beautiful
p.135

Beauty Salons, luxurious spas, sunshine and swimming pools - Qatar has its fair share of pampering pick-me-ups to help you forget your troubles. Whether it's a full-body scrub or an aromatherapy facial at the Bio-Bil Beauty Centre (p.135), or a therapeutic back massage and Turkish bath at The Doha Marriot Spa (p.136), being beautiful needn't be a chore!

Sports & Activities

Qatar is all abuzz in anticipation of hosting the 15th Asian Games in 2006, and all eyes are focused on sport! For 15 days in December 2006, athletes from 45 countries and regions will compete for glory in a total of 423 events. For more information on the games, visit www.doha-2006.com. On a slightly less competitive level, the residents of Doha keep active in many sports and activities on a daily basis. This chapter lists the sports clubs, social groups, hobby societies and general activities that are worth looking into, especially if you've just arrived and want to make the most of life as an expat.

We have hunted high and low to bring you these details, but since it's our first edition we know we might have left somebody out. If you organise or are a member of a group, club or society that doesn't appear in this chapter, we need to hear from you. Send us an email (Info@Explorer-Publishing.com) with all your details, and we'll include your details in the next edition. It's the easy road to fame, and it's free!

Aerobics

Other options → **Dance Classes [p.140]**
Sports & Leisure Facilities [p.138]

Aerobics classes are a good way to exercise – the music is loud and motivating, the instructor will squeeze every last ounce of effort out of you, and you can compare sore muscles afterwards with a group of other fitness fanatics! Step, pump, spinning, aqua and many other kinds of fitness classes are offered at most of the health clubs around Doha – check with each club for their schedule of classes. Prices vary from club to club, but if you are not a member you can expect to pay around QR 35 per class. It is usually necessary to book in advance for the popular classes at peak times.

Bio-Bil Health, Beauty Centre & Spa

Location → Nxt to City Center · Diplomatic District | 493 4433
Hours → 08:30 - 20:30
Web/email → www.ahbqatar.com/biobill.htm   Map Ref → 8-D2

Set in luxurious surroundings and taking up three floors of the prestigious Bilal Suites Building (in the West Bay next to City Center Mall), this amazing salon and spa features the latest equipment and highly trained staff. In addition to beauty treatments and sports therapy, the spa also has a gym for men and women where you get round-the-

clock advice from personal trainers on fitness programmes, nutrition and fat reduction techniques. There are also group fitness classes and yoga classes in the aerobics studio. Other facilities include a swimming pool, Jacuzzi, steam rooms, and Turkish and Moroccan baths. Contact the spa for enquiries about membership. The daily rate is QR 50.

Doha Club

Location → Al Sharq · Al Khulaifat | 441 8822
Hours → Timings on request
Web/email → www.doha-club.com   Map Ref → 11-B4

The Doha Club offers Aqua Aerobics on Tuesdays and Thursdays. You can also do step aerobics and pilates classes. You can either pay per class (QR 35) or per month (QR 350). For more information and a schedule of classes, call Leslie (554 8935).

Funtown

Location → City Center Doha | 483 1047
Hours → 10:00 - 22:00   Fri 13:00 - 22:00
Web/email → na   Map Ref → 8-D2

Funtown is reserved exclusively for women, although boys up to the age of ten can accompany their mothers. Apart from a range of exciting leisure activities (including a bowling alley, ice-skating rink, children's play area and squash courts), Funtown also has a fully equipped gym where you can do aerobics classes. Each class costs QR 35.

InterFitness Club

Location → InterContinental Doha | 484 4979
Hours → Timings on request
Web/email → www.ichotelsgroup.com   Map Ref → 6-D3

The comprehensive health club at this hotel has a 24 hour gym, as well as a range of exciting fitness classes. Choose from something quiet like a stretch class, or something more strenuous like a 'Total Beach-Body Workout'. There is also a running group affiliated to the club, and an active tennis club.

Ramada's Cabana Club

Location → Ramada Doha · Al Muntazah | 441 7417
Hours → 07:00 - 23:00
Web/email → www.ramada-doha.com   Map Ref → 13-B2

Fitness classes at the Cabana Club are open to members and non-members. Choose from step aerobics (a great cardiovascular workout), water aerobics, stretch classes and gym personal training classes (where you can learn the proper techniques for weight training). You can also take classes in yoga and pilates.

The Ritz-Carlton Doha

Location → West Bay Lagoon | 484 8000
Hours → Timings on request
Web/email → www.ritzcarlton-doha.com   Map Ref → 4-D2

If you want high-impact, maxiumum calorie-burning exercise classes, you can try spinning, circuit training, body combat and body pump. If you want something a bit more gentle (but still effective), you can try resistance ball, stretching or body balance classes. And the 'Absolute Abs' class will blitz any wobbly bits you have around the middle! All classes cost QR 35 for non-members; members can join the classes for free.

Badminton   20 QR

Social Sun 7 -10pm,

Doha Club

Location → Al Sharq · Al Khulaifat | 441 8822
Hours → Timings on request
Web/email → www.doha-club.com   Map Ref → 11-B4

Badminton can be played on the multi-purpose outdoor court (also suitable for basketball, football and baseball). The cost for badminton is QR 60 for non-members, and QR 45 for members. Booking is essential. For more information, contact the club at the above number (ext.225), or call Mangala on 526 9338.

Sealine Beach Resort

Location → Mesaieed | 477 2722
Hours → 07:30 - 19:00
Web/email → www.qnhc.com   Map Ref → 1-C3

Sealine Beach Resort has badminton court available for hourly hire. The cost for one hour is QR 10. It is wise to book the court in advance, as it gets quite busy.

Sheraton Doha Hotel & Resort

Location → Sheraton Doha · Doha Corniche | 485 4444
Hours → Timing on request
Web/email → www.starwoodhotels.com/doha   Map Ref → 8-E3

This club has a badminton court but it is for use by hotel guests and club members only. Non-

members can only play if accompanied by a member. The cost per hour is QR 20.

Baseball

Qatar Little League

Location → Various locations | 556 0975
Hours → Timings on request
Web/email → na   Map Ref → na

This baseball league is open to boys and girls (aged 4 – 18). If you have children who are interested in playing, call Ed Dixon (556 0975) for more information on registration, location and timings. There are 20 teams in the league, which began its ninth season in September 2005.

Basketball

Many of the basketball courts in Doha are in health clubs and therefore are reserved for use by members only. However, there are places where non-members can play basketball; some of the health clubs allow non-members to play on their courts, as long as they are accompanied by members. And the Doha Club hires out its court to non-members.

The Diplomatic Club

Location → West Bay | 484 7444
Hours → 07:00 - 22:00
Web/email → www.thediplomaticclub.com   Map Ref → 4-D4

Members can use the half-size basketball court from 07:00 to 22:00. Balls are available from the recreation reception. Regular social sessions are organised so that keen players can practise together.

Doha Club

Location → Al Sharq · Al Khulaifat | 441 8822
Hours → Timing on request
Web/email → www.doha-club.com   Map Ref → 11-B4

Basketball can be played on the multi-purpose outdoor court (which is also suitable for baseball, football and badminton), but obviously the summer temperatures may see you sticking to indoor activities. For more information on prices, timings and reservations, please contact the club on the above number (extension 225) or call Mangala on 526 9338.

COME & JOIN US!

You don't need to be a member
to dine at Doha Club!

 ناديالدوحة

For Membership Inquiries please call on 4418822
Fax No.: 432-7811 • P.O. Box 3666, Doha, Qatar
E-mail : dohaclub@qatar.net.qa • Website : www.doha-club.com

Ramada's Cabana Club

Location → Ramada Doha · Al Muntazah
Hours → 07:00 - 23:00
Web/email → www.ramada-doha.com   Map Ref → 13-B2

Although there is no fee to play basketball on this court, it is for the use of members and hotel guests only (although non-members are allowed to play when accompanied by a member). It is advisable to book one day in advance, especially since there are regular 'Basketball Nights' organised during the week.

Sheraton Doha Hotel & Resort

Location → Sheraton Doha · Doha Corniche
Hours → Timings on request
Web/email → www.starwoodhotels.com/doha   Map Ref → 8-E3

This club has an indoor court that is suitable for basketball – it is open throughout the week from 07:00 - 22:00. It is only for use by members of the club, who have to pay QR 50 to use the court. Booking in advance is required.

Boat & Yacht Charters

Other options → **Dhow Charters [p.124]**

If you aspire to the boating life but can't be bothered with all the hard work of owning your own boat, you can still sail off into the sunset on a chartered boat or a cruise. The companies listed below offer various options depending on how long you want to go for, and how many people are in your group.

Doha Club

Location → Al Sharq · Al Khulaifat
Hours → Timings on request
Web/email → www.doha-club.com   Map Ref → 11-B4

A boat is available for a full-day charter – a daytrip takes seven hours, departing at 10:00 and returning some time after 16:00. It is possible to leave earlier, if required. The boat can carry up to 21 people. A full day's charter will cost QR 800, a trip to Banana Island costs QR 300 and a trip to Safliya Island costs QR 200. Booking is essential – contact Mr. Dawre on the above number (ext. 243) or on 580 0530 – he will be able to tell you if the weather is good enough to sail or not.

Regatta Sailing Academy

Location → Corniche · Diplomatic District
Hours → Timings on request
Web/email → na   Map Ref → 8-E3

The Regatta Sailing Academy has a range of sailing vessels to suit all requirements, including funboats, training boats, dinghies, and even a 28 foot yacht that can be used for pleasure or racing. The academy is staffed with fully qualified British Royal Yacht Academy instructors, who provide instruction in the safety of the lagoon area before venturing out into the waters of Doha Bay. Call for more information on prices and weather conditions.

Bowling

Funtown

Location → City Center Doha
Hours → 10:00 - 22:00   Fri 13:00 - 22:00
Web/email → na   Map Ref → 8-D2

This one-stop fun centre for ladies has a long list of facilities, including a six-lane bowling alley. It costs QR 10 for a game (for one person), and if you need to buy socks, they cost QR 8. Boys are allowed up to the age of ten.

Qatar Bowling Centre

Location → Opp British Embassy · Al Bidda
Hours → 14:30 - 23:30   Thu, Fri 13:00 - 23:00
Web/email → na   Map Ref → 10-B3

The Qatar Bowling Centre has 32 lanes. The entrance fee is QR 10 and then each game costs QR 7 (including shoe rental). Alternatively, you can take out a yearly membership for QR 400. Entrance is free for members. There are some league teams that play regularly (usually on Friday, Sunday and Tuesday evenings) and hold tournaments. Tuesday mornings are reserved for ladies only. The centre has a foodcourt where you can get snacks and soft drinks.

Winter Wonderland

Location → City Center Doha
Hours → 13:00 - 22:00   Fri 13:00 - 23:00
Web/email → na   Map Ref → 8-D2

Winter Wonderland has a ten-lane bowling alley. Prices for a game are flexible: if you play between 10:00 and 14:00, a game costs QR 7. If you play from 14:00 onwards, it costs QR 10. A yearly standard membership costs QR 150 and a yearly league membership costs QR 75 – both standard and league members play QR 7 per game, at any time of day. Alternatively you can pay QR 500 for the 'Strike Gold' membership card, which lets you play 100 games at your leisure. Socks cost QR 6 and you can rent a locker for QR 100.

Boxing

Qatar Boxing Federation

Location ➜ Various locations	**494 4257**
Hours ➜ Timings on request	
Web/email ➜ na	Map Ref ➜ na

The primary function of this federation is to promote Qatar boxing. However, if you are a keen boxer and would like to practise regularly, you can contact them and fill in the information form, and you will be able to use the facilities. You will have to undergo a medical test before you start.

Camel Rides

Other options ➜ **Camel Racing [p.123]**

Sealine Beach Resort

Location ➜ Mesaieed	**477 2722**
Hours ➜ 07:30 - 19:00	
Web/email ➜ www.qnhc.com	Map Ref ➜ 1-C3

This is your chance to experience something that you probably wouldn't get to do in your home country: a camel ride along the beach. It costs QR 15 for a quick ride, and QR 100 for a hour-long ride (padded shorts are recommended for this option!).

Camping

Other options ➜ **Outdoor Goods [p.165]**
Wadi & Dune Bashing [p.134]

To camp in Qatar you will need a well-equipped 4 WD and a group of friends who are experienced campers and know their way around once you get off road. Of course, if you don't have your own 4 WD (or your own friends!), there are companies that can take the hard work out of camping, providing tents that are relatively luxurious, food, water and entertainment.

Qatar International Tours

Location ➜ Various locations	**466 7782**
Hours ➜ Timings on request	
Web/email ➜ www.qit-qatar.com	Map Ref ➜ na

Live the bedouin lifestyle, but without the hardship – QIT will provide all camping equipment including a tent, fully furnished with carpets, cushions, sleeping bags, dressing rooms, and a table and chairs. They even provide sweet water for the showers. A typical night out in the desert starts with the lighting of a huge bonfire, and then while you relax the chef prepares a sumptuous barbecue feast. The minimum number of people required for desert camping is eight. A band and belly dancer are available on request (and for an extra charge).

Cycling

Other options ➜ **Cycling [p.28]**
Sporting Goods [p.169]

Qatar Cycling Federation

Location ➜ Opp Khalifa Stadium · Al Soudan North	**447 5522**
Hours ➜ Timings on Request	
Web/email ➜ www.qatarcf.org	Map Ref ➜12-A3

This cycling group is open to members of the public who are keen cyclists. They organise regular rides and races in the categories of road racing, time trials, individual and team races, mountain biking and triathlons. The federation's official team has participated in many international races and they are training for participation in the 2006 Asian Games. For more information, visit the website or send an email to aljaaass@yahoo.com.

Cycling on the corniche

Dhow Charters

Other options → **Boat & Yacht Charters [p.122]**

InterFitness Club

Location → InterContinental Doha	**484 4979**
Hours → Timings on request	
Web/email → www.ichotelsgroup.com	Map Ref →6-D3

You can charter a dhow for QR 75 per person, including lunch. The trip takes you to the nearby islands, or if you prefer you can just cruise along the corniche. Trips can last anywhere between three and eight hours, depending on your preference (the price will vary accordingly).

Palm Tree Island Boat Company

Location → Nxt to Sheraton · Doha Corniche	**486 9151**
Hours → 09:00 - 22:00 Thu - Sat 09:00 - 23:00	
Web/email → na	Map Ref → 8-E3

A dhow will take you to Palm Tree Island at a cost of QR 20 for adults and QR 15 for children, which includes a soft drink and snack. The trip from the corniche to the island takes about ten minutes; no booking is required. Call Nahed on 486 9151, 486 5178 or 550 9832 for more information.

Diving

Other options → **Snorkelling [p.130]**

Doha Sub-Aqua Club

Location → DSAC Club House · Ras Abu Abboud	**466 1472**
Hours → Timings on request	
Web/email → na	Map Ref → na

The DSAC was founded in Qatar in 1977. It offers a range of diving courses and awards BSAC qualifications. The basic course lasts for six weeks and includes pool practice, lectures and accompanied sea dives. Further qualifications, such as Sports Diver, Diver Leader, Advanced Diver and Instructor, are available. Shore dives are arranged to two artificial reefs that are still under construction by the club. Trips are also arranged to dive sites at Dukhan, Al Khor and the natural coral reefs in the Inland Sea. There are many wreck dives to be found in Qatar's waters. The club owns two boats that are used for offshore trips. On the social side, the club has its own clubhouse and hosts regular barbecues and get-togethers. The club has about 130 diving members. Membership is open to

all, even for those who don't dive. New diver membership costs QR 1920 (this includes the cost of Ocean Diver Training). Annual renewal is QR 1200. Contact the club for more information.

Pearl Divers

Location → Farig Al Nasser Rd · Doha	**444 9553**
Hours → Timings on request	
Web/email → na	Map Ref → na

Pearl Divers is a 5-Star PADI facility – their instructors can help you become a proficient diver in less than a week. After you've completed your training you will get the PADI Open Water Diver certification, which is internationally recognised. Visit the Pearl Divers shop for a comprehensive range of diving equipment and accessories.

QDive Marine Center

Location → Opp Al Fardan Centre · Doha	**437 5065**
Hours → Timings on request	
Web/email → www.qdive.net	Map Ref → 10-E4

This centre offers a full range of diving services, equipment rental and retail. They arrange diving, snorkelling and fishing trips, either with a speedboat or on the classic dhow. They also offer a range of diving courses accredited under PADI. Their shop is the Qatar distributor for renowned brands like Zeagle, Sherwood and Genesis.

Fencing

Qatar Fencing Federation

Location → Nr Independence R/A	**483 8391**
Hours → Timings on request	
Web/email → www.qatarfencing.org	Map Ref → 8-A3

This association caters for those who are serious about fencing – they send a Qatar team to the Fencing World Championships and the Asian Games. The association is also open to members of the public who are interested in fencing though, and beginners can play on Saturdays, Mondays and Tuesdays from 16:00 to 19:00.

Fishing

Other options → **Boat & Yacht Charters [p.122]**

The clear, warm waters of the Arabian Gulf provide rich fishing grounds. From sardines to sailfish, you'll have the chance to catch it in the waters of Qatar's coast. During the fishing season (October to May) you should be able to enjoy some successful fishing trips where your catch might include kingfish, tuna, mackerel and barracuda.

Bringing in the morning catch

Doha Club

Location → Al Sharq · Al Khulaifal | 441 8822
Hours →   Timings on request
Web/email → www.doha-club.com   Map Ref → 11-B4

Fishing trips are available through the club, at a cost of QR 800 for a full-day trip. While the trip is available in summer, it might be more comfortable to go in winter when the weather is cooler. You can expect to catch fish such as hammour, barracuda and kingfish. You have to provide your own fishing equipment and lunch. Trips cannot take place in certain weather conditions, so book in advance and then phone before you go just to make sure that the trip is on.

Qatar International Tours

Location → Various locations | 466 7782
Hours →   Timings on request
Web/email → www.qit-qatar.com   Map Ref → na

A full-day fishing trip with QIT costs QR 180 on the traditional dhow, or QR 200 on the fishing boat. The price includes lunch, fishing line, bait and soft drinks. The QIT captain is highly experienced and guides the boat to locations that yield the best catch.

Flying

Aviation Science Centre

Location → Al Salata Al Jadeeda | 469 6200
Hours →   Timings on request
Web/email → www.qatarflying.net   Map Ref → 16-B1

This aviation centre offers a safe and supervised environment for flying model aircraft. For more information, please contact Mr Khalid Al Khater on the above details or by email (rafco@qatar.net.qa).

Football

Doha Club

Location → Al Sharq · Al Khulaifat | 441 8822
Hours →   Timings on request
Web/email → www.doha-club.com   Map Ref → 11-B4

The multi-purpose outdoor court can be booked for football (as well as other sports such as badminton, basketball and baseball). It costs QR 75 for an hour and QR 125 for two hours. Contact the club for more information, or call Mangala on 526 9338.

Golf

Doha Golf Club

Location → West Bay | 483 2338
Hours → 06:00 - 24:00
Web/email → www.dohagolfclub.com   Map Ref → 4-A2

Doha Golf Club is open daily to members and non-members. It has a 7,312 yard, 18 hole

Doha Golf Club

championship course and a floodlit nine-hole academy course. It is also home to several restaurants, lounges and conference rooms. The club's Golf Academy is a state-of-the-art teaching and practice facility with custom-built chipping, putting and bunker areas. The club is host to the Qatar Masters tournament, which has been a regular feature on the European Tour schedule since 1998.

Hashing

Other options → **Running [p.129]**
Bars [p.204]

Qatar Hash House Harriers

Location → Various locations	**550 7974**
Hours → Timings on request	
Web/email → na	Map Ref → na

The Qatar Hash is a mixed hash, running on Monday afternoons. There is a family barbecue on the first Monday of every month, at which kids are welcome. For more information contact Chris Dommet (dommett_chris@hotmail.com; 585 7491), Keith Davis (davis@qp.com.qa; 447 5783), or Phil York (payork@qatar.net.qa; 582 0684).

Hockey

Other options → **Ice Hockey [p.127]**

Doha Hockey Club

Location → Al Maadeed · Al Khulaifat	**469 0586**
Hours → Timings on request	
Web/email → na	Map Ref → na

The hockey scene in Qatar is an informal affair, but there are enough enthusiasts to make sure newcomers will be able to find a game . There are four clubs – Wanderers, Pakistan HC, Gateway and Doha – and tournaments and matches between the clubs are arranged from time to time. There are currently no dedicated outdoor venues for hockey, but hopefully this will change after the Asian Games in 2006. All interested players are encouraged to join in. Costs are low, covering only the hiring of the ground, if required. Players should bring a stick and shin pads, although beginners can borrow equipment initially. Teams usually play on Tuesday evenings at the Qatar International School. Contact Neville Gibbs for more information.

Horse Riding

Qatar Racing & Equestrian Club

Location → Al Rayyan Farm · Al Rayyan	**480 3098**
Hours → 08:00 - 18:00 Fri closed	
Web/email → www.qrec.net	Map Ref → 2-B3

The QREC offers riding tuition for all ages, conducted by highly qualified instructors. After filling in the application form and paying the monthly subscription fees (QR 300), you can have three lessons per week.

Sealine Beach Resort

Location → Mesaieed	**477 2722**
Hours → 07:30 - 19:00	
Web/email → www.qnhc.com	Map Ref → 1-C3

At this beach resort you can enjoy a horseback ride along the beach for QR 15 (or you can hire a horse for one hour for QR 100). Camel rides are also available.

From the horse's mouth

Ice Hockey

Winter Wonderland

Location → City Center Doha	**483 1047**
Hours → 13:00 - 22:00 Fri 13:00 - 23:00	
Web/email → na	Map Ref → 8-D2

Winter Wonderland has a full-size ice-skating rink that can be used for recreational skating or for training – there are several ice hockey leagues that use the facility. There are qualified coaches on hand to help beginners with their technique. Skate hire is available. For more information, call the above number or 483 9163 (the direct line for the ice rink).

Ice Skating

Funtown

Location → City Center Doha	**483 1047**
Hours → 10:00 - 22:00 Fri 13:00 - 22:00	
Web/email → na	Map Ref → 8-D2

Funtown is for ladies only, although boys are allowed up the age of ten. For an ice-skating session lasting one hour and 45 minutes, it costs QR 35. You can buy a full-day pass for QR 50 and a monthly pass for QR 150.

Winter Wonderland

Location → City Center Doha	**483 1047**
Hours → 13:00 - 22:00 Fri 13:00 - 23:00	
Web/email → na	Map Ref → 8-D2

The full-size rink is available for recreational skating, and a quick spin on the ice certainly provides a novel and welcome respite from the summer heat outdoors. A single skating session costs QR 35 per person, and the entrance fee for non-skaters is QR 10. A full-day pass costs QR 50 from Sunday to Wednesday and QR 100 from Thursday to Saturday. Various membership packages are available: Silver Monthly Membership costs QR 400 and allows unlimited access from Sunday to Wednesday while Gold Monthly Membership costs QR 750 and allows unlimited access at any time. Extra services include skate hire, skate sharpening (QR 75), professional lessons (packages starting from QR 350) and ice hockey classes. The direct number for the ice rink is 483 9163.

Ice Skating at City Center Doha

Kayaking

Other options → **Tours & Sightseeing [p.107]**

Sealine Beach Resort

Location → Mesaieed	**477 2722**
Hours → 07.30 - 19:00	
Web/email → www.qnhc.com	Map Ref → 1-C3

This resort offers many watersports from its beautiful stretch of private beach. You can hire a Kayak for QR 40 per hour.

Martial Arts

Doha Club

Location → Al Sharq · Al Khulaifat	**441 8822**
Hours → Timings on request	
Web/email → www.doha-club.com	Map Ref → 11-B4

Lessons are available in the martial arts of karate, taekwondo and judo. Karate lessons are every Sunday, Monday and Tuesday with Capt Naggar (584 8749). Taekwondo lessons are with Capt Hatem (553 5287) on Mondays and Wednesdays. Karate and taekwondo lessons cost QR 150 per month. Judo lessons are with Capt Hamad (569 6021). All these disciplines are taught at various levels (beginners, intermediates and adults). Call the relevant captain for more information.

IAID

Location → Opp Muntazah Park · Al Muntazah | 432 0974
Hours → 08:00 - 12:00 16:00 - 21:00 Fri closed
Web/email → na   Map Ref → 13-C3

The International Academy for Intercultural Development offers Shotokan karate classes for beginners, intermediate and advanced students. Those who take karate seriously should be able to get to black-belt status in two or three years. Every three months there is an examination to assess your readiness to proceed to the next level. The monthly cost is QR 100 for children and QR 150 for adults.

Ramada's Cabana Club

Location → Ramada Doha · Al Muntazah | 441 7417
Hours → 07:00 - 23:00
Web/email → www.ramada-doha.com   Map Ref → 13-B2

Apart from being able to defend yourself, the benefits of karate and taekwondo include improved physical fitness and energy levels. The Cabana Club has lessons for beginners and advanced students. Call the club for information on prices and lesson times.

Taekwondo Centre

Location → Nr Ramada Doha · Al Muntazah | 465 9066
Hours → 10:30 - 20:30 Fri closed
Web/email → na   Map Ref → 13-B2

Classes are available for men, women and children and are split into three levels: beginners (white and yellow belts), intermediate (green to red belts) and advanced (senior red and black belts). The coach, JK Shin, is a 7th Dan Black Belt, a member of the Qatar National Taekwondo Team and the coach for Korea's National Taekwondo Team.

Motor Sports

Qatar Motor & Motorcycle Federation

Location → Salwa Rd · Doha | 437 9708
Hours → Various timings
Web/email → www.qmmf.com   Map Ref → 13-B2

The QMMF organises rallies and provides advice on driving skills. One of the immediate ways you can get involved is to volunteer to become a marshall at one of their events, held throughout the year. Visit the website to download a volunteer application

form, and to find out more information about the federation's upcoming events.

Motorcycling

Qatar Motor & Motorcycle Federation

Location → Salwa Rd · Doha | 437 9708
Hours → Various timings
Web/email → www.qmmf.com   Map Ref → 13-B2

QMMF promotes two- and four-wheel motor sport in Qatar, organising several events every year. They are always on the lookout for keen volunteers who can help with the organisation of these events, such as marshalling on the day. Visit the website to download the volunteer application form.

Parasailing

The Diplomatic Club

Location → West Bay | 484 7444
Hours → 07:00 - 22:00
Web/email → www.thediplomaticclub.com   Map Ref → 4-D4

Among other watersports and activities available at the Diplomatic Club, you can have a go at parasailing. One round costs QR 100 for adults and QR 75 for children.

Sheraton Doha Hotel & Resort

Location → Sheraton Doha · Doha Corniche | 485 4444
Hours → Timings on request
Web/email → www.starwoodhotels.com/doha   Map Ref → 8-E3

A parasailing session here lasts for about 15 minutes and costs QR 100. It is necessary to book in advance.

Powerboating

The Diplomatic Club

Location → West Bay | 484 7444
Hours → 07:00 - 22:00
Web/email → www.thediplomaticclub.com   Map Ref → 4-D4

The Diplomatic Club has a 21 foot powerboat that can be hired for day trips, fishing trips, water skiing and island drop offs. The hire includes an experienced captain. If you are water skiing, instruction is available, and safety cover is provided by trained lifeguards on jet skis.

Quad Bikes

Sealine Beach Resort

Location → Mesaieed
Hours → 07:30 - 19:00
Web/email → www.qnhc.com

477 2722

Map Ref → 1-C3

As long as you are 16 years old and have a valid driving licence (for identification purposes), you can hire a quad bike from the Sealine Beach Resort. It costs QR 150 per hour for a big bike (160cc) and QR 100 per hour for the medium or small bike (80cc or 50cc). Attendants are helpful and will show you how to operate the bike. If you get stuck in the sand they will hop on a spare bike and come and help you out!

Rugby

Doha Rugby Union Football Centre

Location → Nr Doha College · Al Soudan South
Hours → Timings on request
Web/email → www.doharugbyfc.com

468 3771

Map Ref → 12-C4

This active centre was formed in 1974. Today it has 150 mini rugby players, an U16 side, and first and second XV, a vets' team, a gulf-recognised colts' side and two ladies' teams that have won virtually every tournament in the last two years (including two successive wins at the renowned Dubai Rugby 7s). Perhaps one of the reasons for the centre's success is its dedicated army of supporters, known to number as many as 700 at some local matches. If you would like to join the centre, contact any member of the Executive Committee. Alternatively, you can just show up at the grounds on Sunday or Tuesday evenings at 19:00, with your kit.

Running

Other options → **Hashing [p.126]**

The only two hazards that might hamper your running in Qatar are high temperatures and crazy drivers. On the whole though, the climate is bearable for most of the year (and absolutely perfect in the winter), and there are plenty of routes around the less busy roads allowing you to avoid the cars. Running along the corniche is particularly enjoyable, and proves to be a very popular spot for Doha's joggers.

Runners on the corniche

InterFitness Club

Location → InterContinental Doha
Hours → Timings on request
Web/email → www.ichotelsgroup.com

484 4979

Map Ref → 6-D3

InterFitness aims to gather together running enthusiasts of all fitness levels for an organised run once a week. Runners meet on Wednesday evenings at the corniche - there is no need to book, and no charge; all you need is your running shoes! Call the club for more information.

Sailing

Other options → **Boat & Yacht Charters [p.122]**

The year-round favourable weather conditions and the calm waters off the coast mean that sailing is a popular sport in Qatar. Regular events and regattas are held.

Qatar Sailing and Rowing Federation

Location → Ras Abu Abboud Rd · Al Khulaifat
Hours → 10:00 - 18:00
Web/email → na

443 9840

Map Ref → 11-C4

The Qatar Sailing & Rowing Federation is responsible for promoting sailing in Qatar, with the support of the Doha Sailing Club. The club has a variety of boats suitable for all ages, including the following: Optimist, Laser 4.7, Laser Radial, Laser Standard and Catamaran.

Some boats belong to members, but many are owned solely by the club and the QSRF. To find out more about how you can get involved in the elegant sport of sailing, contact Mr. Abdulla (the president of DSC) or Mr. Rashid (the secretary-general of QSRF) on 443 9840 or 442 0305 respectively.

Regatta Sailing Academy

Location → Corniche · Diplomatic District | 550 7846
Hours → Timings on request
Web/email → na   Map Ref → 8-E3

The academy has a range of equipment suitable for sailors of all ages, including lasers, dinghies and sports boats. You can seek the advice of several fully qualified British Royal Yacht Association instructors, and get some pointers in the safety of the lagoon before progressing to the waters of Doha Bay.

Sand Boarding/Skiing

Other options → **Tour Operators [p.109]**

For thrills and spills, desert style, try sand boarding on the dunes. You won't reach the break-neck speeds of snow boarding, and if you do fall off you'll land in lovely soft sand! This must-try activity is offered by most of the tour operators.

Qatar International Tours

Location → Various locations | 466 7782
Hours → Timings on request
Web/email → www.qit-qatar.com   Map Ref → na

Whether you choose to go on the half-day or full-day desert safari with QIT, you'll have the opportunity to try sand skiing. A half-day tour lasts four hours and costs QR 200 per person. A full-day tour lasts eight hours and costs QR 275. For each tour a minimum of four participants is required.

Shooting

Qatar Shooting Federation

Location → Al Duhail South | 487 0840
Hours → Timings on request
Web/email → na   Map Ref → 3-A3

Although this organisation used to be solely for members of the national shooting team, it is now open to the public. People can practise clay target shooting, skeet shooting and trap shooting, and there will be regular precision shooting events.

Facilities will be the same ones used for training by the national team – the shooting range located on the northern outskirts of Doha (opposite the new North Atlantic College building). The prices are as follows: skeet shooting - QR 50 (25 targets), trap shooting - QR 70 (25 targets), double trap shooting - QR 80 (50 targets).

Snooker

Many major clubs, hotels and resorts in Doha have at least one snooker table. Prices vary from QR 5 to QR 20 per hour of play (not including any entrance fee you may have to pay).

Qatar Bowling Centre

Location → Opp British Embassy · Al Bidda | 444 3355
Hours → 14:30 - 23:30   Thu, Fri 13:00 - 23:00
Web/email → na   Map Ref → 10-B3

The bowling centre has nine snooker tables. Entrance is QR 10, and each game (one hour) costs QR 10. It is not necessary to book in advance, unless you plan to play during peak times or at the weekend. You can become a member – annual membership costs QR 400 and members don't have to pay the entrance fee (just the game fee).

Snorkelling

Other options → **Diving [p.124]**

QDive Marine Center

Location → Opp Al Fardan Centre · Doha | 437 5065
Hours → Timings on request
Web/email → www.qdive.net   Map Ref → 10-E4

Apart from being a top-class dive centre, QDive also offers snorkelling trips. Depending on the weather, there are weekly trips to either the southern or northern waters off Qatar's coast. Day trips are also available to the Banana and Safleya Islands.

Squash

Other options → **Sports & Leisure Facilities [p.138]**

Many hotels and fitness clubs have squash courts, although these may be reserved for use by members and hotel guests only. Member-only courts are available at Ramada's Cabana Club (441 7417), the Sheraton (485 4444) and the InterFitness Club (484 4979).

It's what your 4WD was made for

With 18 incredible off-road routes featuring foolproof directions and crystal-clear maps, the ***Off-Road Explorer*** helps you tame the UAE's wilderness. So forget hitting the kerb in the supermarket carpark, get out there and hit the dunes, mountains and wadis this weekend, and remind yourself why you bought a 4WD.

Phone (971 4) 335 3520 • **Fax** (971 4) 335 3529
Info@Explorer-Publishing.com • www.Explorer-Publishing.com
Residents' Guides • Photography Books • Activity Guidebooks • Practical Guides • Maps

EXPLORER
Passionately Publishing...

Doha Club

Location → Al Sharq · Al Khulaifat | 441 8822
Hours → Timings on request
Web/email → www.doha-club.com Map Ref → 11-B4

The club has air-conditioned squash courts, and lessons are available. For more information on lessons and prices, please contact Essam Faraj on 576 5770.

Duffers Squash League

Location → Various locations | 571 0746
Hours → Timings on request
Web/email → www.squashleagues.com Map Ref → na

This fun squash league is for young and old, men and women, serious players and 'duffers' alike. Depending on your ability, you will be assigned to play at one of five levels, and you will get to play against four different opponents each month. Although it is a fun league, there is a healthy sense of competition and it is a great way to get in or stay in shape. Games are played at various locations in Doha – you will decide with your monthly opponents where to play. To sign up for the league, or get more information, visit the website.

Khalifa Tennis & Squash

Location → Majlis Al Taawon Rd | 440 9666
Hours → Timings on request
Web/email → www.qatarsquash.com Map Ref → 8-B4

The squash courts at this club have recently undergone renovation (due to reopen in November 2005). Timings and prices are subject to change, but the courts are open from 08:00 to 23:00, and to hire a court for one hour costs QR 25.

The Ritz-Carlton Doha

Location → West Bay Lagoon | 484 8000
Hours → Timings on request
Web/email → www.ritzcarlton-doha.com Map Ref → 4-D2

The Ritz Carlton has one squash court that can be used by members and non-members. For members there is no charge, while non-members have to pay QR 50. At present squash lessons are not available. Booking is required in advance - call the hotel for details.

Swimming

Other options → **Sports & Leisure Facilities [p.138]**
Beaches [p.106]

InterFitness Club

Location → InterContinental Doha | 484 4979
Hours → Timings on request
Web/email → www.ichotelsgroup.com Map Ref → 6-D3

Swimming lessons are available here for members and non-members. A private swimming lesson costs QR 100 for an hour and QR 75 for half an hour. It is recommended that people who are serious about learning book a package of ten one-hour sessions at QR 850. Group lessons (maximum four people) are available at a cost of QR 50 per person. Members get a 10% discount off all lessons.

Ramada's Cabana Club

Location → Ramada Doha · Al Muntazah | 441 7417
Hours → 07:00 - 23:00
Web/email → www.ramada-doha.com Map Ref → 13-B2

You can learn to swim here under the watchful eye of qualified instructors and in a temperature-controlled swimming pool. Choose from group or individual lessons. For groups, a package of eight lessons for children (up to 14 years old) costs QR 250 for members and QR 300 for non-members. For adults (over 14 years), packages cost QR 450 for members and QR 600 for non-members. Individual sessions cost QR 35 (members) and QR 45 (non-members) for children and QR 60 (members) and QR 80 (non-members) for adults.

Dive right in, the water's fine

The Ritz-Carlton Doha

Location → West Bay Lagoon
Hours → Timings on request
Web/email → www.ritzcarlton-doha.com

484 8000

Map Ref → 4-D2

The Ritz Carlton is equipped with an attractive 25-metre swimming pool that is ideal for swimming training. Lessons are offered from time to time, both for members and non-members. Swimmers are advised to call the club for details of timings, costs, and lessons.

Table Tennis

Other options → **Sports & Leisure Facilities [p.138]**

Doha Club

Location → Al Sharq · Al Khulaifat
Hours → Timings on request
Web/email → www.doha-club.com

441 8822

Map Ref → 11-B4

Doha Club has three table tennis tables that can be used by non-members for QR 20. Members can use the tables for free. Table Tennis lessons are also available on request.

Qatar Bowling Centre

Location → Opp British Embassy · Al Bidda
Hours → 14:30 - 23:30 Thu, Fri 13:00 - 23:00
Web/email → na

444 3355

Map Ref → 10-B3

There are three table tennis tables at the Qatar Bowling Centre. Entrance costs QR 10, and then an hour of table tennis costs a further QR 10 (including racquet hire). Booking is not required, but it is recommended, especially during busy times. You can become a member of the Bowling Centre annual membership costs QR 400. Members receive various benefits, and once you're a member you won't have to pay the entrance fee.

Ramada's Cabana Club

Location → Ramada Doha · Al Muntazah
Hours → 07:00 - 23:00
Web/email → www.ramada-doha.com

441 7417

Map Ref → 13-B2

Table tennis is available at the Cabana Club from 19:00 to 21:00. Members pay QR 5 per person, and members' guests pay QR 15. Call the club for more information.

Tennis

Other options → **Sports & Leisure Facilities [p.138]**

Doha Club

Location → Al Sharq · Al Khulaifat
Hours → Timings on request
Web/email → www.doha-club.com

441 8822

Map Ref → 11-B4

Private or group tennis lessons are available here on one of seven floodlit courts – contact Alex Rosca on 570 0439 for more information. Members can use the tennis courts for free, and non-members can hire a court for QR 20.

InterFitness Club

Location → InterContinental Doha
Hours → Timings on request
Web/email → www.ichotelsgroup.com

484 4979

Map Ref → 6-D3

There are two courts available for hire at QR 30 per hour (advance booking is recommended). On Fridays and Sundays (18:00 - 20:00) there is social tennis, where you can meet other players. Social tennis costs QR 25 (free for members). Private lessons are available at a cost of QR 120 for non-members and QR 110 for members.

Khalifa Tennis & Squash

Location → Majlis Al Taawon Rd
Hours → Call for timings
Web/email → www.qatarsquash.com

440 9666

Map Ref → 8-B4

The Khalifa Tennis and Squash Stadium, home of the $1 million Qatar Open, has hosted some of the game's greats over the last few years. Tennis courts are available for hire at a cost of QR 25 per hour (booking is required). Lessons cost QR 200 per month (for three lessons a week).

Ramada's Cabana Club

Location → Ramada Doha - Al Muntazah
Hours → 07:00 - 23:00
Web/email → www.ramada-doha.com

441 7417

Map Ref → 13-B2

Private lessons are available and the costs are as follows: Members pay QR 430 for 12 sessions, QR 320 for eight sessions and QR 45 for a single session. Non-members pay QR 550 for 12 sessions, QR 400 for eight sessions, and QR 55 for a single session. Only members can hire a court for non-lesson play. To hire a court costs QR 20 per hour (but there is an extra charge of QR 10 if the member brings a guest).

The Ritz-Carlton Doha

Location → West Bay Lagoon | 484 8000
Hours → Timings on request
Web/email → www.ritzcarlton-doha.com   Map Ref → 4-d2

At the Ritz Carlton there are two indoor tennis courts available for hire. Club members can use the courts for free; non-members have to pay QR 50. Tennis lessons are available at QR 115 per hour.

Sheraton Doha Hotel & Resort

Location → Sheraton Doha · Doha Corniche | 485 4444
Hours → Timings on request
Web/email → www.starwoodhotels.com/doha   Map Ref → 8-E3

Although the facilities here are officially for the use of members only, use of the tennis court and private coaching is possible for non-members during quiet times. There is an indoor and outdoor court, but booking is recommended to ensure availability.

Volleyball

Doha Club

Location → Al Sharq · Al Khulaifat | 441 8822
Hours → Timings on request
Web/email → www.doha-club.com   Map Ref → 11-B4

You can play volleyball on the Doha Club's outdoor court at a cost of QR 150 for two hours. For reservations, call Mangala on 526 9338.

The Filipino Volleyball Association

Location → Nr Qtel · New Rayyan | 537 5994
Hours → See below
Web/email → na   Map Ref → 2-B3

You don't have to be from the Philippines to play with the Filipino Volleyball Association of Qatar. All players are welcome; the only prerequisites are that you are not a professional club player, and you pay the annual membership fee of QR 20. Matches are played on Fridays from 13:00 on the volleyball court at the Philippine International School of Qatar (near the New Rayyan branch of Qtel). For more information contact the chairman (Joey Angeles - 537 5994), vice chairman (Rocky Lumicao - 561 2370), tournament director (Erick Cruz - 520 7785) or tournament secretariat (Ammie Jaca - 536 6972). Team registration forms and membership application forms can be picked up from the tournament secretariat.

Wadi & Dune Bashing

Other options → **Tour Operators [p.109]**
Camping [p.123]

Qatar boasts some impressive sand dunes, reaching heights of nearly 50 metres. With a skilled driver, you can spend a thrilling afternoon racing up sand dunes and navigating your way down the other side. Unless you are extremely experienced, it is safer to enlist the help of one of the tour operators than to attempt dune bashing yourself. If you do go off into the desert in your own vehicle, always adhere to safety precautions and most importantly, travel in convoy!

Qatar International Tours

Location → Various locations | 466 7782
Hours → Timings on request
Web/email → www.qit-qatar.com   Map Ref → na

Experience the thrill of riding up and over dunes and through rugged wadis on an organised trip with QIT. You can choose from a half-day tour (lasting four hours and costing QR 200 per person) or a full-day tour (lasting eight hours and costing QR 275 per person). There must be a minimum of four participants per trip.

Wakeboarding

Other options → **Water Skiing [p.135]**

The Diplomatic Club

Location → West Bay | 484 7444
Hours → 07:00 - 22:00
Web/email → www.thediplomaticclub.com   Map Ref → 4-D4

A range of watersports is available here, and non-members can pay an entry fee to use the facilities (QR 75 on weekdays, QR 100 on weekends). Wakeboarding is available for adults and children. The club has wakeboarding coaches on hand, so you can become a wakeboarding pro – perhaps even learn how to jump three metres high off the specially installed pylon! Wakeboarding costs QR 100 per hour; there is no extra charge

Explore the GCC

If you want to drop in on your neighbours then go prepared with one of the Explorer Insider Guide series. Be it for a shopping spree in Dubai, a luxury holiday in Abu Dhabi, a get-back-to-nature trip to Oman, a long weekend to Kuwait or a sporting event in Bahrain, don't leave Qatar without an Explorer!

for instruction. All watersports are available from 09:00 to just before sunset.

Water Skiing

Other options → **Beach Clubs [p.138]**
Wakeboarding [p.134]

The Diplomatic Club

Location → West Bay
Hours → 07:00 - 22:00
Web/email → www.thediplomaticclub.com

| 484 7444
Map Ref → 4-D4

An hour of water skiing costs QR 100, and coaching is available at no extra cost. Members can enter the club for free, but non-members have to pay an additional QR 75 on weekdays and QR 100 on weekends. Water skiing is available from 09:00 until just before sunset.

Jet skis on the coast

Water Sports

Sealine Beach Resort

Location → Mesaieed
Hours → 07:30 - 19:00
Web/email → www.qnhc.com

| 477 2722
Map Ref → 1-C3

This resort offers a range of watersports activities from kayaking and pedal boating to jet skiing and aqua cycles. Contact Sealine for more information on prices.

Windsurfing

Regatta Sailing Academy

Location → Doha Corniche · Diplomatic District
Hours → Timings on request
Web/email → na

| 550 7846
Map Ref → 8-E3

Regatta Sailing Academy offers windsurfing lessons at Sheraton Lagoon. An hour-long lesson costs QR 150, and all equipment is supplied. Beginners are welcome.

Well-Being

Beauty Salons

Other options → **Hairdressers [p.72]**
Perfumes & Cosmetics [p.166]

Beauty Salons

Al Kazem Beauty Centre	443 2417
Al Majedah Beauty Saloon	444 8508
Al Malika Ladies Salon	444 3448
Bio-Bil Health, Beauty Centre & Spa	493 4433
Cannelle	444 3255
Dona Beauty Salon	444 1301
Donia Beauty Salon	436 2254
Femme Hair & Beauty Salon	467 1684
Hilda Beauty Centre	431 0900
Int' Hair Mode	468 9211
Lucena	467 3217
Manila Beauty Saloon	443 6164
Meche d'or Beauty Parlour	444 1995
Sally Beauty Centre	435 5868
Sara Beauty Center	442 5111
Special Touch Beauty Center	441 3801
Stylo Salon	436 3626

Health Spas

Other options → **Sports & Leisure Facilities [p.138]**
Massage [p.136]

Bio-Bil Health, Beauty Centre & Spa

Location → Nxt to City Center Doha
Hours → 08:30 - 20:30
Web/email → www.ahbqatar.com/biobill.htm

| 493 4433
Map Ref → 8-D2

Bio-Bil offers head-to-toe pampering in luxurious surroundings. Some of the treatments on offer are aromatherapy facials, treatment facials (for wrinkles or sun spots), body scrubs and massages. After your treatment you can use the swimming pool and other facilities such as steam room, spa bath and relaxation room. Monthly and yearly memberships are available.

The Doha Marriott Spa

Location → Marriott Doha · Al Khulaifat | **443 2432**
Hours → Timings on request
Web/email → www.marriotthotels.com   Map Ref → 11-D4

This spa offers treatments to pamper every inch of your body, from therapeutic back massages and Turkish baths to body scrubs and facial treatments. Other treatments include body wraps, fitness counselling, foot baths, manicures, pedicures, therapy baths and waxing. Call the spa directly to make an appointment (429 8520).

The Spa

Location → Ritz-Carlton Doha · West Bay Lagoon | **484 8173**
Hours → Call for timings
Web/email → www.ritzcarlton-doha.com   Map Ref → 4-D2

This luxurious spa has separate facilities for men and women. There are seven private treatment rooms, as well as a sauna, a steam room and roman baths. Treatments include Oriental massage and hydrotherapy.

The Spa and Wellness Centre

Location → Four Seasons Hotel · Diplomatic District | **494 8888**
Hours → 09:00 - 21:00
Web/email → na   Map Ref → 8-E2

This state-of-the-art spa boasts unique facilities including a hydrotheraphy lounge, a hydrotherapy pool, cool and warm plunge pools, a Kneipp foot bath, heated laconium beds, a laconium room, a colour therapy room and a meditation room. Other treatments offered include wraps, scrubs and Thai massage. There are separate areas for men and women. Complimentary refreshments are offered in the relaxation areas.

Massage

Other options → **Sports & Leisure Facilities [p.138]**
Health Spas [p.135]

The following hotels offer massage services in their spas: InterContinental (484 4979), Marriott (443 2432), Ritz-Carlton (484 8000) and Sheraton (485 4444). Additionally, the Doha Club's Health &

Fitness Centre has a specialist masseur and masseuse on hand (441 8822).

Bio-Bil Health, Beauty Centre & Spa

Location → Nxt to City Center Doha | **493 4433**
Hours → 08:30 - 20:30
Web/email → www.ahbqatar.com/biobill.htm   Map Ref → 8-D2

Bio-Bil offers luxurious massages starting from QR 200 for a full body massage. There are separate massage rooms for men and women. Facial massages are also available, including aromatherapy facials. Monthly and yearly memberships are available.

Lady Siam Massage

Location → Nxt Toys R Us · Al Mirqab Al Jadeed | **435 4115**
Hours → Call for timings
Web/email → na   Map Ref → 12-E1

The main massage treatments offered here are Thai massage and aromatherapy massage using essential oils. The regular price is QR 120 for a full body massage, but look out for monthly promotions where the price comes down to QR 100. Ladies only.

Pilates

Other options → **Yoga [p.137]**

InterFitness Club

Location → InterContinental Doha | **484 4979**
Hours → Timings on request
Web/email → www.ichotelsgroup.com   Map Ref → 6-D3

If you are new to pilates, you need to take two beginners' classes before moving on to other sessions. It is advisable to do two or three classes a week in addition to other aerobic activity in order to get the full benefit of pilates. No special equipment is required; just wear comfortable clothes, socks (no shoes) and bring water. An exercise mat is supplied. Classes take place at various times, and cost QR 30 for members and QR 35 for non-members. Ladies only.

Ramada's Cabana Club

Location → Ramada Doha · Al Muntazah | **441 7417**
Hours → 07:00 - 23:00
Web/email → www.ramada-doha.com   Map Ref → 13-B2

The gentle exercise of pilates is offered at the Cabana Club. Pilates is suitable for all ages and all levels of fitness, and can assist with rehabilitation of injury or strain, and correction of poor posture that is often associated with lower back problems. A package of eight one-hour sessions costs QR 200 for members and QR 250 for non-members. A single session costs QR 30 for members and QR 35 for non-members.

Reiki

Reiki Therapy

Location → Various locations	591 5925
Hours → Timings on request	
Web/email → na	Map Ref → na

One hour of Reiki is the equivalent of four hours of deep sleep; it is an effective natural stress reliever and can be used to heal both physical and emotional problems. A treatment usually lasts for one hour and involves the practitioner placing their hands in a sequence of positions over the body. The recipient does not have to remove any clothing. A reiki session costs QR 150. Call for more information and directions.

The Beauty Room

Location → Al Adl Rd · Doha	467 0409
Hours → Timings on request	
Web/email → na	Map Ref → na

Karen Roche is a beauty therapist, reflexologist and reiki master and works from her home. Reiki and reflexology treatments can help alleviate stress, allergies, asthma, irritable bowel syndrome (IBS), and menstrual problems. They can also boost the immune system.

Yoga

Other options → **Pilates [p.136]**

Al Dana Club

Location → Majlis Al Taawon Str	483 4700
Hours → Timings on request	
Web/email → www.aldanaclubqatar.com	Map Ref → 8-B4

Al Dana Club offers yoga classes for ladies only. Classes are predominantly for members of the club, but non-members can participate if they are accompanied by a member. The class lasts for an hour and costs QR 30 for members and QR 35 for non-members. Classes take place on Mondays and Wednesdays.

InterFitness Club

Location → InterContinental Doha	484 4979
Hours → Timings on request	
Web/email → www.ichotelsgroup.com	Map Ref → 6-D3

Yoga classes are held twice a week, and only morning classes are available. The price is QR 30 for members and QR 35 for non-members. Booking is recommended, especially for non-members.

IAID

Location → Opp Muntazah Park · Al Muntazah	432 0974
Hours → 08:00 - 12:00 16:00 - 21:00 Fri closed	
Web/email → na	Map Ref → 13-C3

The International Academy for Intercultural Development offers yoga classes for men and women. Before you sign up for classes, you are encouraged to have a one-on-one session with an instructor, who will assess your level of fitness and the benefits you wish to gain from taking up yoga. Classes take place at various times throughout the day early birds can do the early morning class from 06:30 to 07:30, ladies can do the mid-morning class (10:30 - 11:30), and there is also an evening class. You can sign up for the monthly package, which includes three classes a week and costs QR 200 per month. Alternatively, a single session costs QR 25.

Ramada's Cabana Club

Location → Ramada Hotel · Al Muntazah	441 7417
Hours → 07:00 - 23:00	
Web/email → www.ramada-doha.com	Map Ref → 13-B2

Yoga classes take place on Sunday and Tuesday evenings. A block of eight sessions costs QR 300 for non-members and QR 250 for members. A single class costs QR 35 for non-members and QR 30 for members.

Valerie Jeremijenko

Location → Various locations	na
Hours → Timings on request	
Web/email → vjeremij@yahoo.com	Map Ref → na

Valerie offers yoga classes at the Sheraton and other locations in Doha. The classes at the Sheraton take place on Friday and Saturday mornings at 08:30 and cost QR 35 per class. She has taught internationally for 15 years and teaches astanga vinyasa yoga, a physically challenging form that builds strength, flexibility and endurance but that is also deeply relaxing.

Sports & Leisure Facilities

As the host of the 15th Asian Games, to be held in December 2006, Doha has gone sports mad. Even though it already has its fair share of sports and leisure facilities, particularly at the luxurious hotels and at clubs such as the Doha Club, there is a massively funded drive to improve facilities and construct new sports grounds in time for the games.

Beach Clubs

Other options → **Beaches [p.106]**

The various beach clubs in Doha offer the best of everything; not only can you use the gym facilities, swimming pools and spas (where available), but you can also use the private beach and try out various watersports on offer. Most beach clubs also house a number of food outlets.

Health Clubs

There are plenty of health clubs in Doha, most of them attached to the various five-star hotels. Standard facilities that you can expect include a swimming pool (or more than one in some cases), well-equipped gyms (usually separate for men and women), tennis and squash courts and aerobics studios.

Doha Club

Sports Clubs

Al Dana Club

Location → Majlis Al Taawon St |483 4700
Hours →   Timings on request
Web/email → www.aldanaclubqatar.com   Map Ref → 8-B4

The Al Dana Club is a great family club, offering a range of exciting activities for kids and adults alike. Facilities include tennis courts, swimming pools (indoor and outdoor), a fitness centre, squash courts, a massage room and snooker tables. Fun events, such as football tournaments and volleyball matches, are held regularly.

Doha Club

Location → Al Sharq · Al Khulaifat |441 8822
Hours →   Timings on request
Web/email → www.doha-club.com   Map Ref → 11-B4

Doha Club is a popular destination for expats, and they have a long list of facilities. There are heated and chilled swimming pools, a children's pool, seven floodlit tennis courts, two squash courts, a well-equipped fitness centre and aerobics studio, a multi-purpose outdoor court (suitable for football, volleyball, badminton, etc) and a games room. There is also a baby and toddler area, a recreation hall, a 100 berth marina, a private beach, a beauty salon and a sports centre. Coaching is available for many of the sports played at the club, including badminton, billiards, squash, swimming, tennis and karate. Visit the website for even more information on this comprehensive club.

> **Down the Club!**
>
> *Doha Club is a firm favourite with expats living in Qatar. As well as excellent leisure facilities they have a number of popular restaurants and the good news is you don't have to be a member to dine there.*

Sports & Health Clubs

Al Dana Club	483 4700	8-B4
The Diplomatic Club	484 7444	4-D4
Doha Club P.121	441 8822	11-B4
Doha Golf Club	483 2338	4-A2
The Doha Marriott Spa	443 2432	11-D4
InterFitness Club	484 4979	6-D3
Ramada's Cabana Club P.191	441 7417	13-B2
The Ritz-Carlton Doha P.v	484 8000	4-D2
Sealine Beach Resort	477 2722	1-C3
Sheraton Doha Hotel & Resort	485 4444	8-E3

Expand Your Horizons

One of the best things about being an expat living and working in a foreign country is the community feeling among other expats. You'll find a lively network of social clubs and hobby groups who welcome new members of all nationalities. Alternatively, you could try your hand at something new and take a course in a variety of topics. Whether it's learning a new language, taking a dance class or going to a cooking workshop, you'll have plenty of opportunities to do it in Qatar, and if your desired activity isn't already catered for, then why not go ahead and organise a club or society yourself?

Art Classes

Other options → Art Supplies [p.152]

Ceramics Galore

Location → Nr Jarrir Bookstore · Al Muntazah | 435 2598
Hours → Timings on request
Web/email → na | Map Ref → 13-B2

Pottery classes are offered for adults and children, at a cost of QR 30 for a three-hour session. Children's classes take place on Saturday mornings and are suitable for children aged four and up. You can choose to make one of 1500 designs.

French Cultural Centre

Location → Al Nuaija East | 483 5090
Hours → Timings on request
Web/email → na | Map Ref → 16-D2

Li Chevalier offers painting classes at the French Cultural Centre (evenings) and the Al Jazi Garden Club House (Wednesday mornings). The classes explore various techniques in mixed media painting. Classes are open to all, and teaching is available in English, French, Italian and Chinese. For a course of ten classes (one class per week), the fee is QR 1000. Contact Li for more information and to register.

Virginia Commonwealth University School of Art

Location → Btn Wajba & Garafa · Education City | 492 7200
Hours → See below
Web/email → www.qf.edu.qa | Map Ref → 2-B2

The Virginia Commonwealth University School of Art is located on the Education City Campus on Luqta Street, and offers various community classes including portrait drawing, history of art, jewellery making, watercolours and Islamic art. Costs vary, but courses generally start at QR 350 and go up to QR 1000 per course. Call the school to check for timings, but as a general guide, classes are usually held in the evenings between 17:00 and 21:00. The school also arranges various exhibitions, which are free to the public. The school gallery is open from Sunday to Thursday, 10:00 – 18:00.

Ballet Classes

Other options → Dance Classes [p.140]

The International Centre for Music

Location → Nr The Mall · Al Matar Al Qadeem | 467 1354
Hours → Timings on request
Web/email → na | Map Ref → 16-E1

Ballet classes are offered for all ages. Students can take their Royal Academy of Dance examinations to get certification. Please call to get more information on class fees and times.

Isabelle Mojansky

Location → Various locations | 521 6579
Hours → Timings on request
Web/email → na | Map Ref → na

Isabelle Mojansky offers jazz, modern and classical ballet classes suitable for children aged four to 16 years. All disciplines are taught twice a week, either at Doha College or the Sheraton Hotel. Each hour-long class costs QR 30. Call for more information.

Ramada's Cabana Club

Location → Ramada Doha · Al Muntazah | 441 7417
Hours → 07:00 - 23:00
Web/email → www.ramada-doha.com | Map Ref → 13-B2

Traditional classical ballet classes are available at the Ramada's Cabana Club. The dance techniques are taught with enjoyment in mind, and classes are suitable for children aged five to 15 years. Classes cost QR 35 for non-members and QR 20 for members. Advance booking is required. To speak to someone in the dance section directly, call the above number and request extension 2393 or 2013.

Belly Dancing

Other options → **Dance Classes [p.140]**

Oriental Dance

Location → Sheraton Doha · Doha Corniche | 483 6363
Hours → See below
Web/email → www.starwoodhotels.com Map Ref → 8-E3

Belly dancing is not just an ancient Arabian artform, it's also a great way to keep fit, not to mention a good way to impress your friends when you go back home! Oriental dance classes at the Recreation Centre are suitable for people aged 15 and upwards, and take place on Sunday and Wednesday evenings at 19:00. Booking is essential – a class costs QR 25 for members and QR 35 for non-members.

Birdwatching Groups

Other options → **Environmental Groups [p.141]**

Not only does Qatar have a range of local bird species resident throughout the year, it is also a stop-off point for migrating birds moving to new climates during spring and autumn. The mangrove-rich area just north of Al Khor is an area particularly rich with birdlife.

Qatar Natural History Group

Location → Various locations | 493 1278
Hours → Timings on request
Web/email → na Map Ref → na

Birdwatching is just one of the interests of the Qatar Natural History Group. The group has regular meetings (on the first Wednesday of the month), when there is usually a slide show and discussion on various topics. They organise birdwatching trips to Al Khor or other Doha locations. Annual membership costs QR 20 and the group currently has over 250 members. Call Margaret Robertshaw (493 1278) or Fran Gillespie (467 5991) for more information.

Clubs & Associations

Other options → **Scouts & Guides [p.144]**

There are many clubs and associations for you to join, and since you are an expat, a good place to start is to find a club based on your nationality. It can be reassuring to mingle with your fellow country-folk, who will probably be able to pass

Clubs & Associations

American Women's Association	556 3517
Dutch-speaking Women in Qatar	549 8978
Egyptian Women's Association	468 4581
French Women's Association	483 9430
German Stammtisch	487 6959
Indian Women's Association	443 8945
Silver Dhow Association	435 2598
South African Ladies Group	465 7220
South African Social Committee	447 2136
Spanish Speaking Ladies Group	551 8358
Tuesday Ladies Group	458 1487

some of their Qatar experience on to you. Or you can just get together and share memories of your homeland. Check with your embassy whether there is a group you can join.

Cookery Classes

The Ritz-Carlton Doha

Location → West Bay Lagoon | 484 8000
Hours → Timings on request
Web/email → www.ritzcarlton-doha.com Map Ref → 4-D2

The Ritz Carlton offers a monthly cooking class, under the watchful eye of one of the hotel's many expert chefs. The theme varies, but classes in French and Italian cuisines are always in demand. Each class costs QR 120 (plus 17%), which includes a three-course meal. They also offer a children's cooking class, where kids can try their hand at cake decorating and making easy meals. The children's class costs QR 66 (+ 17%), which includes a children's buffet.

Dance Classes

Other options → **Belly Dancing [p.140]**
Music Lessons [p.143]

IAID

Location → Opp Muntazah Park · Al Muntazah | 432 0974
Hours → 08:00 - 12:00 16:00 - 21:00 Fri closed
Web/email → na Map Ref → 13-C3

Specialising in Indian classical dance, the classes at the International Academy for Intercultural Development are affiliated to the Nalanda Dance Research Centre of Mumbai. The academy offers seven years' worth of certificate courses for children, who can progress to Prarambhika after four years and Kovida after seven years. Examinations are conducted on a regular basis by a visiting professor from Nalanda. For an individual, a month's package of Indian classical dance lessons (two per week) costs QR 175. The monthly cost for a couple (one two-hour lesson a week) is QR 200. The academy also offers dance classes in jazz, Latin American, ballet and ballroom.

The International Centre for Music

Location → Nr The Mall · Al Matar Al Qadeem | 467 1354
Hours → Timings on request
Web/email → na | Map Ref → 16-E1

The International Centre for Music offers classes in ballet, salsa, ballroom dancing, tap, hip hop and modern dance. Please call to get more information on timings and costs.

Line Dancing

Location → Doha Rugby Club | 468 3771
Hours → Timings on request
Web/email → na | Map Ref → 12-C4

There is one line-dancing class every week, on Mondays, at the Doha Rugby Club. It is not necessary to book in advance. Call for information on costs and times.

Scottish Country Dancing

Location → DESS · Kulaib | 465 5823
Hours → 19:00 - 21:00 Mon
Web/email → na | Map Ref → 7-D4

This dance class takes place at the Doha English Speaking School (DESS), and it is all about having fun – anyone with a sense of humour is welcome. Classes take place on Mondays at 19:00 and last for about two hours. All you need to wear is comfortable clothes and soft shoes, and all you need to bring is a soft drink and the class fee of QR 10.

Skills Development Centre

Location → Opp Muntazah Hall · Al Muntazah | 442 5100
Hours → 08:00 - 12:00 16:00 - 20:00 Fri closed
Web/email → na | Map Ref → 13-C2

This centre specialises in Indian dance forms, concentrating on folk dance, classical dance and cinematic dance. To learn an Indian dance style, it is recommended that you attend three classes a week. Beginners are welcome, but it will take quite a lot of time and effort before you can compete with the Bollywood stars!

Drama Groups

Doha Players

Location → Kulaib | 487 1196
Hours → Timings on request
Web/email → www.dohaplayers.com | Map Ref → 7-D4

The Doha Players were an extremely active amateur dramatics group, staging regular productions at their theatre that were well-supported, both in terms of participants and audiences. Tragically, in March 2005 the Doha Players Theatre was the target of a suicide bomb attack and is no longer in use. With the help of the authorities, alternative locations have been identified and things are starting to get back to normal – the Doha Players Executive Board and members are actively following up on plans to build a new theatre. As always, the players welcome new members. Full membership costs QR 100 per year. Student membership is QR 50, and family membership is QR 150. Log onto their website for more information on how you can join this community-driven organisation.

Environmental Groups

Other options → **Voluntary & Charity Work [p.48]**

Qatar Animal Welfare Society (QAWS)

Location → Nr Race Club R/A | 528 6335
Hours → See below
Web/email → www.qaws.org | Map Ref → 12-A3

Qatar Animal Welfare (QAW) was formed to improve the lives of the many abandoned or mistreated cats and dogs in Qatar. As with any volunteer-run organisation, they need lots of help from people who care about animal welfare. Whether you can donate money or time, they gratefully appreciate all the help they can get. QAW is always looking for people who can sponsor an animal or foster a pet temporarily. Alternatively, you can be an official 'Friend of the Shelter' by becoming a member – for just QR 25 per quarter you will receive a regular newsletter keeping you up to date with the current issues, as well as a a badge and car sticker. There are plans underway to develop a discount scheme for members at participating outlets.

Timings: 15:00 - 18:30, Sat 10:00 - 18:00, Fri by appointment only.

Qatar Natural History Group

Location → Various locations	**493 1278**
Hours → Timings on request	
Web/email → na	Map Ref → na

This society is open to anyone interested in the environment. There are four interest groups: birdwatching, flora & fauna, ramblers and astronomy. Regular meetings are held (on the first Wednesday of every month), and field trips are organised to different places in Qatar. Membership is QR 20 per year, and there are currently over 250 members. For more information call Margaret Robertshaw (493 1278) or Fran Gillespie (467 5991).

Flower Arranging

Other options → **Gardens [p.160]**
Flowers [p.159]

The Ritz-Carlton Doha

Location → West Bay Lagoon	**484 8000**
Hours → Timings on request	
Web/email → www.ritzcarlton-doha.com	Map Ref →4-D2

Flower arranging at the Ritz Carlton is a popular activity among Doha's residents of leisure. Participants learn at least three arrangements per workshop, which cost QR 99 (plus 17%). Lunch is included, and participants are allowed to take the flowers home afterwards.

Gardening

Other options → **Gardens [p.160]**

Doha Garden Club

Location → Bin Mahmoud South	**479 3952**
Hours → 15:30; Second Sunday of every month	
Web/email → na	Map Ref → 13-B1

It may at times seem like an impossible task, but this group of keen gardeners (both men and women) explore the possibilities of growing beautiful gardens in the challenging weather conditions of the region. The club meets on the second Sunday of every month (September to May) at 15:30. Every year there is a Charity Garden Tour, which features various gardens in Doha. For more information, please contact Raka Singhal on 469 0545. The membership fee is QR 50 per year.

Qatar Horticultural Society

Location → Various locations	**486 7044**
Hours → Timings on request	
Web/email → na	Map Ref → na

Guest speakers give regular talks on horticultural topics such as landscaping, propagating houseplants, plants that can survive Qatar's climate and flower arranging. The group has built up a fairly large library of books on various gardening subjects, which members can borrow. Every year the society hosts the annual Flower and Vegetable Show, where people from all over Qatar exhibit their vegetables, pot plants, roses and gardens.

Language Schools

Other options → **Learning Arabic [p.78]**

British Council

Location → Opp Tivoli Furniture · Al Mirqab Al Jadeed	**442 6193**
Hours → 08:00 - 20:00 Sat 08:00 - 16:00	
Web/email → www.britishcouncil.org	Map Ref → 12-D1

The British Council has a presence in many countries around the world, with the purpose of spreading information about the United Kingdom and improving relations. One way they do that is by offering some excellent courses in the English language. So whether you want to study in the UK or improve your english, they can get you on the right road. The British Council in Qatar is situated in a large villa on Al Sadd St, opposite Tivoli Furniture. Courses offered include English for Adults, English for Youngsters and Business English. Call for more information and class timings.

French Cultural Centre

Location → Al Nuaija East	**493 0862**
Hours → Timings on request	
Web/email → http://qatarfrancophonie.free.fr	Map Ref → 16-D2

Learn to speak the language of love at the French Cultural Centre, where there are classes for adults, teenagers, children and even infants. They offer preparation courses for the following French exams: TEF (test assessing French language skills) and DELF (Diploma in French Language). Ladies-only classes are available. The centre also offers Arabic classes and computer lessons in Word, Excel, PowerPoint and web design.

Qatar Centre for the Presentation of Islam

Location ➜ Madinat Khalifa South | 441 1122
Hours ➜ Timings on request
Web/email ➜ na | Map Ref ➜ 7-C3

This centre offers free Arabic language classes. You can choose to learn either classical Arabic (which will help you communicate with Arabs all over the world), or Qatari Arabic, so that you can communicate using the special vocabularies and pronounciations that Qataris use. Classical Arabic classes are held in the mornings (two classes per week) and evenings (one class per week). There are also classes in Islamic culture and Qatar life. All classes are separate for men and women. For more information, contact the men's section (441 1122) or the women's section (488 5915).

Be Famous

If you'd like to see your very own club or association featured in this chapter, send us an email to Info@Explorer-Publishing.com and we'll give you a mention in the next edition.

Qatar Guest Centre

Location ➜ Opp Aisha bin Abu Bakar Mosque · Kulaib | 486 1274
Hours ➜ Timings on request
Web/email ➜ na | Map Ref ➜ 7-C4

The Guest Centre offers Arabic language and Islamic classes (the Islamic classes are particularly useful for those who have recently converted to Islam). All classes are separate for men and women. The basic Arabic Course runs for three months. Call for more information (men's classes – 486 2390; women's classes – 486 1274).

Libraries

Other options ➜ **Second-Hand Items [p.168]**
Books [p.153]

British Council

Location ➜ Opp Tivoli Furniture · Al Mirqab Al Jadeed | 442 6193
Hours ➜ 08:00 - 20:00 Sat 08:00 - 16:00
Web/email ➜ www.britishcouncil.org | Map Ref ➜ 12-D1

The library and information centre of the British Council is open from Sunday to Thursday (10:00 - 12:00 and 16:00 - 19:30) and on Saturdays (10:00 - 16:00). It is an ideal place to study for your exams, get relevant online information, seek advice on UK culture or just browse through the collection of books – over 10,000 in total. Annual family membership costs QR 400, and you can borrow up to eight items at a time.

Music Lessons

Other options ➜ **Singing [p.144]**
Music, DVDs & Videos [p.165]
Dance Classes [p.140]

IAID

Location ➜ Opp Muntazah Park · Al Muntazah | 432 0974
Hours ➜ 08:00 - 12:00 16:00 - 21:00 Fri closed
Web/email ➜ na | Map Ref ➜ 13-C3

The International Academy for Intercultural Development offers music classes in instruments such as keyboards and guitar. It also offers voice classes in disciplines such as carnatic and hindustani vocals. Call the academy for more information.

The International Centre for Music

Location ➜ Nr The Mall · Al Matar Al Qadeem | 467 1354
Hours ➜ Timings on request
Web/email ➜ na | Map Ref ➜ 16-E1

This centre offers classes in piano, guitar, violin, keyboards, flute, clarinet and saxaphone. They also offer singing lessons. Students can take examinations and get certificates under the Associated Board Royal Schools of Music. To get more information about class timings and costs, call the above number or 555 7976.

Photography

Qatar Photographic Society

Location ➜ Nr Indian Cultural Ctr · Al Hitmi Al Jadeed | 467 7793
Hours ➜ Timings on request
Web/email ➜ www.qpsimages.com ✳ | Map Ref ➜ 9-D2

The amateur photographic scene is alive and well in Qatar with the Qatar Photographic Society. It has over 200 members and aims to promote photography in Qatar, encourage new talent and provide a forum where photographers can share knowledge and showcase their work. From time to time there are courses on various aspects of photography including still life, portrait and digital photography. The society organises exhibitions of members' work throughout the year. Log onto the website for more information.

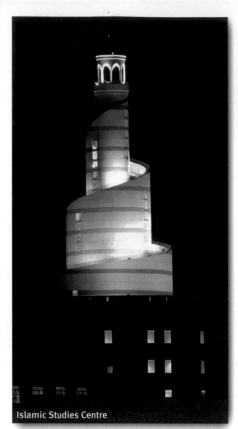

Islamic Studies Centre

Scouts & Guides

Other options → **Clubs & Associations [p.140]**

1st Doha Scout Group

Location → DESS	431 8776
Hours → See below	
Web/email → na	Map Ref → 7-D4

The 1st Doha Scout Group is a 'British Group Abroad' and runs the same exciting Scout and Brownie programmes as UK scout groups. It currently has a Beaver Colony for children aged six to eight, and a Cub Pack for eight to ten year olds. Meetings are every Wednesday from 16:00 to 17:30 at Doha English Speaking School (during term time only). Each term includes a wide range of supervised activities, such as trips, games, crafts and badge work. Places are limited and there is a waiting list. For more information, contact the group leader on 432 3703.

Singing

Other options → **Music Lessons [p.143]**

Doha Singers

Location → Doha College · Alwaab	442 4329
Hours → See below	
Web/email → na	Map Ref → 12-C4

This group of singers gets together at the Doha College every Monday at 19:30 to practise. For more information, call Ian Young (442 4329).

Social Groups

Other options → **Clubs & Associations [p.140]**
Support Groups [p.73]

Life as an expat can get lonely and you need a long list of activities and social gatherings to keep those homesick feelings at bay. Below are just some of the social groups available in Qatar.

The Doha Debates

Location → Education City	492 7000
Hours → Call for timings	
Web/email → www.thedohadebates.com	Map Ref → 2-B2

The Doha Debates publicly promote dialogue and freedom of speech in Qatar. Renowned international journalist Tim Sebastian (former host of BBC's *Hard Talk*) invites four speakers a month to address controversial issues facing the Arab and Islamic worlds. Past topics have included women in Islam, the Israeli/Palestinean roadmap to peace, and the role of the US. They follow the traditional Oxford Union style of debate, where two teams argue over a central motion, the audience is invited to participate, and at the end a vote is taken and the chairman announces the result. If you would like to attend the debates as a member of the audience, visit the website and fill in the information form.

International Pot Luck Group

Location → Various locations	483 0142
Hours → Timings on request	
Web/email → na	Map Ref → na

Monthly meetings are held at members' houses. Each member prepares a traditional dish from their home country to share with the others. The Pot Luck Group has over 100 current members from 40 countries, so it's a great way to mingle with other cultures, meet new people, and taste exotic food.

Qatar Centre for Voluntary Activities

Location → Various locations | 467 5999
Hours → Timings on request
Web/email → na Map Ref → na

The QCVA was established in 2001 and aims to train and prepare volunteers for participation in Qatar's social development projects. All you need to do to sign up as a volunteer is fill in the special application form and provide the required documents. Volunteers should be over 16 years old. The QCVA helps charities with their projects, including taking care of people who have illnesses, the elderly and those with special needs.

Qatar Scientific Club

Location → Al Salata Al Jadeeda | 469 6200
Hours → Timings on request
Web/email → na Map Ref → 16-B1

The Scientific Club has over 4,000 members who are split into various interest groups. Interests include model aircraft, scuba diving and astronomy, but there are many other topics covered. Call the above number for more information on joining the club.

Qatar Toastmasters

Location → Rydges Plaza · Al Bidda | 435 6300
Hours → Twice a month
Web/email → na Map Ref → 10-C3

Qatar Toastmasters currently has 47 members, who meet twice a month at the Rydges Plaza Hotel. Membership costs QR 350 for six months,

Fun for the kids

which covers a public speaking manual, a leaflet, a monthly magazine and the meeting fee. Beginners will be given training on how to improve their public speaking techniques, and to alleviate common public speaking problems, such as nervousness.

Kids' Activities

Kids

Aladdin's Kingdom

Location → Al Istiqlal · New District of Doha 66 | 483 1001
Hours → 16:00 - 22:00 Sun closed
Web/email → na Map Ref → 6-D2

This one-stop fun destination has a great big rollercoaster, a ferris wheel and go-karts. There are separate rides for smaller children, so it is a suitable place to take all members of the family. Entry to the park is free, and then you just pay for each ride as you go. There are several food outlets available inside the park should all the fun and frolics leave you peckish. Mondays and Wednesdays are for women and children only.

Girls Creativity Centre

Location → Al Madeed Rd · Doha | 468 8835
Hours → Timings on request
Web/email → na Map Ref → 2-C3

Helping girls to explore their creativity, this centre runs up to ten courses at any one time. Courses are available in various artistic techniques, including pottery, drawing, painting and sculpture. Many of the classes are taught in Arabic, but teachers will teach in English if there is a demand for it.

Jungle Zone

Location → Hyatt Plaza · Alwaab | 469 4848
Hours → 13:00 - 22:00 Sat 10:00 - 22:00
Web/email → na Map Ref → 12-A4

Entrance to the Jungle Zone costs QR 45 on weekends (Thursday, Friday, Saturday) and QR 30 from Sunday to Wednesday. It is packed with activities (all jungle-themed) to keep kids occupied. Apart from the usual attractions, they will also organise your child's birthday party or school outing.

**MARKS &
SPENCER**

DUBAI • ABU DHABI • SHARJAH • OMAN • KUWAIT • QATAR • BAHRAIN

Al-Futtaim sons

www.marksandspencerme.com

Shopping
EXPLORER

Shopping

Highlights...

Souks
Pg 176

While shopping in Qatar may have all the mod-cons, with shiny shopping malls and international brands by the dozen, the souks and markets still pay homage to a time-honoured shopping tradition. The Fish Market is a must for the catch of the day as well as being an interesting (if a little smelly) experience.

Clothing Sizes

Women's Clothing

Aust/NZ	8	10	12	14	16	18
Europe	36	38	40	42	44	46
Japan	5	7	9	11	13	15
UK	8	10	12	14	16	18
USA	6	8	10	12	14	16

Women's Shoes

Aust/NZ	5	6	7	8	9	10
Europe	35	36	37	38	39	40
France only	35	36	38	39	40	42
Japan	22	23	24	25	26	27
UK	3.5	4.5	5.5	6.5	7.5	8.5
USA	5	6	7	8	9	10

Men's Clothing

Aust/NZ	92	96	100	104	108	112
Europe	46	48	50	52	54	56
Japan	S	-	M	M	-	L
UK	35	36	37	38	39	40
USA	35	36	37	38	39	40

Men's Shoes

Aust/NZ	7	8	9	10	11	12
Europe	41	42	43	44.5	46	47
Japan	26	27	27.5	28	29	30
UK	7	8	9	10	11	12
USA	7.5	8.5	9.5	10.5	11.5	12.5

Measurements are approximate only; try before you buy

Shopping

The shopping scene in Qatar is usually a great experience, full of surprises and bargains, and it should keep most shopaholics happily swiping their credit cards. There may be a few items that you can't find, but you'll get over your disappointment by discovering a whole new world of things to buy. Big shopping centres all house international brands, and because there is no sales tax or VAT you might find some things cheaper than in your home country. The Qatar construction industry has a full calendar over the next couple of years, with plans for several new shopping centres in the pipeline.

Malls are not concentrated in one area of Doha in particular; you'll find them scattered around. As it is a small city, everything is relatively close together anyway, so mall-hopping is as easy as jumping in your car or a taxi.

The traditional markets (souks) are a must-do and they are all clustered together so you can wander from one to the other quite easily. They are particularly enjoyable for shoppers who enjoy a good rummage and there are unbelievable bargains to be had if you've got the time to look. They sell a range of items including jewellery, Arabian souvenirs, perfume, power tools, clothes and much, much more.

Shopping outside of Doha is less appealing; luxury malls and interesting souks are few and far between. If you can't find what you're looking for in Doha, chances are you won't find it outside the capital and a quick shopping trip to nearby Dubai might be the answer.

Refunds and Exchanges

Larger shopping outlets have fairly generous return policies, similar to reputable shops in your home country. Major chains, like Carrefour or Home Centre, will return your money if the merchandise is returned in its original condition, as long as you present your receipt and return the item within the deadline (seven days in most cases). Sometimes you will have to insist on speaking to the manager if you want a cash refund rather than a credit note. He or she will always have the final say and will have to sign the paperwork if a cash refund is given.

You'll always get a better result if you stay calm and don't let yourself get frustrated with the shop assistants. Be firm but reasonable and aim for an amicable resolution. If you are making a purchase, always make a note of the returns policy before you hand over your money; it should be displayed somewhere in the shop, but if it isn't then ask to see it.

Some international shops, like Marks & Spencer, Debenhams and Monsoon, will often exchange across international borders, so if you are sent something from M&S in the UK, you can exchange it here; or if you buy something here, you can exchange it in the UK store. Conditions do apply though – the item must be part of the current range and you should be able to produce the original receipt.

Exchange policies at the souks are non-existent; shop owners may exchange an item for you or simply refuse to do so. Getting an item exchanged depends on each shop owner and your rate of success might even fluctuate from one day to another! Souk vendors are usually friendly and helpful, but the fact that any returns are going to affect the money that goes into their own pockets at the end of the month may make them inflexible when it comes to giving you your money back. For this reason, and also because some items may be of lower quality than at large, reputable shops, it is probably not wise to make any large or expensive purchases at the souks.

Consumer Rights

Your rights as a consumer in Qatar are not protected. If you are purchasing from a large store in a shopping centre, then your rights are at the discretion of the manager. If you feel you are not being heard or you have been treated unfairly, you can try approaching the mall management offices and laying a complaint. Put your complaint in writing and request an appointment with the manager. Even at this stage, it is always better to aim for an amicable resolution. Until such time as there is an official consumer watchdog organisation in Qatar, your best bet is to be careful where you make your purchases, be aware of return policies, and always keep your receipts – without them you won't have a leg to stand on.

Shipping

If you want to buy something and have it shipped back to your home country, there are a number of reputable shipping companies that can assist you. This is not a common practice however; some goods in Doha might be cheaper, but if you add the shipping and insurance costs on top you won't be saving any money at the end of the day. Air freight is much quicker than sea freight, but it is also more expensive. If you are lucky enough to know someone who is shipping something back to the same country, you can share a container and this will translate into significant savings. The following shipping companies are reputable and offer a worldwide service:

Shipping

Air Sea Cargo Qatar	Air & Sea	462 2266
Allied Pickfords (IFS) P.61	Air & Sea	466 7100
Crown Relocations P.41	Air & Sea	462 1115
Global Shipping Svc	Air & Sea	432 3975
Gulf Agency Company (GAC) P.63	Air & Sea	431 5222
International Freight Services P.61	Air & Sea	466 7100
Qatar Logistics P.36	Air & Sea	455 0991

How to Pay

Shops in the malls accept cash, debit cards and credit cards. Cheques are not accepted, even if from a local bank. Smaller retailers, including souks, usually only accept cash in the local currency.

Virtually all credit cards are accepted here, including Visa, Mastercard, American Express and Diners Club. Banks actively encourage you to use your credit card whenever possible by offering discounts and loyalty programmes. It is up to you to decide whether these perks are worth the interest.

Debit cards are becoming a very popular way to pay, saving you the trouble of drawing cash but without having to incur credit card interest charges. The most common debit card system is Visa Electron.

Some shops may accept foreign currencies as payment, which is handy if you are in town for a short while and don't want to change your money into riyals. The downside is that shops may add a surcharge or use a less favourable exchange rate. Currencies accepted may include US dollars, pounds sterling, euros and other GCC currencies, but each shop will vary in its foreign currency policy. You'll find money exchanges in all the main malls, in the souks or in banks.

ATMs or cash machines are also widely available in malls, petrol stations, banks and even in some government buildings. If you are on holiday you will probably be able to draw money out of your bank account at home, as most ATMs are now linked to an international network.

Bargaining

Bargaining may seem strange to you at first, but it is an accepted way of doing business in this region. Most shop owners in the souks expect you to bargain with them, so the first price they quote you is usually a vastly inflated one. Offer half of what they ask and work upwards from there. The key to being a good bargainer is to remain pleasant at all times, but be firm. Don't get flustered or irritable – the friendlier you are the more likely you are to get a good discount. A great technique is to say you are going to have a look around for a better price and walk out of the shop – shop owners have been known to follow customers out into the street offering lower prices!

It is not normal practice to ask for discounts in shopping centres or department stores, as prices are fixed, but if you feel comfortable doing so, there is no harm in asking. An exception is jewellery shops, where you will almost always get a discount on the first price quoted.

The calculator is often used as an important bargaining tool. Shop owners will tap away at the keys with great flourish, making you think they are using a complicated set of formulas to give you the best discount possible, and then show you the calculator. At this stage, you can simply clear the screen and type in your price and hand the calculator back to the vendor who will engage in more furious tapping away. Eventually you will reach a price that you both agree on; once this happens it would be considered bad form to leave the shop without making the purchase.

There will be times when you love the fact that you can bargain and times when you just want to buy something at a fair price without going through the whole negotiating rigmarole. Just remember that it is supposed to be fun, so enjoy it and remember that a skilled bargainer gets the best bargains!

Traditional shopping in Qatar

AMOUAGE

The most valuable perfume in the world

www.amouage.com

Doha has a wide variety of places to shop. There are traditional souks which sell everything from jewellery to fabrics. There are modern shopping centres selling international brand names that you will probably be familiar with from your home country. There are also hypermarkets where you can buy electronics, luggage, clothes, bed linen and food all under one roof. Hypermarkets offer a variety of non-branded or out-of-season items at cheaper prices to those found in the shopping centres. No matter what price range you can afford, you will find plenty on offer in the various shopping areas throughout Doha.

DSF

If you fancy a weekend shopping break then why not head to Dubai for the Shopping Festival. Not only can you stock up on bargains galore, but also there is a whole host of exciting entertainment going on. Pick up a copy of the Dubai Explorer for more information.

You may have trouble finding certain items, particulary when grocery shopping. If you can't live without a particular item but can't find it in Qatar, enlist the help of friends who are travelling back to their home countries or neighbouring GCC countries and ask them to bring back a stockpile for you.

This section lists common purchases and points you in the right direction to find them. Hopefully it will make your initial shopping trips in Doha a lot less stressful. If you happen across an undiscovered shopping gem during your travels in the city and you want to tell us about it so we can include it in our next edition, send us all the details to Info@Explorer-Publishing.com.

Alcohol

Other options → **Drinks [p.181]**
On the Town [p.202]
Liquor Licence [p.45]

As Qatar is a Muslim country, the sale of alcohol is closely monitored and restricted to licenced establishments. Most of the hotels have a licence to sell alcohol for consumption on the premises. When drinking alcohol in hotels, you pay an additional tax of 17.5% on top of menu prices. Bars and restaurants will serve alcohol to anyone over 21. Independent restaurants (those not in hotels) don't usually have liquor licences, so don't expect to have a glass of wine with your street-cafe pizza.

Doha has one liquor store where you can buy alcohol for personal consumption at home. It is called the Qatar Distribution Company (QDC) and it is the sole importer of alcohol. To buy alcohol for your personal use, you need to have a special liquor permit, which can be applied for once you have a Qatar residence visa (for the procedure, see p.45).

QDC offers a wide range of alcohol and a great selection of wines from all over the world. Prices are definitely not cheap, although not totally unreasonable either. QDC is closed during the holy month of Ramadan, so stock up in advance.

It is illegal to bring alcohol into the country, but you can buy it from the airport duty free as you leave.

QDC can be contacted on 469 9412
10.30-7.30 Sat - Thurs
closed Friday

Art

Other options → **Art Classes [p.139]**

While it may not match New York or London, Qatar's art scene should offer enough to sustain most art lovers, with a few galleries holding exhibitions every month both by local and international artists.

The recently opened Four Seasons Hotel has a good collection of artworks in its foyer and restaurants, which are worth viewing if you are an avid art lover.

The Museum of Islamic Art, due to open in 2006, will display Qatar's national collection of Islamic art, making it a great place to discover and learn about the country's heritage and culture with a particular focus on art.

Art

Al Dana Club	Mesaieed	483 4700
Al Mezzan Gallery	Al Muntazah	574 6342
Apollo Furniture	Salwa Road South	442 6664
Fawzi Abdulla Ibrahim	Ibn Mahmoud South	555 2992
Four Seasons Hotel	Diplomatic District	494 8888
Qatar National Museum	Al Diwan	443 8123
Virginia Commonwealth University School of Art	Education City	492 7200

Art Supplies

Other options → **Art Classes [p.139]**

There are a few shops selling art supplies here in Doha. The Jarir Bookstore has a good selection of art items, including supplies for specialist hobbies such as silk screening, mosaics and canvas painting. The bookshop in The Centre has a small collection of arts and crafts pieces, with the likes of stencils, canvases and paints. One of the better places is Colour Note, located on Al Marqab Street. They have a great selection of art materials from Europe and will be happy to order things from their suppliers, if you can't find what you're looking for.

Art Supplies

Colour Note	Al Marqab St	441 8548
Jarir Bookstore	Salwa Road South	444 0212
The Centre Bookshop	The Centre	443 4782

Beachwear

Other options → **Sporting Goods [p.169]**
Clothes [p.156]

There are no specialist beachwear shops in Qatar, although luckily you will still find a good range in larger stores like Marks & Spencer, Debenhams and Bhs. Sports shops also sell swimming costumes, bikinis and the related accessories. There is a good selection of children's swimwear in the market, although you'll have to hunt high and low to find UV-protective items; it is probably best to bring these from your home country. The Qatar sun is harsh, and swimsuits made from UV-protective fabrics make a big difference in protecting your children from sun damage.

Beachwear

BHS	Landmark Mall	487 4271
Debenhams	City Center	483 2668
Etam Lingerie	The Mall	468 3374
Galaxy Sports	City Center	483 0322
Marks & Spencer	Landmark Mall	P.146 ► 488 0101
Monsoon	LandMark Mall	487 1128
Next	The Mall	467 8222
Robina	Royal Plaza	413 1000
Sports Corner	The Mall	483 1304
Sun & Sand Sports	City Center	483 7007

As Qatar is blessed with a warm climate, you will possibly be swimming throughout the year. As a result, swimwear is always on display in department stores, sports shops and lingerie shops. Keep your eyes peeled for sales and promotions, which are held regularly.

Bicycles

Skate Shack on Salwa Road offers a good selection of bicycles and accessories, as well as other

Bicycles

Skate Shack	Alwaab, Salwa Rd	469 2532
The Baby Shop	City Center	483 9082
	Musheirib	442 1766
Toys R Us	Al Mirqab Al Jadeed	443 5904

sporting goods. They only sell TREK bikes, but have a so~~...~~ and recreational mo~~...~~nge of safety gear, such as lights, ~~...~~ protective pads for shins, knees and elbows (you'll be needing these if you brave Qatar's roads!). You'll also find a range of clothes, spare parts and padlocks. The shop assistants are helpful and knowledgeable and they are willing to order a specific model of bike if they don't already stock it (as long as it is TREK). Prices are reasonable compared to Europe and the US.

For children's bikes try Toy-R-Us or Babyshop; the prices at Babyshop may be cheaper but make sure you are not compromising on quality.

Books

Other options → **Libraries [p.143]**
Second-Hand Items [p.168]

Qatar has a limited number of English bookshops, so if you're the type that likes to while away the weekend hours browsing through a multi-storey bookshop, you might be a bit disappointed. The Jarir Bookstore, which also sells electronics and stationery, has a moderate collection of English books and magazines. Apart from fiction, you will also find books on cooking, IT, travel, science and reference. Prices are reasonable, although may be higher than in your home country. The bookshop will order a book for you if it is available at one of their branches elsewhere, but they will only order a minimum of 30 copies. Alternatively you can order books online through the well known websites such as Amazon. You can expect delivery to take two to three weeks. Carrefour stocks a limited selection of magazines and books. International magazines are very expensive and subject to the

GCC

Whether you're travelling around the Gulf or further afield, Explorer Publishing produces a range of books for visitors and residents, full of useful information and advice. Be it for a shopping spree in Dubai, a luxury holiday in Abu Dhabi, a get-back-to-nature trip in Oman, a long weekend in Kuwait or a sporting event in Bahrain, don't leave Qatar without an Explorer!

censor's approval, so don't be surprised to find black marker across any exposed body parts. Every now and again you may stumble across a bestseller or two on Carrefour's shelves, but this is more a matter of good luck than literary judgement on behalf of the hypermarket!

Other supermarkets and some hotels also stock a small range of books and magazines, but these rarely deserve a visit in terms of range and astronomical prices.

Many people tend to swap books around once they have read them; with all the travelling in and out of Qatar you'll usually find someone who has picked up the latest bestseller in a foreign airport.

Books		
Carrefour	City Center	484 6222
Family Bookshop	City Center	485 4049
Jarir Bookstore	Salwa Road South	444 0212

Camera Equipment

Other options → **Electronics & Home Appliances [p.158]**

The photography equipment market in Doha is fairly good, with most of the latest models available (although they may arrive a bit later than they do in other markets). There are numerous dedicated photography shops offering a good range of cameras and equipment. You will find camera shops in the souk area near the Sofitel that are reasonably stocked and priced, although they may not have the latest models. Al Mushri Co. specialises in Minolta cameras and even stocks a few underwater cameras.

Hypermarkets such as Carrefour and Lulus stock a range of cameras and you may find they are cheaper than the individual retailers. Jarir Bookstore also stocks cameras and some accessories. Wherever you buy your camera equipment, be sure to keep your receipt and check that the warranty you get is an international one (an international warranty is especially important if you are buying a camera to take home).

When you need to get your pictures processed there is no shortage of places where you can drop off your film or memory card for processing. Gulf Colours has many branches around Doha, and there are also some internationally recognised shops such as Kodak and Fuji. This service is probably cheaper than in your home country and

whenever you have a roll of film developed you will get a free replacement film and photo album. Most processing shops now have the ability to print digital photos, either from your memory card or a CD. They can also transfer photos onto a CD for you, both from memory card and film.

Camera Equipment		
Al Mushiri Co.	Abdul Aziz	442 3030
Fuji Film	Landmark Mall	487 5077
Gulf Colours	Abdul Aziz	443 4772
Kodak	City Center	483 9522
Qatar Studio	Abdul Aziz	442 2953

Cards & Stationery

Other options → **Books [p.153]**
Art Supplies [p.152]

This is one shopping category where you may find yourself longing for your home country – the range in Doha is a poor comparison. The best place is Gulf Greetings, a distributor of Hallmark cards, which has branches in all the major shopping malls. They provide a limited selection of cards for all special occasions (Christmas, Easter, Eid, Mother's Day, birthdays, etc), as well as wrapping paper, postcards and a small range of toys.

A limited collection of cards can be found in Marks & Spencer, Carrefour, Jarir Bookstore and Events. Some expats actually stock up on cards and paper when travelling on business or on annual leave.

Jarir Bookstore has a good range of stationery. Al Rawnaq has a fairly good selection of items such as cards, folders and office stationery, with prices being slightly cheaper than Jarir. Carrefour also has a small stationery section.

Cards & Stationery		
Al Rawnaq Stationery	Al Hilal East	466 9555
	Al Markhiya	432 8973
Carrefour	City Center	484 6222
Events	Royal Plaza	413 1155
Family Bookshop	City Center	485 4049
Gulf Greetings	City Center	483 8117
	Landmark Mall	486 2889
	The Centre	444 0202
	The Mall	467 8383
Jarir Bookstore	Salwa Road South	444 0212
Marks & Spencer p.146	Landmark Mall	488 0101
Wrap It	Hyatt Plaza	468 5497

Carpets

Other options ➔ **Souvenirs [p.169]**
Bargaining [p.150]

Most carpets sold in Qatar have been made in countries such as Iran, Pakistan or China. Persian carpets are regarded as being the best investment. The price of an original Persian carpet can reach tens of thousands of riyals. They are usually extremely pretty, with intricate designs and a myriad of colours. A good Persian carpet can take up to five years to make, so if you divide the price by five years' worth of labour, you can understand why they are so expensive.

Hand-made carpets are more valuable than machine-made ones, and silk is usually more expensive than wool. The more knots per square metre, the better the carpet.

The best places to buy carpets are the major shopping malls like City Center and Royal Plaza. To make sure the carpet you are buying is original, ask for a certificate of authenticity. Oriental Carpets also has a nice selection. You can get cheaper carpets in the souks, but to get a good bargain you really need to know a lot about carpets – the shop owners are very convincing and will make you believe you are getting a great carpet at a low price.

If you are looking for cheaper carpets and rugs, try Al Ramez International on Salwa Road (located next to Eli France Cafe), Home Centre, THE One or Apollo.

Carpets

Al Ramez International	Al Mirqab Al Jadeed	435 6556
Apollo	Salwa Road South	468 9522
Bradan Carpets	Al Matar Al Qadeem	467 8886
Home Centre	City Center	483 9400
Oriental Carpet Co.	Al Muntazah	413 1850
Original Art	Al Sadd	413 1325
Reshi	Ras Abu Abboud	486 4795

Bag a carpet

Cars

Other options ➔ **Buying a Vehicle [p.78]**

If you're lucky enough to be in the market for a new car, most major brands are available from Daihatsu to Bentley and everything in between. Keep an eye on the local press for promotions and special offers, particularly during Ramadan and Eid. While these may not save you much on the price of the car, you might find you get a good deal on insurance, finance or on a warranty; and some dealers might even offer a raffle draw where you can win back the price of your car!

New cars are made affordable with long finance periods (up to five years) and low interest rates (typically 4%). Insurance is usually based on the value of your car and rates range from 4% to 6% depending on what kind of car you have (saloon, 4 WD, sports, etc). Some models are blacklisted by some insurance companies (such as the Mitsubishi Lancer Evolution, which is built for speed), but you might be able to get assistance with insurance through the dealer (although it will cost you).

If you are looking for a good deal on a second-hand car, there are a few reputable dealers around. Many of the second-hand cars in the market are imported from other Gulf countries or are of dubious origin – the golden rule when buying second-hand is to steer clear of anything that doesn't have a full service history and a comprehensive warranty. You do have the option of buying privately from somebody who is leaving Qatar or upgrading their car. However, as most large companies have a local intranet for their employees, a lot of private sales don't make it to the public domain. Used cars for sale in the newspaper classifieds are few and far between, but you will probably find quite a range advertised on supermarket notice boards.

Importing a car is straightforward if you can buy the car for cash, as Qatar recently dropped the 5% import tax. The car has to be less than three years old.

Off-Road Pioneers

Once you've conquered the challenging desert terrain that Qatar has to offer, continue your quest for off-road domination of the region by heading for the natural delights of the UAE. With maps and suggested routes, off-roading tips and safety recommendations, the **UAE Off-Road Explorer** is the essential accessory for modern-day adventurers.

Clothes

Other options → Beachwear [p.153]
Kids' Items [p.162]
Lingerie [p.164]
Shoes [p.168]
Sporting Goods [p.169]
Tailoring [p.169]

The latest international fashions are available at Doha's many clothes shops. Prices may be higher than in your home country, but on the upside there are usually fantastic sales at least twice a year.

Various designers have a presence in the shopping malls – Karen Millen, MaxMara, Massimo Dutti and Valentino mingle with Calvin Klein, Gucci and Prada. If high-street shopping is your thing, then you'll feel right at home in Next, Debenhams, Monsoon, Marks & Spencer and Bhs, all of which can be found in various shopping malls. You'll find cheaper fashions in Splash or Sana. No matter what your budget, you'll be spoilt for choice.

There are hundreds of tailors and fabric shops around Doha, so you can always have things made if you want something specific. The tailors here can copy any garment, picture or pattern, and once you find a tailor you are happy with then you'll be thrilled with the results.

Clothes		
Benetton	The Mall	467 7088
BHS	Landmark Mall	487 4271
Debenhams	City Center	483 2668
French Connection	City Center	493 0774
Giordano	City Center	483 9221
Guess	Royal Plaza	413 1334
Highland	City Center	467 8678
Karen Millen	Landmark Mall	486 7752
Levis	Royal Plaza	413 1301
Marks & Spencer P.146	Landmark Mall	488 0101
Massimo Dutti	Landmark Mall	487 6860
MaxMara	Emporium	437 5796
Monsoon	Landmark Mall	487 1128
Next	City Center	483 7615
	The Mall	467 8222
Oasis	The Mall	467 8881
Pull and Bear	Landmark Mall	487 6856
Roots	Royal Plaza	413 1110
Salam Studio	The Mall	467 8467
Sana	City Center	483 9173
Splash	City Center	483 1139
Stradivarius	Landmark Mall	486 1756
Ulla Popken	Royal Plaza	413 1302
Valentino	Royal Plaza	413 1441
Zara	Landmark Mall	487 4654

Window shopping

Clothes – Nearly New

There are no second-hand clothes shops in Qatar. The Centre has a factory outlet that sells branded clothing at reasonable prices, and Sana, Splash and Carrefour have really cheap ranges of clothes. Carrefour often sells branded clothing that are over-runs – the labels have been cut out but it is not uncommon to find clothes by Gap or George if you have a good rummage.

If you are having a wardrobe clearout you can donate your unwanted clothes to one of the four charity organisations in Doha: Qatar Charity (466 7711), Qatar Red Crescent (443 5111), Sheikh Eid Bin Muhammad Al Thani Charity Association (487 8061) and Sheikh Jasim bin Jaber Al Thani Charity (441 1011).

Computers

Other options → Electronics & Home Appliances [p.158]

Most computer shops in Qatar are located in the Musheirib area near the Sofitel. Most of these retailers can either sell you the latest off-the-shelf technology, or build a machine to your personal specifications (having a computer built up for you is usually cheaper; the disadvantage is that you won't get an international warranty). If you do buy an international brand, make sure you get a warranty card and that it is stamped by the dealer, otherwise the warranty will be void if you leave Qatar. Most computer shops will be able to perform repairs at a reasonable rate. Lulus, Carrefour, Modern Home and the Jarir Bookstore offer international brands of computers and accessories.

ABU DHABI
Experience The Magic

Abu Dhabi offers all the attractions of a top class
international resort ... plus a taste of something
extra. It combines year-round sunshine and
superb facilities for leisure and recreation with
the spice and mystique of an Arabian adventure.
Abu Dhabi is a dynamic 21st century city with
unspoiled beaches, the tranquility of the desert,
rugged mountain scenery and lush green oases.

هيـئـة أبوظبـي للسيـاحـة
Abu Dhabi Tourism Authority

P O Box 94000 Abu Dhabi, United Arab Emirates, Tel +971 2 4440444, Fax +971 2 4440400
info@abudhabitourism.ae

Prices of computers are likely to be quite similar to those in your home country, although you can bargain a few riyals off the marked price here. Look out for regular promotions; these will usually take the form of bundled software or accessories (like a free printer or webcam).

Computers		
Al Afdhal	Musheirib	435 4755
Carrefour	City Center	333 3333
Family Computers	Musheirib	432 4070
Hi Tek Computer	Musheirib	443 9235
LuLu Hypermarket	Al Hilal East	466 7780
Modern Home	Al Mirqab Al Jadeed	442 2815

Costumes

You can buy children's costumes in shops like Toys R Us and the Babyshop. Party Mania has a small selection of both adults' and children's costumes. The Party Balloon has some costumes for hire, or you can request one of the shop's entertainers to wear a particular costume for your child's birthday party.

If you can't find the costume you are looking for, you could try shopping online. Alternatively, take a picture to your tailor and get them to make your costume.

Costumes		
Party Balloon	Al Mansoura	431 8205
Party Mania	Al Muntazah	441 8810
The Baby Shop	Musheirib	442 1766
	City Center	483 9082
Toys R Us	Al Mirqab Al Jadeed	443 5904

Electronics & Home Appliances

Other options → **Camera Equipment [p.154]**
Computers [p.156]

Carrefour and LuLus both have good selections of household names like Black and Decker, Kenwood, Sanyo, Sony and LG to name a few. These hypermarkets tend to be a little bit cheaper than retailers in major shopping malls, although they may not offer the very latest models. Both offer home delivery.

In the souks you'll find a street dedicated to electronic shops, with hundreds of televisions, stereos and other electronics lining the shopfronts. Some of the goods will be well-known brand names

and some may be brands you've never heard of, which may be cheaper but slightly lower quality. Techno Q on Salwa Road offers a selection of high-end goods from brands like Yamaha and Denon.

Noticeboards in supermarkets and schools are a good source of information for second-hand items, as people leaving usually post a list of goods for sale.

A large share of rented accommodation will be leased on a semi-furnished basis, so most kitchen appliances will be fitted. There is no standard system for cookers in Doha; some houses use gas cookers and some use electric. If you have a gas cooker you can order gas cylinders for home delivery.

Electronics & Home Appliances		
Al Muftah	Al Sadd St	444 6868
Bang and Olufsen	Landmark Mall	487 3240
Carrefour	City Center	484 6265
Darwish Trading	Salwa Road South	442 2781
Jumbo Electronics	City Center	442 3303
LuLu Hypermarket	Al Matar Al Qadeem	466 7780
Modern Home	Al Mirqab Al Jadeed	442 2815
National Panasonic	Musheirib	441 7575
Techno Blue	Al Muntazah	437 0756
Techno Q	Salwa Road South	468 9494
Technotrade	Salwa Road South	432 1242

Eyewear

Other options → **Sporting Goods [p.169]**
Opticians [p.71]

Unless you want to spend all your time outdoors shielding your eyes from the sun with your hand, a good pair of sunglasses is a necessity. In a country where it is almost always sunny, the demand for sunglasses is high and fortunately the supply is plentiful. Every shopping mall has at least one sunglasses shop, stocking a wide range of designer sunglasses. Cheaper options are available in supermarkets and the souks sell endless cheap knock-offs. While with sunglasses it is not always true that the more expensive they are, the better protection they give (sometimes you are paying more for the designer logo on the side than for the lens quality), it is safe to say that a ten-riyal pair of plastic sunglasses from the souk may not give you the UV protection you need from the harsh sun.

You'll also find an impressive range of opticians in Doha. Located in shopping malls, you can just walk in and get your eyes tested (some offer this service for free, even if you don't make a purchase).

Eyewear

Al Jabor Vision Technology	Al Muntazah	442 7152
Bahrain Optician	City Center	483 8848
Carrefour	City Center	484 6265
Giant Stores	Hyatt Plaza	469 2991
Ibn al Haytham Optics	Bin Omran	487 8119
Optic Gallery	The Mall	467 8100
Qatar Optics	Landmark Mall	486 6649
Royal Optician	City Center	483 7724
Royal Optician	Royal Plaza	413 1300
Sunglass Hut	City Center	483 0501
Yateem Optician	Royal Plaza	413 1363

Flowers

Other options → **Gardens [p.160]**

There are many independent florists in Doha. Some, such as Larissa and Gardenia, sell both flowers and chocolates. Many supermarkets have in-house florists where you can get fresh flowers, arranged in a nice bouquet, at reasonable prices. You can expect to pay around

Flowers

Casa Flora	Al Mirqab Al Jadeed	432 8111
Gardenia	Al Mirqab Al Jadeed	444 0789
Home Centre	City Center	483 9400
Interflora	Umm Ghuwailina	432 2717
Larissa	Bin Omran	487 5664
Mega Mart	Landmark Mall	488 3001
Riviera	Al Sadd	432 0120

QR 50 and upwards for a decent arrangement. Interflora makes lovely bouquets and offers a delivery service both locally and internationally. Shop around online if you want to send flowers to someone overseas, as it is sometimes more expensive to send flowers to a neighbouring country than to Europe.

Food

Other options → **Health Food [p.160]**

Food shopping can be challenging; supermarkets stock a good range of international items for many different nationalities, but you may have to traipse through several shops before you can tick off every item on your shopping list. The joy of discovering your favourite product from back home can turn to despair a few days later when you discover that it has all sold out, never to reappear on the shelves again. So if you see something that you use often, stock up! Q-Mart stocks a range of Tesco products

(a popular UK brand) and quite a few expats shop here, even though the prices are on the expensive side. Mega Mart also has a great range of international products and they have a good selection of fruit, vegetables and meat. The Landmark branch of Mega Mart has a Bateel Bakery where you can get the best breads in town.

Carrefour, in City Center, has a variety of products from around the world at reasonable prices. They have excellent fish and vegetable sections. Carrefour's prices are good and it's a great place to buy your cleaning products and toiletries. If you park at the Carrefour end of City Center you can also get your car washed while you shop, for QR 8!

The Family Food Centre on the Airport Road stocks a good range of food for special dietary requirements. Lulus and the Dasman Centre both have their own supermarkets which are popular with Asian expats.

Discount Cards

There are a few stores in Qatar that offer discount cards: at Jarir Bookstore you can first apply for a blue card that gives you 10% discount, and then as your purchases increase you will be entitled to 15% discount through the silver card, then to 20% though the gold card.

The Home Centre privilege card gives you points based on your purchases. As your points grow, the shop will mail you credit vouchers which you can use anytime except for when the store is having sales. Remember always to apply for these cards. In some stores if you don't ask, no one will remind you.

Food

Carrefour	City Center	484 6265
Dasman Centre	Al Hilal East	467 4055
Family Food Centre	Al Hilal East	442 2456
Giant Stores	Hyatt Plaza	469 2991
Mega Mart	Landmark Mall	488 3001
	Al Muntazah	444 0018
Q-Mart	The Mall	467 8822

Mega Mart

Gardens

Other options → **Hardware & DIY [p.160]**
Flowers [p.159]

The harsh environment and extreme temperatures hardly make Qatar an ideal location for keen horticulturists, but with plenty of water and TLC it is possible to make your garden grow. While there are no big garden centres in Doha with everything under one roof, the Omani Market (located behind the central markets just off Salwa Road) is worth a visit. Here you can get plants, pots, soil, and various other items like woven mats and baskets. In the same area there are also a number of nurseries selling plants and a small selection of pots. You could happily spend a few hours rooting around in these markets and nurseries, and when you do see something you like don't forget to negotiate the price as a spot of haggling is expected.

While they may be more expensive, many supermarkets sell a range of plants, flowers and pots. You'll find some great garden furniture in Carrefour, the Home Centre, THE One and Apollo. Prices vary from reasonable (Carrefour) to expensive (Apollo). Although Apollo's furniture is more expensive, the quality and beauty is excellent. Alternatively you can get something made according to your specifications at carpentry shops in Najma and the industrial area. All you need is a picture of what you want and the carpenters will copy it. Use word of mouth to find a carpenter you are happy with.

Gardens		
Apollo	Salwa Road South	468 9522
Carrefour	City Center	484 6265
Floranza	Abu Hamour	469 9982
Green House	Abu Hamour	469 7403
Home Centre	City Center	483 9400
THE One	Landmark Mall	488 8669

Hardware & DIY

Other options → **Outdoor Goods [p.165]**

There are no dedicated DIY shops in Doha... yet. Carrefour in City Center Mall (484 6265) has a good selection of tools and hardware, but it is a poor comparison to international DIY superstores like Ace and B&Q. The tool souk (Souk Al Waqif) sells every kind of tool you might require for simple DIY jobs in the house and garden, with the

exception of hand drills (which you'll find at Carrefour). To find the tool souk, drive along the corniche and turn right at the traffic lights between Qatar Central Bank and HSBC, onto Grand Hamad Street. After the first set of lights, take the first slip road on your right and turn right and the tool souk will be in front of you. The best place to find parking is in the basement carpark on the corner as the road bends to the left. It is not advisable to visit the tool souk if you are a woman; you are not in any danger but you might get annoyed by the slack-jawed stares of the shop-owners and passers-by!

If you need paint, there are a number of shops around Doha selling various colours and all the accessories you'll need. They can mix thousands of colours, but unfortunately they don't offer tester pots. You just have to take your chances by buying a litre (luckily it isn't that expensive).

Health Food

Other options → **Health Clubs [p.138]**
Food [p.159]

Qatar isn't awash with specialist food shops, but some of the supermarkets (including Mega Mart, Q-Mart and the Family Food Centre) stock a range of items for special dietary requirements. Some health foods will be kept in the medicine aisles, so just ask an assistant if you can't find what you're looking for. You should be able to get your hands on wheat-free products (pasta, bread, biscuits, cereal), sugar-free sweets and chocolates, and soya milk. Prices are usually high, with Family Foods and Q-Mart tending to stock the least expensive products. Stock doesn't last long, so buy in bulk whenever you can.

The Nutrition & Diet Centre on Al Kinana Street can help you with any special dietary requirements. Their qualified dieticians will assess you and provide a specific dietary programme according to your individual needs. They have their own kitchen and can cook your daily meals according to the amount of calories you need. They also stock a range of sweets and chocolates for various dietary requirements.

Health Food		
Family Food Centre	Al Hilal East	442 2456
Mega Mart	Landmark Mall	488 3001
Nutrition & Diet Centre	Al Mirqab Al Jadeed	436 8831
Q-Mart	The Mall	467 8822

What & Where to Buy

Shopping

Scenes from the souks

Home Furnishings & Accessories

Other options → **Hardware & DIY [p.160]**
Furnishing Accommodation [p.60]

Home Furnishings & Accessories		
Almana Maples	Salwa Road South	432 8812
Apollo Furniture	Salwa Road South	468 9522
Bombay	Al Matar Al Qadeem	466 6869
Carrefour	City Center	484 6222
Debenhams	City Center	483 2668
Final Touches	Royal Plaza	413 0188
Home Centre	City Center	483 9400
Homes R Us	Hyatt Plaza	469 3454
ID Design —	The Mall	467 8777
Living in Interiors	Al Salata	437 0042
Oriental Furniture	Al Matar Al Qadeem	465 5123
The Home Centre	Abdul Aziz	435 5300
THE One	Landmark Mall	488 8669

Home furnishings

Jewellery & Watches

Other options → **Souks [p.176]**

There are numerous outlets selling watches and jewellery, many of which are located in shopping malls. Most major international watch brands are available and price tags range from under QR 100 to over QR 100,000! You will also find plenty of watches on sale in the souks, including some pretty convincing imitations.

Jewellery & Watches		
Al Fardan Jewellery	City Center	483 0110
	Landmark Mall	486 1400
Al Jaber Watches	Royal Plaza	413 1717
Al Wajba Jewellery	City Center	483 3535
Ali Bin Ali Establishment Jewellery	City Center	483 8153
Allied	Royal Plaza	413 1100
Blue Salon	Ibn Mahmoud North	446 6111
Cartier	Royal Plaza	442 9900
Charriol	Royal Plaza	413 1332
Damas	Landmark Mall	487 7882
Damas Exclusive	The Mall	467 7200
Damascus Jewellery	City Center	443 4828
	Hyatt Plaza	468 2506
Diamond & Diamond	Royal Plaza	413 1010
Jaber Watches	The Mall	467 8484
Makki Gallery	Royal Plaza	413 1212
	The Mall	467 8006
Makki Jewellery	Landmark Mall	486 5344
Marzooq Al Shamlan & Sons	The Mall	467 8883
	Hyatt Plaza	469 7267
Muftah Jewellery	City Center	483 3000
Paris Gallery	Hyatt Plaza	468 2626
Rado Watches	City Center	483 9442
Raymond Weil	City Center	447 7800
Rivoli	Landmark Mall	487 3190
	City Center	483 3679
Royal Jewellery	City Center	444 9244
Shahla Jewellery	City Center	483 9182
Tag Heuer	The Mall	467 8866
Tiara Jewellery	Royal Plaza	413 1777
Tzarina	Royal Plaza	413 1361
Watch Corner	City Center	493 0758
	Landmark Mall	487 2707
Wazni Jewellery	City Center	493 3311

Jewellery is sold by weight and you may find that prices are cheaper here compared to your home country. Every mall will have at least one jeweller and of course the gold souk is a wall-to-wall wonderland of glittering gold shops. If you don't find anything you like, it is easy to find a jeweller who will make a piece of jewellery to your specifications. Cases of jewellers conning their customers by selling fake gold at real-gold prices are few and far between; nevertheless it is a good idea to ask for a certificate of authenticity (especially important when buying diamonds).

Kids' Items

Other options → **Clothes [p.156]**

There is a definite 'kiddy culture' in Doha, with a huge selection of shops selling clothes, toys and furniture for kids. Kids' clothing brands from around the world are available, including Pumpkin Patch, Premaman, OshKosh and Reset. There are also great children's departments in shops like Marks & Spencer, Debenhams, Bhs and Monsoon, all of which can be found in major shopping malls. For baby items, you should be able to find all the necessities in Mothercare and the Babyshop. Jacadi Paris is on the pricey side, but they sell a beautiful range of items for newborns.

You'll find toys on sale everywhere, although be mindful of safety standards if you are buying from the cheaper end of the scale. Toys R Us is a reputable shop with a large selection at reasonable prices, but just one word of warning – if you see something you like, buy it when you see it as it may not be there on your next visit. Popular items sell out like hotcakes and it can take ages for that item to reappear on the shelves. The Early Learning Centre has a few branches throughout Doha and stocks some fantastic toys and arts-and-crafts items. Prices may be higher than in the UK. Babyshop has a good range of clothes (at excellent prices) as well as a huge toy section and a selection of necessities for babies (bottles, breast pumps, nappy-changing accessories, toddlers' cutlery, etc).

Shopping for your child's party is a bit more challenging, particularly if they want a themed party. Events and Toys R Us sell a range of invitations, decorations and party accessories, choices are limited (think Mickey Mouse and Winnie the Pooh rather than Fimbles, Teletubbies or My Little Pony). If your three-year old insists on a Strawberry Shortcake or Bob the Builder party, you might have to order your paper plates, party hats, cups and decorations online.

Al Rawnaq (in the 'button and bow' souk) is great for party gifts. They stock an unbelievable range of cheap-and-cheerful toys and hair accessories that are ideal as party bag fillers.

Kids' Items		
Al Rawnaq Stationery	Al Hilal East	466 9555
BHS	Landmark Mall	487 4271
Debenhams	City Center	483 0582
Early Learning Centre	City Center	483 9782
	Hyatt Plaza	469 7964
	Landmark Mall	486 6579
Events	Royal Plaza	413 1155
Jacadi	Nr Royal Plaza	432 1725
Marks & Spencer P.146	Landmark Mall	488 0101
Mothercare	City Center	483 0475
	Landmark Mall	488 0578
Osh Kosh	Landmark Mall	486 2012
Premaman	The Mall	467 8800
Pumpkin Patch	The Mall	466 1597
Reset	City Center	483 0102
	Landmark Mall	486 8585
The Baby Shop	City Center	483 8508
Toys R Us	Al Mirqab Al Jadeed	443 5904

Just add kids

Other options → Clothes [p.156]

	Landmark Mall	487 4271
∴nhams	City Center	483 2668
Etam Lingerie	Hyatt Plaza	468 3374
	The Mall	465 9679
La Senza	City Center	483 3862
	The Mall	467 8800
Marks & Spencer P.146	Landmark Mall	488 0101
Nayomi	City Center	483 1299
Triumph	Royal Plaza	413 1319
Woolworths	City Center	483 9352

Luggage & Leather

Other options → Shipping [p.149]

You can purchase luggage from various retail shops, supermarkets and souks. Salam Studio and Highland have a good selection of Samsonite and Delsey products, Roots and Blue Salon both have extensive ranges of Samsonite luggage and the supermarkets such as Mega Mart and Carrefour sell ranges of cheaper luggage. The souks are great if you want a full set of fake Louis Vuitton luggage, but don't be surprised if the handles fall off the first time you use it.

Luggage & Leather		
Blue Salon	Ibn Mahmoud North	446 6111
Highland	The Mall	467 8678
Mega Mart	Landmark Mall	488 3001
Roots	Royal Plaza	413 1110
Salam Plaza	City Center	483 2050
Salam Studio	The Mall	467 8467

Maternity Clothes

Other options → Maternity [p.70]

Maternity Clothes		
Debenhams	City Center	483 0582
Marks & Spencer P.146	Landmark Mall	488 0101
Mothercare	City Center	483 0475
	Landmark Mall	488 0578
	The Mall	467 8844
Woolworths	City Center	483 9352

Medicine

Other options → General Medical Care [p.68]

There are plenty of pharmacies in Doha, but they are not as prevalent the further you travel outside of the capital. They are found as stand-alone shops, or linked to petrol stations, or in souks, and all the main shopping centres have at least one pharmacy. The Middle East region as a whole has a fairly relaxed attitude to medication and there are many items available over the counter here that would be more expensive and require a prescription in your home country. The only downside is that stocks often run out and it could be a few weeks (or more) before they are replaced, so make sure you always have a back-up supply of any medication you depend upon. You should also make sure you're not allergic or sensitive to any medicines you buy, as the pharmacist may not always ask.

There are several 24 hour pharmacies available, and these will be indicated by a clearly visible sign. You can get a list of them by contacting the Ministry of Health on 446 8468.

Medicine		
City Center Pharmacy	City Center	483 9200
Good Life	City Center	483 1245
Tylosland Pharmacy	Landmark Mall	486 6599

Mobile Telephones

Other options → Telephone [p.65]

Just like in all Gulf countries, it seems that every person in Doha has a mobile phone permanently stuck to their ear. Due to the high demand, there are plenty of places to buy the most up-to-the-minute phones and accessories.

All the main shopping centres have at least one or two phone outlets. Carrefour and Lulus also offer the latest models at reasonable prices. You'll also find a number of independent phone shops around Doha; shopping at one of these or at one of the hypermarkets might result in slightly lower prices. In general though, prices are quite affordable and cheaper in comparison to many other countries. No matter where you buy your phone, make sure that you get the warranty card stamped and attached to your receipt. Your phone should come with a one-year warranty, and if it breaks during the year you can get it fixed by the dealer for free as long as you have the paperwork.

There are some second-hand mobile shops on Al Nasr Street and Al Sadd Street. You can often pick up a nearly new phone at a great prices, since mobiles are seen as a fashion accessory and some people upgrade whenever a new model arrives on the market. Negotiate on the price and you should be able to save a few riyals.

Most mobile phone shops also offer repair services. Just remember to ask for a quote before they do any work, as the repairs may end up costing more than a new phone.

Mobile Telephones		
Carrefour	City Center	484 6222
Consolidated Gulf Co.	Al Nasr	443 0666
Modern Home	Al Mirqab Al Jadeed	442 2815
Nokia	City Center	483 5352
Voda Group	Hyatt Plaza	469 7290

Music, DVDs & Videos

You can buy DVDs, CDs, audio cassettes and videos at various independent shops around Doha, and there are also a few outlets in some of the shopping malls. Unfortunately, internationally renowned superstores like Virgin Megastore have not arrived on Doha's shores yet and the range available is currently quite disappointing. You can usually get the latest mainstream releases, although these tend to sell out quite quickly. Hypermarkets like Carrefour and Lulus sell a fairly good selection of DVDs and CDs at excellent prices, although they may not have the latest releases.

Thank goodness for online shopping! If you band together with your friends for a big order and share the shipping costs, shopping online is a viable option. Shipments usually take around three weeks to arrive, but chances are your package will be stopped by customs and sent to the censorship department for inspection (this is especially true with large online retailers, such as Amazon, because their packaging is branded).

If you are the type of person who can't watch the same movie twice, you have the option of renting DVDs and videos from several rental shops around Doha. You might have to pay a hefty deposit, but rental charges are reasonable and return times are quite flexible.

If your conscience permits, you can get the latest releases on pirated DVDs. Just take a wander around the souk area and you'll no doubt be approached by someone offering you 'DVD copies'.

They're as cheap as chips, but the risk is that you could get them home and discover that the quality is terrible. Piracy is illegal in Qatar (as in virtually every country in the world), but it is unlikely that the police will raid your house to bust you for that dodgy copy of *Finding Nemo*.

Music, DVDs & Videos		
Carrefour	City Center	484 6222
The Center	Salwa Road South	444 0202
Falcon Video	Al Markhiya	486 9988
Music Center	City Center	483 9900
Music Master	Landmark Mall	487 0500
Star Music	Royal Plaza	413 1131

Musical Instruments

Other options → **Music Lessons [p.143]**

There isn't a huge range of musical instruments to be found here. The branches of Modern Home stock Yamaha instruments. They sell trumpets, saxaphones, flutes, keyboards, trombones and miniature drums. Some music shops may be able to repair instruments, especially string, and order a specific instrument for you from overseas if you can't find what you're looking for in Doha.

Musical Instruments		
Modern Home	Al Mirqab Al Jadeed	442 2815
	City Center	493 0000
X-po Center	Diplomatic District	483 6474

Outdoor Goods

Other options → **Camping [p.123]**
Hardware & DIY [p.160]
Sporting Goods [p.169]

If you're after decent outdoor goods then Carrefour has a good selection of tents, cool boxes and barbecues at reasonable prices. Apollo stocks an Australian range of barbecues – they look great and have many added features, but then again they are on the expensive side, with prices ranging from QR 1700 to QR 8000. Apollo and Home Centre both have good selections of high-quality garden furniture.

Outdoor Goods		
Apollo	Salwa Road South	468 9522
Carrefour	City Center	484 6265
Home Centre	City Center	483 9400
The Home Centre	Abdul Aziz	435 5300

A spot of quiet shopping

Party Accessories

For party accessories, most supermarkets stock a range of balloons, candles, paper plates and party bags. Gulf Greetings sells a limited selection of invitations and party favours. In addition to providing party goods, many card shops also provide a gift-wrapping service during special occasions like Valentine's Day and Christmas. Events in the Royal Plaza sell a wide range of party items, especially for kids' parties. They sell balloons, invitations, wrapping paper and decorations, and they have future plans to start a party organising service.

The Party Balloon organises parties and has a range of items and activities for you to choose from. They have bouncy castles for rental, with prices varying according to size (as a guide, you can expect to pay anything from QR 300 upwards). They can also arrange face painting, entertainers, bulk quantities of balloons and catering. Try negotiating on the first price quoted, as they will often give discount.

Ramada Hotel is popular for kids' parties. One feature in particular that kids (and adults) love there is the amazing chocolate fountains available in milk, dark or white chocolate.

Party Accessories

Carrefour	City Center	484 6222
Events	Royal Plaza	413 1155
Gulf Greetings	City Center	483 8117
	Landmark Mall	486 2889
	The Centre	437 2830
	The Mall	467 8383
Party Balloon	Khalifa St	431 8205
Party Mania	Al Muntazah	441 8810
Toys R Us	Al Mirqab Al Jadeed	443 5904
Wrap It	Hyatt Plaza	468 5497

Perfumes & Cosmetics

Other options → Souks [p.176]

With so many 'ladies of leisure' in the region, there are plenty of shops selling perfumes and make-up. Paris Gallery is well known throughout the GCC, selling virtually every brand of make-up and perfume. Their prices are reasonable and they often have good promotions, especially around Eid and Christmas. Department stores, such as Debenhams, Highland, Merch and Salam Studios also stock a huge range of cosmetics, with all the major houses (Estee Lauder, Clinique, Clarins, Lancome, etc) represented.

While in the Middle East you should try some authentic Arabian perfume, such as Amouage which is regarded as the most valuable in the world. Modern Home and Ajmal are good for Arabian scents. Souk Wafiq has numerous shops selling ready-made perfumes, or they can blend a signature fragrance for you. Other souks have perfume shops, although keep an eye on whether the fragrance you are buying is authentic – more than a few fakes are sold to unsuspecting shoppers.

If you have special make-up requirements (for sensitive or teenage skin, for example) and can't find what you need in the shops, all the top hotels have excellent salons and spas where you may find ranges of speciality make-up.

Perfumes & Cosmetics

4U	City Center	483 9240
	Royal Plaza	413 1307
Ajmal International	City Center	483 7664
Al Muftah	Al Mirqab Al Jadeed	444 6867
Blue Salon	Ibn Mahmoud North	446 6111
Body Shop	Landmark Mall	488 5109
Debenhams	City Center	483 2668
Faces	Landmark Mall	487 9519
Highland	The Mall	467 8678
Merch	The Mall	467 4314
Modern Home	Al Mirqab Al Jadeed	442 2815
	City Center	493 0000
Paris Gallery	Royal Plaza	413 1310
	Hyatt Plaza	468 2626
Salam Studio	The Mall	467 8467

What & where to Buy

Shopping

Copper wall panel (5m high) · Art paint effects

MacKenzie Associates

ART & SPECIALIST DECORATION

MURALS · GILDING
CREATIVE COMMISSIONS

'no 2 sterility, yes 2 creativity…'

F. MacKenzie – Artist · Designer · Feline fan

Art details · gold panel (1.5m high)

Tel 04 396 2698 Fax 04 396 2698 PO Box 34275 Dubai UAE
mackenziart@yahoo.com

Pets

Other options → Pets [p.64]

Pet shops throughout the GCC region are notoriously poor, and Doha is no exception. Animals are kept in small, often unclean, cages and are not properly looked after. Animal Kingdom on Al Mirqab Street (441 9998) is probably one of the better shops, where you can buy birds, fish, terrapins, cats and dogs, to name a few. The birds in particular are well looked after (especially large birds, like parrots, as they are very valuable and sold for high prices). The dogs in Animal Kingdom may be pedigreed, but check their health before you take them home.

If it's just a friendly family pet you're after, try the animal shelter. The Qatar Animal Welfare Society rescues cats and dogs, many of whom are left behind when their owners leave Qatar. The animals are generally well-trained and affectionate, and have been checked by a vet and vaccinated. For more information, and to view the pets needing homes, check their website www.qaws.org, or contact Janet Berry on 528 6335.

The Qatar Cat Coalition rescues cats from the streets. There is a huge stray cat population in Qatar and the QCC hopes to improve the problem with a neutering scheme.

If you are looking for a specific breed of dog or cat, it is probably best to order from overseas. A vet will be able to advise you on this procedure. Check with a government vet first though, as there is a list of breeds that have been banned in Qatar.

Portraits

Aim of Dreams (435 3030) next to Toys R Us do lovely portraits for adults and children, and they are planning to open a digital studio so that clients can have numerous shots taken and then select the best one. QatShoot, in the Landmark Mall, takes excellent portrait shots of children and families. Dream Memories on Al Kinana Street (436 9955) is renowned in Lebanon and has recently opened their Doha branch. They specialise in weddings and special events, but they also take portrait photos. Gulf Colours, with several branches around Doha, have photographers that can cover special occasions. You can expect to pay similar prices to what you would pay for these services in Europe.

If you would like a painted portait, contact the Al Mezzan Art Gallery (574 6342). They do portrait paintings using water colours or oil paints; you'll pay around QR 400 for a water-colour portrait and up to QR 1,500 for an oil painting.

Second-Hand Items

Other options → Cars [p.155]
Books [p.153]
Furnishing Accommodation [p.60]

The second-hand souk in the Najma area (also known as Souk Al Haraj, on Al Mansoura Street) sells furniture, although the quality may not be that good. If you have a good rummage around you might uncover some unusual items worth buying. The souk is only open Fridays and gets quite overcrowded. THE One (located in the Landmark Shopping Mall, 488 8669) has a damaged goods section where you can buy shop-damaged furniture at reduced prices.

Keep an eye open for garage sales held by people leaving Qatar, or for notices pinned up on supermarket noticeboards, at schools or offices. There are no thrift shops in Qatar, although if you have unwanted items that you want to donate you can call one of the four charity organisations: Qatar Charity (466 7711), Qatar Red Crescent (443 5111), Sheikh Jasim bin Jaber Al-Thani Charity Association (441 1011), or Sheikh Eid bin Muhammad Al-Thani Charity Association (487 8061).

Shoes

Other options → Sporting Goods [p.169]
Clothes [p.156]
Beachwear [p.153]

Most shopping malls have numerous shoe shops, and as long as you know where to go you'll be able to find shoes for any occasion. There is a great selection of international and local brands available. Apart from dedicated shoe shops, such as Milano, Nine West and Dune, you will also find large selections in department stores such as Debenhams and Marks & Spencer. Salam Studios is where to head if you're after designer-label shoes, although many design houses also have their own shops in the malls. Outlets such as Next, Oasis and Monsoon have limited collections, with Monsoon being particularly good for pretty flipflops. Brantano and Shoe Mart have shoes wall-to-wall, with prices to suit every budget. These shops are good for all styles of shoes, whether you're after strappy sandals, sports shoes, kids' shoes or school shoes.

Shoes

Boudoir	Royal Plaza	432 5350
Brantano	Landmark Mall	487 3161
Debenhams	City Center	483 2668
Dune	Landmark Mall	486 4183
Marks & Spencer p.146	Landmark Mall	488 0101
Milano	City Center	493 2229
Monsoon	Landmark Mall	487 1128
Next	City Center	483 7615
	The Mall	467 8222
Nine West	City Center	483 9543
Oasis	The Mall	467 8881
Salam Studio	The Mall	467 8467
Shoe Mart	City Center	483 8560

Souvenirs

Other options → **Carpets [p.155]**

Don't fall into the 'My grandma went to Doha and all I got was this lousy T-shirt' souvenir trap; Doha has a wide range of interesting souvenirs on offer that reflect the special character of Arabia. Souvenirs tend to be similar throughout the GCC countries. Intricately carved wooden trinket boxes, Arabian incense, shisha pipes, fluffy singing camels and miniature brass coffee pots have all found their way into many a suitcase on its way out of the GCC and Doha is no exception. There are also numerous souvenirs made using the regions most abundant resource: sand (such as sand art and little glass jars holding different colours of sand). Most hotels have little lobby shops that sell a limited range of the standard souvenirs, but for the best souvenir shopping in Doha, head for the souks. Here you'll find wall-to-wall souvenirs and negotiable prices, so you can just about take something back for everyone you've ever met! There is a shop called Traditional Corner, located at the beginning of Al Mirqab Street, which has a good selection of interesting knick-knacks from India, China and the Arab world. It's well worth taking the time to browse through all the items there, but the shop only opens after 18:00. There are a few souvenir shops along Abdulla Bin Thani Street such as Arts and Crafts, which sells a good range at reasonable prices. Most shopping malls have souvenir shops and there are often in-mall exhibitions that showcase the region's favourite souvenirs.

Souvenirs

Arts and Crafts	Musheirib	442 5525
Jarir Bookstore	Salwa Road South	444 0212
Traditional Corner	Al Mirqab Al Jadeed	524 2599

Sporting Goods

Other options → **Outdoor Goods [p.165]**

In December 2006, Qatar is going to be in the international spotlight as it hosts the 15th Asian Games. Doha also hosts many other international sporting events, such as the men's and women's ATP tennis championships and the Qatar Masters golf tournament. On a more local level there are many sports clubs and activities, including football, rugby and golf, that keep many expats both physically and socially active.

Whatever sport you choose to participate in, you'll be able to find all the kit you need in Doha's many sports shops. You'll find major shops like Sports Corner or Sun and Sand Sports in the major shopping malls, whereas Sport Mart and Galaxy Sport are huge independent shops that you'll find around town. Prices of clothing and shoes can be on the expensive side, unless you shop in the sales (which usually take place at least twice a year and offer substantial discounts). Carrefour stocks a limited range of sports equipment, and Skate Shack has a wide range of watersports equipment such as water kites, wind surfers, wake boards and water skis. They also sell wet suits, life jackets and safety helmets, as well as bikes, skateboards, ice hockey equipment and roller blades. If it's scuba gear you're after, try Pearl Divers, which has a PADI-certified equipment shop on the premises.

Sporting Goods

Carrefour	City Center	484 6222
The Center	Salwa Road South	444 0202
Galaxy Sports	City Center	483 0322
Pearl Divers	Farig Al Nasser St	444 9553
Skate Shack	Salwa Road South	443 8395
Sport Mart	Opp City Center	443 0311
Sports Corner	The Mall	483 1304
Sun & Sand Sports	City Center	483 7007

Tailoring

Other options → **Clothes [p.156]**

There's no shortage of tailors in Doha and once you find a good one he will be able to make up anything you want. Word of mouth is the best way to find a good tailor who is competent and reliable. Prices don't vary much from one tailor to another, although highly skilled tailors who can produce more intricate garments, like wedding dresses, are

What & Where to Buy

Shopping

more expensive. Once you have chosen your fabric, you can show your tailor a picture of what you want or even just take in a garment for him to copy.

Tailoring

Tailoring		
Al Misk	Musheirib	432 1141
Organza	Al Sadd	442 6848
Sterling	Musheirib	432 2975

Textiles

As a stopover on major trading routes, the Middle East region has always had a thriving textile market. No matter what colour or type of fabric you are looking for, there are numerous dedicated fabric shops around Doha. Souk Al Dira and Souk Al Aseiry have a collection of shops inside air-conditioned buildings, selling all types of fabrics. Prices tend to be a little more expensive than in individual shops, with prices ranging from QR 30 to QR 800 per yard.

Textiles		
Bombay Silk	Musheirib	441 2715
Century Textiles	Musheirib	442 1283
Fashion Corner	Musheirib	443 8908
Tash Textiles	Al Sadd	432 9449
Tayef Textiles	Al Jasra	441 7157

Toys, Games & Gifts

Toys R Us should be one of your first stops for toys. They stock all the latest gimmicks and gadgets that your kids will have seen on the telly and just have to have. So whether it's a Bratz pencil case, a Spiderman figurine or a pair of Incredible Hulk hands, you'll find them at Toys R Us. Another good toy shop is the Early Learning Centre, with branches in City Center, Landmark and Hyatt Plaza.

Toys, Games & Gifts		
Claire's Accessories	Landmark Mall	487 1964
Dasman Centre	Umm Ghuwailina	431 3115
Early Learning Centre	City Center	483 9782
	Hyatt Plaza	469 7964
	Landmark Mall	486 6579
Gulf Greetings	Landmark Mall	486 2889
	The Mall	467 8383
Royal Toys	Al Mirqab Al Jadeed	443 2220
The Baby Shop	Al Khaleej St	442 1766
	City Center	483 9082
Toys R Us	Al Mirqab Al Jadeed	443 5904

They sell a range of lovely toys, many of which are educational or used for arts and crafts. They have toys suitable for all ages of children, including newborns. Their exchange policy is excellent: if you buy a gift for a child from ELC, the child can exchange that gift without a receipt. Other places to try are the Babyshop, Royal Toys (on Al Mirqab Street), the Dasman Centre and Lulus. Gulf Greetings has a limited selection of toys and gifts. Claire's Accessories has a great range of hair accessories, jewellery and other funky knick-knacks for slightly older girls.

Places to Shop

The following section will help you discover the various shopping destinations in Qatar. As it is such a small country, and there is not much in the way of shopping outside the capital city, all of the outlets recommended below are in Doha. Of course our lists are not exhaustive, and every astute expat quickly finds their own heavenly 'hidden gems' when it comes to shopping. If you don't see your favourite shop in here and feel it deserves a big shout-out, email us at Info@Explorer-Publishing.com

Shopping Malls

Shopping Malls		
City Center Doha	Diplomatic District	493 3355
Emporium	Suhaim Bin Hamad	437 5796
Hyatt Plaza	Al Waad	469 4848
Landmark Mall	Al Shamal	487 5222
Royal Plaza	Al Sadd	413 0000
The Mall	Al Matar Al Qadeem	467 8383

Shopping Malls - Main

Shopping centres are popular venues with both expats and locals, not only for the wonderful selection of shops, but as meeting places for catching up with friends over a nice cup of tea. There are malls located across the capital city of Doha, some of which are always busy and some of which are not. What the centres all have in common though, are attractive interiors, a good range of shops, and plenty of air-conditioning (comes in handy during summer!). Some of the centres have cinema complexes, food courts, and children's entertainment areas.

Most of the malls tend to have huge sales twice a year, at the beginning of summer and towards the end of the year. There is a festival held over the summer and most shopping centres will have shows and family entertainment running throughout the festival. During this time, Qatar residents try their luck in prestigious raffles where the top prize is usually a brand new, luxury car.

Parking is free at the shopping malls, but trying to find a parking spot in the evenings and at weekends brings the words 'needle' and 'haystack' to mind. Parking gets even more hectic during public holidays and Eid. Even though car parks are full though, the centres themselves never feel overcrowded. At some malls, Thursday evenings are reserved for families only, so no single men are allowed in.

One thing to remember when out shopping is that supermarkets close at 10.45 for Friday prayers and re-open at 12.00.

City Center Doha

Location → Diplomatic District · Doha   483 0582
Hours → 10:00 - 22:00   Friday 2pm - 10pm
Web/email → na   Map Ref→8-D2

This is one of the largest shopping complexes in the Middle East – you could spend an entire day in City Center and still not get to experience everything it has to offer! Situated in the Diplomatic Area, it has become a well-known landmark in Doha. The shopping centre has three levels of outlets selling a variety of international and local merchandise. With its lovely interior, which is spacious and well-lit, the centre is welcoming for the whole family. Numerous cafes are scattered throughout the mall if you need to take a break. There is an ice-skating rink situated on the basement level; shoppers can stop and watch from the upper levels. Also on the basement level there is a ten pin bowling centre and a children's indoor water park. The third level is home to 'Extreme World' (a great children's entertainment centre), and two foodcourts. There is an additional bowling centre, ice rink, spa and salon, all exclusively for ladies, on the third floor. The centre also has a large multiplex cinema that screens the latest movies from around the world. City Center even has a ballroom and function hall and it hosts various exhibitions and special events. They also have a business centre that offers state-of-the-art facilities including all equipment and software required for presentations. There are also a number of prayer rooms situated throughout the centre.

Apart from the main shops, there are a number of other small shops and offices. Banks are available in the centre and there are a number of cash machines (ATMs) located on each floor. You'll also find travel agents, pharmacies and a Qtel Customer Service Centre.

City Center Doha

The parking area is huge, with over 3,000 parking spaces. However, at weekends and on public holidays you will still find it hard to find an empty space. If you park your car at the Carrefour end of the centre, you can get it washed for QR 8.

City Center is open from 10:00 - 22:00 (Saturday to Thursday), and from 14:00 - 22:00 on Fridays. Carrefour opens at 08:00.

Outlets include: Accessorize, Adam's, Adidas, Al Fardan, Al Jaber Watches, Al Muftah , Apple Center (opening soon), Arabian Oud, Baby Shop, Bateel, B-Bushh, Body Shop, Carrefour, Claire's Accessories, Debenhams, Early Learning Centre, French Connection (FCUK), Gant, Gerry Weber, Giordano, Gulf Greetings, Gulf Optics, Home Centre, Hush Puppies, Jumbo Electronics, La Senza, Mac, Milano , Mont Blanc, Mother Care, Nayomi, Next, Nine West, Nokia, Pierre Cardin, Promod, Qtel, Raymond Weil, Sana , Shoe Mart, Splash, Sun & Sand Sports, Sun Glass Hut, Swatch, United Colors of Beneton, Woolworths, Yateem Optician. There is also a Qtel Customer Service Centre, an internet cafe, no end of food outlets, and a large number of banks and ATMs

Landmark Mall

Location → Al Shamal	**487 5222**
Hours → 09:00 - 22:00 Fri 15:00 - 22:00	
Web/email → www.landmarkdoha.com	Map Ref →7-A1

Since opening, Landmark has undergone two extensions. It is a popular mall and features a variety of international and local stores that are suitable for all kinds of shopper. You'll find renowned brands like Monsoon, Marks & Spencer, Mango, Mexx and Karen Millen, all stocking the latest fashions. Mega Mart offers fantastic grocery shopping and the in-store Bateel Bakery has some of the best bread in town. Stop for refreshments at one of the mall's many cafes, including the first Starbucks in Doha. The centre also has a foodcourt housing many fastfood outlets like MacDonalds, Hardees, Pizza Hut and Subway.

Throughout the year, Landmark hosts a number of art exhibitions and events, and during special occasions and festivals (like Eid), there is plenty of family entertainment within the mall.

Parking is free and can be found around the perimeter of the centre. Mega Mart opens at 08:00, and the rest of the shops open at either 09:00 or 10:00 (On Fridays, all shops open at 15:00, except for Mega Mart which opens at 08:30). The centre closes at 22:00 every night.

Outlets include: Accessorize, Adams, Bang & Olufsen, Bhs, Body Shop, Brantano Shoe City, Claire's Accessories, Damas, Dune, Early Learning Center, Esprit, Evans, Faces, Fujifilm, Gant, Givenchy, Godiva Chocolatier, Gulf Greetings, Jennyfer, Karen Millen, Mango, Marks & Spencer, Mega Mart, Mexx, Milano, Miss Sixty, Monsoon, Mothercare, Nine West, Nokia, Patchi, Rivoli, Sunglass Hut, Swatch, THE One, Trucco, Wedgwood, Zara.

Landmark Mall

Royal Plaza

Location ➜ Al Sadd Rd · Al Sadd	**413 0000**
Hours ➜ 09:00 - 22:00 Fri 15:00 - 22:00	
Web/email ➜ www.royalplazadoha.com	Map Ref ➜ 12-E1

Royal Plaza is one of the newest shopping centres to open in Doha, and while it is not as big as the others it has a great selection of shops. The centre has no children's play area, and isn't really the kind of place that welcomes kids with open arms. But it is home to a variety of shops selling clothes and accessories for ladies and children. There are a few furniture shops that sell some interesting pieces. There are a few shops for men, and several jewellery and watch shops. If you need a rest there is a cafe, and a Japanese restaurant is set to open soon. The following shops should open in the centre soon: Givenchy, Morgan, Godiva Chocolates and Clockwise. It is still early days for Royal Plaza, but with planned improvements and new additions, it is set to become one of the busiest places in town.

Outlets include: Al Jaber Watches, Al Muftah Jewellery, Amiri Gems, Arabian Oud, Budy Shop, Cartier, Clair De Lune, Dupont, Givenchy (Opening Soon), Guess, Hang Ten, Levi's, L'Occitane, Makki Gallery, Mont Blanc, Morgan (Opening Soon), Nails, Onyx, Paris Gallery, Ray's Reef, Red Earth, Roots-Gap, Royal Opticians, Smart Kids, Star Music, Thalgo Spa, Titto Bluni, Triumph, Valentino, Voda Group, Yateem Optician. 41 30322 .

Shopping Malls - Other

The following shopping centres are smaller than the main ones and not as popular. Emporium is worth going to if you like designer clothes and Hyatt Plaza has a great children's play area. Doha is growing rapidly and you can already see a number of new shopping centres under construction; give it a few years and there should be plenty more places to spend, spend, spend!

Emporium

Location ➜ Suhaim Bin Hamad St	**437 5796**
Hours ➜ 09:00 - 13:00 16:00 - 22:00 Fri 16:00 - 22:00	
Web/email ➜ na	Map Ref ➜ 13-A2

Emporium is one of the smaller shopping centres, but has a number of designer shops. It is located near the Ramada Junction, making it easy to find. They have Kenzo, Escada, Betty Barclay, MaxMara, Laurel, More & More, Babycare and Ciel. The latest lines may not appear on the shleves as quickly as they do in other countries. There is parking at the front and back and it never really seems to gets busy.

Hyatt Plaza

Location ➜ Alwaab · Doha	**469 4848**
Hours ➜ 09:00 - 22:00 Fri 14:00 - 22:00	
Web/email ➜ na	Map Ref ➜ 12-A4

You really can't miss Hyatt Plaza: you'll recognise it from the enormous shopping trolley in the car park, which you can see from the roundabout by Khalifa Stadium. The trolley is an advert for Giant, the supermarket located in the centre. This mall is not on the same scale as Landmark or City Center, and has a limited selection of shops and boutiques, but the big furniture shop Homes R Us is popular.

There is a large foodcourt situated next to the children's play area, with a fair selection of food outlets, and weary shoppers will also find a couple of coffee shops in which to sit and relax.

To get to Hyatt Plaza, drive west along Salwa Road and turn right at the fourth roundabout (Tebah Gardens) from the Ramada Junction. Then go straight till you reach the next roundabout and turn left (by Khalifa Stadium) then straight over the next roundabout and the mall is on your right-hand side. Finding parking, especially at weekends, can be challenging to say the least.

The Mall

Location ➜ Al Matar Al Qadeem · Doha	**467 8383**
Hours ➜ 09:00 - 22:00 Fri 14:00 - 22:00	
Web/email ➜ na	Map Ref ➜ 16-E1

The Mall has the distinction of being the first shopping centre to open in Doha, in the mid 1990s. Since then it has grown into one of the most popular places for shopping and meeting friends. You can find international and local fashions in the various clothes shops. A number of new outlets are set to open shortly in The Mall: Radio Shack, Paul Frank, Birkenstock and Monsoon. They are also opening a new children's play area which will make the centre even more exciting for mums and their little ones. There is a cinema inside the mall, showing the latest American, European and Arabic films.

The mall has an American feel, with spacious avenues lined with shops. A foodcourt houses KFC, MacDonalds and a Chinese restaurant. Chili's, the popular American restaurant, is due to open soon. The Mall is host to a number of exhibitions and special events throughout the year. It is very popular with families during festival time, when there is plenty of entertainment.

Department Stores

Doha has plenty of department stores, most of which are internationally recognisable names. Almost without exception, department stores can found inside the major shopping malls. The department stores here may pale in comparison to the huge ones you find in Europe or America, but they are still good places to go for one-stop shopping. None of them have big food sections, although Marks & Spencer does have a selection of biscuits, sweets and chocolates.

Debenhams

Location → City Center Doha · Diplomatic District | 483 0582
Hours → 10:00 - 22:00   Friday 2pm - 10pm
Web/email → na   Map Ref → 8-D2

Debenhams is located in the City Center Doha and is very popular. It houses a great selection of fashion and accessories for the whole family. There is a good home furnishing section, where you can get bed linen, kitchen goods, towels, tablecloths and accessories (like candlesticks and photo frames). They also have a wide variety of cosmetics and perfumes, including counters for all the big names like Clinique, Clarins and Estee Lauder. The sales assistants are friendly and always eager to assist you.

Highland

Location → The Mall · Al Matar Al Qadeem | 467 8678
Hours → 09:00 - 22:00
Web/email → na   Map Ref → 16-E1

Highland is a two-level department store located in The Mall. They sell a variety of items such as cosmetics and perfumes, luggage, bed linen, household items such as lamps, photo frames, mirrors, and bedding. You'll find the household section and the children's department upstairs. The bedding is expensive, but the designs are beautiful and the quality is good. The children's section caters more for younger children, and even has a small collection of nursery items (cots and bedding). On the first level you'll find cosmetics, clothes for men and women, and the luggage department, featuring Samsonite luggage and a selection of ladies' handbags.

The Mall

Marks & Spencer

Location ➜ Landmark Shopping Mall · Al Shamal
Hours ➜ 09:30 - 22:00
Web/email ➜ na | 488 0101
Map Ref ➜7-A1

Those not famliar with Marks & Spencer are in for a treat – it is a great department store that is well known and much loved by British people. The Doha branch is not as big as you might find in other countries, but plans for expansion are in the pipeline. The store is located in Landmark and has a great selection of fashion items for the whole family.

Marks & Spencer

They have a wide selection of mens suits, and a particular bonus is that they make the trousers in various lengths - short, medium and long - which is great if you have very short or very long legs! The ladies section has a lovely selection of the latest fashion and clothes are available in a wide range of sizes, from petite to plus-size. They have a variety of childrens clothes, ranging from beautiful things for newborns right up to trendy teens. The underwear section is famous: here you'll find underwear for everyone; but the women's section is a haven of pretty colours and styles ranging from sexy to sensible. Most of their underwear is 100% cotton, which is great for hot climates.

They also do a small range of household items such as photo frames, cushions, candles and vases. In the UK, M&S is renowned for its food hall, and while in this branch the food section is relativeley small, they do sell quality non-perishables like biscuits, chocolates and teabags. Apparently this section will get bigger soon, and will eventually have a frozen food section.

Marks & Spencer is very popular with both expats and locals, and definitely somewhere to add to your shopping list.

Salam Plaza

Location ➜ Opp City Center · Diplomatic District
Hours ➜ 10:00 - 13:00 16:30 - 22:00 Fri 16:30 - 22:00
Web/email ➜ na | 483 2050
Map Ref ➜ 8-D3

Salam is a well-known name in this part of the world: their department stores, Salam Plaza and Salam Studios, sell wide ranges of designer clothing and accessories. Other items you could tick off your shopping list in Salam are cosmetics, perfumes, luggage, household goods and shoes. You'll find Salam Studios in The Mall (see p.173), and Salam Plaza is situated in the Diplomatic District.

If it's upmarket merchandise you want, Salam is the place to go. All of their items are made by internationally famous brands, and the quality is excellent. Of course this is reflected in the prices, so it's not the ideal shopping destination for avid bargain hunters (except during the sales).

Streets/Areas to Shop

Some areas in Doha are more popular than others for shopping. In general, malls are the most popular areas for expats to do their shopping; not just because of the variety of well-known shops, but also because in summer they are nice and cool thanks to powerful air conditioning!

Salwa Road is home to various independent outlets that are visited frequently by all kinds of shoppers. You'll find Jarir Bookstore, Modern Home, Apollo Furniture and Skate Shack, to name just a few. Salwa Road is famous for its many furniture shops, although a significant amount of the furniture is for those with rather flamboyant tastes! One of the nice things about shopping on Salwa Road is the easy availability of parking spaces.

Al Mirqab Street is another popular shopping destination. It has several fabric shops and tailors, a great art shop, shops where you can get upholstery or curtains made, phone shops, toy shops and a few pharmacies.

Al Sadd Street also has many shops of interest, as well as the newly opened Royal Plaza shopping centre.

The souk areas are popular, and offer a vibrant glimpse into traditional life. The food and fabric souks are popular with all nationalities. In the Musheireb area (better known as the Sofitel shopping complex) has numerous shops selling

Places to Shop

Shopping

Inspecting the goods

On the whole, souks are fascinating not only from the point of view of the sheer variety of items on sale (you could spend an entire morning rummaging around), but also because of the cultural experience – it's a good chance to get up close and personal to local folk doing business in a traditional way.

Bargaining is a skill that should be practised and enjoyed – vendors are friendly and eager to make a sale, and they expect a bit of negotiating from their customers. A good bargaining tool is to shop around first so that you know what something is worth, and use that as a starting point for your negotiations.

Remember that souks are traditional areas often predominately populated by men, so it's wise for ladies to dress conservatively, with shoulders and legs covered. If you wear something tight or revealing then be prepared to be gawped at – it's just the way things are!

All of Doha's main souks (Omani Market, Fruit & Vegetable Market, Fish Market, Animal Market) are situated in the same area.

Animal Market

Location → Salwa Road · Al Maamoura	na
Hours → 08:00 - 13:00 17:00 - 22:00	
Web/email → na	Map Ref → 15-C3

The animal market doesn't get too many expat visitors, and since most westerners are not in the market for camels or goats, it is the kind of place you would go to simply for interest's sake rather than to shop around! The vendors are friendly and eager to talk to you, although their English is very basic. Just in case you are interested (and you have a big back garden!) a young camel will set you back around QR 5,000, and you can get an adult one for QR 10,000 upwards. It would certainly make an interesting souvenir to take back home with you, if you could get it past customs. Sheep and goats go for about QR 500 each, and if you pay a bit extra they will prepare the animal for eating.

> **Looking for a Pet?**
>
> *If you're looking for a new family member, the Qatar Animal Welfare Society (528 6335, www.qaws.org) always has cats, dogs and other animals in need of a loving home.*

The animal market is next to the fish market, and along with livestock they also sell pets. However, a big word of warning: these animals are usually kept in very poor conditions and many carry diseases. Unless you have a heart of stone, it's best to stay away.

everything from cheap fabric to top-of-the-range TVs. It is very busy at weekends, and the parking situation is a nightmare, but the municipality is in the process of installing parking meters that should make it easier to find a spot. Despite the bustling activity of the souks, many people choose to go to shopping malls, especially in the summer, for the convenience of having everything under one roof. But there is no doubt that souks should definitely be on the list of things you do with visitors from out of town! The Central Market area is where you will find the food and livestock markets, and these are well worth visiting now and then to stock up on fruit, vegetables and fresh fish.

Souks

Other options → **Bargaining [p.150]**

The souks in Doha sell a huge range of items. Many things that you can buy in the souks may also be found in shopping centres and supermarkets, but as a general rule you can get them cheaper at the souks because you have the power of bargaining!

Fish Market

Location → Salwa Road · Al Maamoura | na
Hours → 04:00 - 01:00
Web/email → na   Map Ref → 15-B2

You can't miss the fish market: just walk along Salwa Road until you see loads of people walking along with blue plastic bags, and it won't be long before you recognise the smell. It is not a place for those with weak stomachs; the smell is enough to make you turn around and go to the supermarket instead. But the fish is fresh daily and is slightly cheaper than from a supermarket (and can be significantly cheaper if you can drive a hard bargain). The market opens at 04:00, and the earlier you get there the better choice you have (and the less overpowering the smell is). The stalls are all set up in an air-conditioned building and a cleaning/gutting service is provided for QR 1.

Catch of the day

Fruit & Vegetable Market

Location → Salwa Road · Al Maamoura | na
Hours → 06:00 - 22:00
Web/email → na   Map Ref → 15-B2

At this market you'll find a good selection of fresh fruit and vegetables, and the prices are usually cheaper than at supermarkets. Buying in bulk is cheaper than buying by the kilogram, but if you are buying in bulk make sure you check the fruit at the bottom of the box to make sure it hasn't been squashed. Vendors are happy to let you sample the fruit before you buy it. As you enter the souk a man will follow you around with a trolley or wheelbarrow,

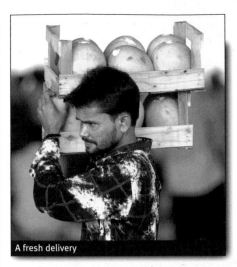
A fresh delivery

collecting all your purchases as you go. Once you've finished shopping he will then take it all to your car and help you load it in! It's up to you how much to pay, but anything from QR 5 upwards is appreciated. All the market stalls are covered, providing shade all day, so it doesn't matter what time you go.

Omani Market

Location → Salwa Road · Al Maamoura | na
Hours → 08:00 - 13:00 16:00 - 21:00
Web/email → na   Map Ref → 15-B2

The Omani Market sells plants, pots, garden materials and a selection of woven mats and baskets. They also have a few stalls selling nuts and dates. There isn't a huge choice of pots, but it is worth taking the time to browse through all the plants. Don't forget to bargain with the vendors, all of whom are friendly and enthusiastic, for a better price. There are a number of plant nurseries in the surrounding area selling pots and plants.

Thursday & Friday Market

Location → Salwa Road · Al Maamoura | na
Hours → 17:00 - 22:00   Thu & Fri Only
Web/email → na   Map Ref → 15-B2

Located opposite the Fish Market, this market is only operational on two days of the week (Thursday and Friday, obviously!) in the evenings. They sell assorted goods such as perfume, clothes, carpets, fabric and household items. There are a few permanent shops in the area selling similar items, but the selection is poor compared to what you will find in the market.

DINE **IN**

LET **OUT!**

Going Out

EXPLORER

Going Out

Highlights...

Go Local [p.186]

Qatar's restaurant and cafe scene has something for just about every taste, with cuisines from around the world all well represented. However, while you're in the Middle East you should certainly try the local fare. Whatever your mood, there are plenty of fine dining Arabic restaurants and street side shawarma stands and before long you may just find yourself hooked on hummus, tabouleh, arabic breads and falafel.

Sample the Shisha [p.201]

When in Rome... or Qatar...you have to sample the shisha. Not just for the sweet taste but also for the atmospheric experience of a shisha cafe. There are plenty of places where you can try shisha, from specific cafes to various restaurants that will serve shisha with or after a meal. Alternatively you can pick up your own shisha pipe and fruity selection and host a dinner/shisha party. Ifyou have family or friends in town it is also an excellent cultural experience for them.

Posh Nosh

If you're planning on some gourmet gallivanting to Dubai, then make sure you consult *Posh Nosh, Cheap Eats and Star Bars* from Explorer Publishing. This new title contains reviews of the city's best outlets for eating and drinking, so whether you're looking for seven-star extravagance or cheap and cheerful chow, pick up a copy and peruse the options before you pick the venue for your big night out.

Going Out

Although Doha is a relatively small city there never seems to be enough time for the various social activities that take place. If restaurants are your thing then this is the place to be, with Doha boasting an impressive selection of dining options and price ranges. With the exception of the Sealine Beach Resort, there are few restaurants or hotel outlets located outside of Doha, so the eating and socializing action is very much centered in the capital. People tend to eat lunch at home with family, or grab something while at work, so the evening is the time for most people to eat out. Folks in Doha tend to go out late, rarely before 20:00, and dinner is rarely served before 21:00. During the week most restaurants will close by midnight, although at weekends they tend to stay open a bit later. Qatar is not a dry country, with alcohol available in the outlets of the major hotels.

Eating Out

Eating out and venturing to new restaurants in Doha is a popular pastime, as food and entertaining is relatively inexpensive compared to many other parts of the world. The quality of food can often be on a par with some of the best restaurants in the world. The range of culinary options is limitless and there is a great selection of price ranges depending on your budget.

Restaurants can be busy most nights of the week although Wednesday, Thursday and Friday tend to be the busiest and in many instances will require you to confirm a reservation to ensure a table. Nearly all restaurants are family-friendly, with many having designated family sections that are off limits to single men unless they are in the company of at least one female.

Delivery

On the whole food is quite inexpensive in Qatar, so it is much simpler to entertain outside without the hassle of home cooking and cleaning. Many people do order from independent outlets and have food delivered to the house, and this is not simply limited to pizza joints or fast food outlets. A lot of the hotel restaurants also have off-site catering services, which are especially popular for larger gatherings.

Drinks

Other options → Alcohol [p.152]

The serving of alcohol is strictly limited to those outlets within hotels and clubs. There are strict fines for consuming alcohol other than on licensed premises or within your own private dwelling. Drink driving is considered a serious offence and Qatar has a zero tolerance law against it.

Qatar Distribution Company (or QDC) is the only company operating a liquor store in Qatar. The store is open to non-Muslims who have been provided with a letter from their sponsor detailing their monthly income. QDC will allocate a specific amount or quota of alcohol you are allowed to purchase based on your monthly income. For more details see Liquor Licence on p.45.

The hotels purchase their alcohol supplies from QDC, so there tends to be a common range of drink available in the hotels that does not go much further than what the liquor store sells.

In terms of soft drinks, all brands are available. One can purchase both Pepsi and Coca Cola products in addition to Red Bull and Mountain Dew.

Fruit cocktails are a main staple in many restaurants as it is a favourite beverage amongst the locals.

Not many people drink the tap water, although you shouldn't become ill from doing so. Instead, many residents buy bottled water if purchased from a convenience store a large bottle will cost approximately QR 2, while a restaurant or hotel may charge QR 10. Imported and brand name waters such as Pellegrino, Perrier and Evian are readily available, but these are obviously more expensive than the local bottled water.

Hygiene

The Health Authority is the official body responsible for hygiene standards in Qatar's eateries, and most outlets are quite hygienic so you shouldn't be concerned about food poisoning in any of the local establishments.

Tax & Service Charges

Depending on the type of establishment, you may find that your bill includes a few additions. A 7% government tax is added to many hotel restaurant bills, and a service charge of 10% (and sometimes more) could also appear. Sometimes these charges are incorporated in the prices, but this should be clearly explained on the menu either way. Be aware that this service charge is not voluntary, so cannot be withheld for poor service.

Tipping

If you are using a food outlet in a hotel, service charges are often included in the bill. It is important to note that the service charge is not the tip that is going to your server. Thus, if you are interested in leaving a tip add an additional 10% to your bill. To ensure that the tip goes to the server try to leave a cash amount rather than charging it to your credit card.

With the independent outlets, tipping is certainly appreciated although it is not mandatory. Taxi drivers, doormen and those who pour the petrol in your car certainly appreciate being tipped but it is not an expectation. Porters at the airport will request QR 10 for helping with your luggage. This is the flat fee that is charged and they will even provide you with a receipt.

Independent Reviews

We undertake independent reviews of all restaurants and bars that we include in this book. The following outlets have been visited by our freelance reporters and the views expressed are our own. However, if we have unwittingly led you astray, please do let us know. We appreciate all feedback, positive, negative and otherwise. You can contact us via our website – www.explorer-publishing.com.

Restaurant Listing Structure

The food outlets in this section are categorized by cuisine type. Restaurants that serve varying cuisines or styles have been listed either under their prominent cuisine, or under 'International' if the mix is truly varied. If you want to know what outlets are in a particular hotel you can flip to the index at the back of the book and look up the hotel, under which there will appear a list of all the outlets with their corresponding page numbers.

To avoid any confusion concerning a particular restaurant's listing, as a rule, any non English names retain their prefix (ie, Al, Le, La and El) in their alphabetical placement, while English names are listed by actual titles, ignoring prefixes such as 'The'. Bon appetit!

Quick Reference Explorer Icons

👍	Explorer Recommended!
💳	NO Credit Cards Accepted
🎸	Live Band
🍷	Alcohol Available
🛵	Will Deliver
👶	Kids Welcome
☎	Reservations Recommended
👔	Dress Smartly
⚒	Outside Terrace
Ⓥ	Vegetarian Dishes

Vegetarian Food

You will find that most restaurants are very accommodating and will make any necessary menu changes if they do not already have a specific vegetarian selection. With many of the American or European chain restaurants, vegetarian sensitivities are already established and they always have a designated vegetarian menu. Also, many of the appetizers in Arabic cuisine, such as hummus, babba ganoosh and the various traditional Arab salads, are suitable for vegetarians. There is also a large number of independent Indian restaurants that serve only vegetarian food, often very cheaply.

Restaurants

American

Other options → Tex Mex p.199

Applebee's

Location → Suhaim Bin Hamad Rd
Web/email → www.applebees.com

436 0747
Map Ref → 13-A1

Applebee's offers American style dining that is completely family oriented. The menu is full and will surely please all tastes. The restaurant has a young vibrant feel to it with happy energetic staff that are extremely knowledgeable about the menu. You can even catch up on the latest television

Everything you expect. Each beyond expectation.

What makes Grand Regency magnificent is not its complete array of facilities,
but the extravagance placed into each of them.

GRAND REGENCY
HOTEL • DOHA

Welcome to a world of luxury. Welcome to Grand Regency.

TEL: (+974) 434 3333 FAX: (+974) 434 3444 www.grand-regency.com

action as there are screens by the bar for all to enjoy. Their shared appetizer dishes are always a fun way to kick off the dining experience, but the portions are so generous you may not even make it on to the mains.

Chilis

Location ➜ Ramada Junction · Al Muntazah **444 5335**
Web/email ➜ www.chilis.com Map Ref ➜ 13-B2

The famous American chain known for its full menu and signature hamburgers has made its mark on Qatar. As well as the very generous food portions, the soft drinks are bottomless and the refills continue until you make them stop! The atmosphere is relaxed with western background music to enjoy, and you could be forgiven for thinking you've left the Middle East and been transported to somewhere in the US. The friendly and knowledgeable staff lend to a great overall experience.

Fuddruckers

Location ➜ Khalifa Complex · New District 62 **483 3983**
Web/email ➜ www.fuddruckers.com Map Ref ➜ 8-B4

The Doha branch of this US restaurant chain is a firm family favourite. Children are provided with an elaborate play space outside, allowing the grown ups some relative peace and quiet in the Americana themed dining area. The menu is big and varied, with Fuddruckers particularly priding themselves on their steaks and burgers. You'd better be hungry as portions are certainly on the large side, and all washed down with bottomless sodas and shakes.

Johnny Rockets

Location ➜ Al Emadi Centre · Al Muntazah **455 2792**
Web/email ➜ www.johnnyrockets.com Map Ref ➜ 13-B2

Johnny Rockets is a classic American diner, complete with colourful booth-seating, a well-stocked jukebox and enthusiastic singing staff! The menu is loaded with traditional favourites including burgers with all the trimmings, hot dogs and chicken dishes. Milkshake fans are also well

catered for. If it's a little early in the day for the full burger experience, between 07:00 and 13:00 the restaurant offers a breakfast menu featuring such delights as French toast and pancakes.

Johnny Rockets

Ponderosa

Location ➜ Ramada Junction · Al Muntazah **465 5880**
Web/email ➜ www.ponderosasteakhouses.com Map Ref ➜ 13-B2

This firmly established restaurant chain offers an enjoyable dining experience for children and families, as well as being a great place to catch up with large groups of friends. The menu features good quality fare with the emphasis on steak, chicken and seafood dishes. The all you can eat buffet is also a popular option throughout the day, covering all areas of North American cuisine from the salad bar to the self serve ice cream. Additional location: Dafna Cooperative Society, 483 6206.

TGI Friday's

Location ➜ Landmark Mall · Al Duhail South **486 6602**
Web/email ➜ www.tgifridays.com Map Ref ➜ 7-A1

TGI Friday's opened their first Qatar branch at Landmark Mall in late 2005. This ever-popular American theme restaurant offers a fun and unique

American

Going Out

IS FINALLY HERE!

Open at Land Mark Mall, Tel: 4866602

dining experience where friends and family can get together and enjoy great food, flowing drinks, and a lively atmosphere. While dining is obviously the main focus, the square bar area is always busy, and a perfect spot to meet for a drink before making for your table. If you're the first to arrive, the uniformed bar staff will keep you entertained - tossing and twirling bottles as they serve.

Arabic/Lebanese

Other options → Moroccan **p.197**
Persian **p.197**

Al Batross

Location → Al Bustan Hotel · Al Salata
Web/email → na

432 8888
Map Ref → 11-A4

This pleasant Eastern styled restaurant is popular with local families and visitors alike. The cuisine is international with a Lebanese flavour, and the generous portions of beautifully cooked food are served in a relaxed atmosphere by friendly and knowledgeable staff. Alcohol is not served in the restaurant, however for a different experience there is an adjacent tented section where you can relax on typical Arabic seating and enjoy a 'Hubbly Bubbly' (or shisha) pipe – great fun, even if you don't normally smoke.

Al Hamra

Location → Al Rayyan Rd · Al Hitmi Al Jadeed
Web/email → na

443 3297
Map Ref → 9-D3

Al Hamra offers casual dining with a full Arabic/Lebanese menu and makes a great place to stop by for a quick bite alone, or to catch up with friends. It is centrally located close to the souks (behind Al Reem Pharmacy) and is frequented by those who have just left the shopping world and need to regain their energy. The fresh juices are certainly a good way to get your sugar levels back up. This is also a good spot for morning breakfast, with the thyme

Food Restrictions

Qatar is a Muslim country and independent, chain and hotel outlets do not serve any dishes containing pork. There is a zero tolerance towards pork items and one cannot bring it into the country for personal consumption.

flavoured breads and traditional mint tea recommended.

Al Khaima

Location → Al Sadd Rd · Al Mirqab Al Jadeed
Web/email → na

444 6962
Map Ref → 12-E1

Al Khaima literally translated means the tent, and diners here can relax in traditional tented surroundings around the clock as the restaurant is open 24 hours. Known for its quality Arabic cuisine, each dish is accompanied by fresh warm oval shaped bread. The food is quite addictive and if you can't finish your meal you can always ask the helpful staff to wrap it up for you to take home. There is ample space in the restaurant making this a great venue for families with children.

Al Majlis

Location → Al Sadd Rd · Al Mirqab Al Jadeed
Web/email → na

444 7417
Map Ref → 12-E1

This popular local restaurant is known not only for its cuisine but also for the authentic dining experience that goes with it. The upstairs level has intimate cubicles that even have curtains that can be drawn for extra privacy, but for the real deal you should opt for the area where you dine seated on traditional Arabic cushions and carpets. The food is also traditional Arabic, with assorted mezzes and grilled meats. Al Majlis is known for its dish of hammour fish with baby shrimp on a sizzling iron pan smothered in onions and cheese – a must try for all seafood lovers!

Al Shaheen

Location → Sheraton Doha · Doha Corniche
Web/email → www.starwoodhotels.com

485 4444
Map Ref → 8-E3

Set on the top floor of the pyramid-shaped Sheraton Hotel, this restaurant enjoys impressive views of the city and coastline from all sides. The service can be disorganised and the traditional live entertainment a little overbearing, but don't let this put you off too much as the menu offers a good chance to try some great Arabic dishes in luxurious surroundings. The food is beautifully presented and portions are ample, and for less adventurous diners there is a selection of western dishes too.

Automatic

Location → Al Sadd Rd · Al Mirqab Al Jadeed
Web/email → na
442 5999
Map Ref → 12-E1

The Automatic chain of restaurants has been serving great quality Arabic food in a casual setting across the Middle East for years. The menu sports a good selection of great value mezzes, salads, and grilled meat, fish and kebabs. The portions are of a good size and are served hot and fresh to your table by efficient and friendly waiting staff. Automatic is also a good takeaway option, and several offices in the vicinity are known to order breakfast pastries to enjoy with their morning coffees.

Balhambar

Location → Corniche · Doha
Web/email → na
483 7807
Map Ref → 8-C4

Situated on the corniche and enjoying panoramic waterfront views, Balhambar is a well-known Doha restaurant offering traditional Qatari cuisine in an equally traditional setting. The waiting staff, all in National dress, are extremely attentive and friendly, and the building's windtowers outside and gypsum walls inside are typical of the region. The restaurant is known for two Qatari speciality dishes – Ghuzi, a whole roasted lamb served on a bed of rice with pine nuts, and Harees, a slow cooked wheat and lamb dish. With seating areas inside and outside depending on your taste and the weather, a trip to Balhambar is recommended for visitor and residents alike.

Beirut

Location → Electricity St · Al Jasra
Web/email → na
442 1087
Map Ref → 10-D3

This restaurant is located on the busy Electric Street near the heart of the souk area. It is predominantly a takeaway style restaurant, where you can actually drive up close to the door and a staff member will run up to the car window to take your order. Serving a good selection of tasty local fare, Beirut is known to many residents of Doha for

its fabulous Foul, the traditional bean dish popular throughout the Arab world that can be eaten for breakfast, lunch, or as a midnight snack.

Kebab King

Location → Ras Abu Aboud · Al Khulaifat
Web/email → na
441 0400
Map Ref → 11-D4

This is a typical style kebab house with brightly coloured chairs surrounding Formica tables. The staff are friendly and helpful but you may have to brush up on your Arabic if you fancy a chat. The menu caters to carnivores and vegetarians alike and even the health conscious will be happy with the wide range of dishes on offer. Grilled fish and meat of various kinds are served with rice, salad or vegetables. With takeaway and home delivery available, this really is fast food Arabic style.

Layali Restaurant

Location → Salwa Rd · Al Mirqab Al Jadeed
Web/email → na
431 0005
Map Ref → 13-A2

If you are looking for a truly authentic Lebanese experience, then this is a must. Layali, literally translated, means many nights, and the service and food here will ensure repeat visits. In their smart black uniforms the staff are polished and extremely attentive and the food is impeccable. Many people go for the wide selection of Arabic mezzes, either hot or cold, but the mains too take grilled meats and fish to a new culinary level in both presentation and taste. Layali is also known to have some of the best shisha flavours in town.

The Tent

Location → Al Bustan Hotel · Al Salata
Web/email → na
432 8888
Map Ref → 11-A4

As soon as you enter, the traditional design of the furniture, the soft lighting, and the aroma of shisha will totally awaken your senses to this truly Middle Eastern experience. Here you can sample delicious Arabic fare in real Arabic style. The food is a great example of local cuisine, and if you are not familiar with this style of menu the waiters are more than happy to advise. It's a good spot for a romantic evening or to refresh yourself after a long day, and reservations are recommended if you are planning to come after 22:00.

Chinese

Other options → Far Eastern **p.188**

Beijing

Location → Salwa Rd · Al Mirqab Al Jadeed
Web/email → na

435 8688
Map Ref → 13-A2

This independent restaurant is nestled in a private villa off of the busy Salwa road. It has both indoor and outdoor seating which is suitable for large groups, or you could choose to dine more intimately in the private dining areas separated by cubicles. Beijing has friendly, knowledgeable staff that can assist you in selecting from the extensive menu, which features a good selection of great tasting traditional Chinese favourites.

Chopsticks

Location → Grand Regency Hotel Doha · Al Sadd
Web/email → www.grand-regency.com

434 3333
Map Ref → 9-E3

In a pleasant setting befitting this smart new hotel, Chopsticks is located on the lobby level of the Grand Regency. The restaurant serves all the usual favourites from the orient, expertly prepared in an authentic style. The menu features a good selection of rice and noodle dishes, suitable for both vegetarians and non vegetarians. The staff are friendly and able to assist diners with their choices. Chopsticks is open for lunch and dinner.

Chopsticks

Far Eastern

Other options → Japanese **p.196**
Chinese **p.188**

Thai Noodles

Location → Opp Souq Asiery · Musheirib
Web/email → na

443 4220
Map Ref → 10-C4

Tucked away in the heart of the souq area, you may need a hand to find this little piece of Thailand in Doha, but it's well worth the effort. As you enter you are greeted with big smiles and the aromas of traditional Thai cooking. Open for breakfast, lunch and dinner, the extensive menu offers a huge choice of Thai and oriental dishes to eat in or take away. The popularity of this place speaks volumes about the excellent food.

French

Brasserie on the Beach

Location → Four Seasons Hotel · Diplomatic District
Web/email → www.fourseasons.com

494 8888
Map Ref → 8-E2

You may be a little disappointed that the Brasserie is not actually on the beach, but it does overlook the attractive Four Seasons resort. Open throughout the day, this buffet style restaurant serves the usual array of soups, salads and a variety of meat and fish dishes. Considering it is slightly more expensive than its neighbours you may expect more from the experience, but the service cannot be faulted with thoughtful staff waiting to fill your glass and offer advice. This would certainly be a suitable venue for a business lunch or dinner with clients.

Fauchon

Location → Salwa Rd · Al Mirqab Al Jadeed
Web/email → www.fauchon.fr

432 4888
Map Ref → 13-A2

Although they market themselves as a true Salon de Thé, Fauchon actually specialise in various areas. As well as serving gourmet teas, coffees and pastries, they are known to create some of the most decadent desserts in the city, and their cakes

A square book but not for squares

Explore Dubai's decadent range of restaurants, bars, cafes and clubs in this beautiful book with stunning images and informative reviews. More than just a guidebook, it's at home on a coffee table while you're out on the town.

Phone (971 4) 335 3520 • **Fax** (971 4) 335 3529
Info@Explorer-Publishing.com • www.Explorer-Publishing.com
Residents' Guides • Photography Books • Activity Guidebooks • Practical Guides • Maps

EXPLORER
Passionately Publishing...

make for impressive gifts. This cafe is also respected for its immaculate off-site catering facilities. Simply provide your budget and they will tailor a full scale menu that even includes the china, silverware, and a team of uniformed staff to ensure your event impresses the guests.

La Mer

Location → Ritz-Carlton Doha · West Bay **484 8000**
Web/email → www.ritzcarlton.com Map Ref → 4-D2

Located on the top floor of the Ritz Carlton Hotel and offering exceptional views of Doha's waterfront and the Pearl development, La Mer is synonymous with indulgence and class. Its unmatched interior (with shining silverware, finest china, and sparkling chandeliers) and faultless French cuisine make this a contender for the ultimate dining experience in Qatar. The restaurant's layout allows you to simply enjoy a drink in the bar area whilst listening to the house pianist, or experience the full dining extravaganza following a few cocktails. The service, as you'd expect, is first class and discreet.

Maxim

Location → Ramada Doha · Al Muntazah **441 7417**
Web/email → www.ramada-doha.com Map Ref → 13-B2

The plush decor of this French style restaurant features dark paneled walls, red carpets, white

Local dining

linen table cloths, silver cutlery and chandeliers. The menu offers a good choice of traditional continental dishes such as Steak Diane, with sorbet served between courses to refresh the palate. The main courses are wheeled to your table and served very formally from a trolley, and the service is good and not too intrusive. Live entertainment is provided every evening by the resident pianist.

Dress

The dress code for going out in Doha is quite varied. During the summer months people seem to be more relaxed in their attire due to the extreme levels of heat and humidity, but at other times of the year it is fair to say that most people do dress up a little. It is important to note that Doha is a conservative Muslim country, so it is always better to be sensitive to the local culture and traditions. That means nothing too tight or revealing. You should also keep in mind that many restaurants and venues have super-efficient air-conditioning, so it is wise to have a few layers on hand such as a shawl or light jacket. Finally, unless you are of Qatari origin you should not wear their local clothing, as this is considered disrespectful.

Indian

Bukhara

Location → Khalifa Complex · New District 62 **483 3345**
Web/email → www.bukhara.com Map Ref → 8-B4

Bukhara is well-known for its authentic Indian cuisine. It is a softly lit restaurant that has friendly staff, and the tandoor oven is visible for all to see as the chef works his magic in the open air kitchen. The food is delicious and the presentation, in traditional copper pots, is impeccable. To accompany the varied curry and grilled meat dishes, the freshly baked naan breads are mouthwateringly good. If you enjoy great tasting, good value Indian food, then this is a must visit.

Chingari

Location → Ramada Doha · Al Muntazah **441 7417**
Web/email → www.ramada-doha.com Map Ref → 13-B2

Chingari is one of the most popular Indian restaurants in Doha. It is known for its plush red

Qatar's most exciting cocktail!

Restful rooms & suites. Business facilities. Sports & leisure. Relaxing cafés.
Lively lounges. Mouthwatering restaurants. Take your pick. Enjoy good times.

℞ RAMADA.
P.O. BOX 1768, DOHA, STATE OF QATAR
TEL. (974) 4417417, FAX (974) 4410941
EMAIL: ramada@qatar.net.qa

room with cozy red cushions that allow you to sit close to the ground comfortably. Chingari is an Indian word that describes the sound of cracking charcoal that comes out of a tandoor oven, and the rich curries that come from the kitchen are absolutely cracking too! This venue has a wonderfully exotic ambience with a live traditional Indian band playing soft background music. If you are being joined by a large group you can request a private room.

Chingari

Star of India

Location ➔ Al Markhiya · Doha
Web/email ➔ na

486 4440
Map Ref ➔ 7-D2

Star of India is a popular restaurant among the city's locals and expats. They offer an extensive menu that incorporates Chinese cuisine in addition to the wide ranging Indian selections including curries and biryanis. This is definitely a family oriented dining facility that also has a separate party hall for groups of 35 or more guests. The decor of the restaurant is simple and relaxed, with ample space for enjoying the satisfying, value-for-money food.

The Garden

Location ➔ Shara Al Kaharba · Musheirib
Web/email ➔ www.thegarden-online.com

36 5676
Map Ref ➔ 10-C4

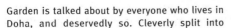

Garden is talked about by everyone who lives in Doha, and deservedly so. Cleverly split into separate dining areas catering to different tastes, downstairs is famous for its vegetarian dishes, while upstairs you can eat al a carte or buffet style and all at very reasonable prices. The rich reds and golds of traditional Indian restaurants are abundant and seating is in separate booths or at open tables. The waiters are full of smiles and welcome you at the door. On the menu you will find all your favorites and many more dishes to tempt you, and the food is excellent. You can also order takeaway, and they even deliver.

International

Al Bandar

Location ➔ Corniche · Doha
Web/email ➔ www.albandarrestaurant.com

431 1818
Map Ref ➔ 8-C4

Al Bandar is a definite favourite with residents and for all those visiting Qatar. Designed to resemble three individual wooden dhows, each is home to a separate restaurant serving a different cuisine. So depending on your taste and mood, you can opt for Indian, seafood, or more traditional Arabic food. Set on the scenic corniche the restaurant complex offers both indoor and outdoor seating, and enjoys beautiful views of the Doha bay and the city backdrop. It always has a fun, summer feel to it, and the friendly staff make it a thoroughly enjoyable experience.

Al Hubara

Location ➔ Sheraton Doha · Doha Corniche
Web/email ➔ www.starwoodhotels.com

485 4444
Map Ref ➔ 8-E3

Situated in the far side of the lobby at the Sheraton Hotel, Al Hubara restaurant is open for breakfast, lunch and dinner. Serving a buffet style menu, there is a good range of international cuisine to chose from, including Arabic, Japanese and Italian dishes. The helpful staff ensure you can relax and enjoy your meal. The restaurant has a separate room for families which doubles as a non smoking area. This is a popular venue for lunchtime meetings and for those seeking a lingering break from work.

Amwaj

Location → InterCon Doha · West Bay
Web/email → www.ichotelsgroup.com
484 4444
Map Ref → 6-D3

Serving breakfast, lunch and dinner, this is the Intercontinental's buffet restaurant, and what a buffet! An incredible display of international cuisine with something for everybody, children are welcome and on a Friday brunch you will even find a clown to entertain them while you eat in peace. The food is excellent, superbly presented and the choices never ending, and the set price means you can try as much as you like and not worry about the bill. The surroundings are fresh and bright and the service is first rate.

Café Batteel

Location → Salwa Rd · Al Nasr
Web/email → na
444 1414
Map Ref → 12-E3

As you head out of Doha on Salwa Road, Café Batteel is easy to miss but you really should try not to. Menu options include superb salads, soups and sandwiches, plus heartier main courses that lean towards Indian but also include Italian, Arabic and seafood. The interior complements the food, with inlaid wooden alcoves, gypsum walls, Arabic cushions and barasti palm ceilings. Upstairs is the family room, plus a computer games room where the kids will keep themselves entertained for hours. Batteel's other great selling point is that once you've finished eating you can stock up on sweets, cakes, pastries, bakery products, and even ice cream.

Crepaway

Location → Al Mouthanna Complex · Salwa Road
Web/email → www.crepaway.com
465 5830
Map Ref → 13-B2

The menu at Crepaway, as the name suggests, features a large and lip smacking selection of sweet and savoury crepes, but that is by no means the limit to their culinary creativity. Open for breakfast, lunch and dinner, they also serve salads, burgers, sandwiches, pizzas, pastas, and desserts. The good food is definitely matched by the good mood, with the restaurant having the feel of a fun, young, and upbeat diner. There's a jukebox, a live DJ who can inspire sporadic outbreaks of dancing, and occasional karaoke nights too. Crepaway is a lively venue popular with families and Doha's hip and happening crowd, but if it all sounds too energetic you can even take advantage of free delivery.

Crepaway

Diva Downtown

Location → Al Emadi Center · Al Muntazah
Web/email → na
467 7748
Map Ref → 13-B2

Despite being situated in the busy dining hub that is the Ramada Junction, Diva Downtown has managed to tuck itself away from all the other restaurants and is considered something of a getaway. After climbing the stairs, you'll be met by soft lighting, a cozy interior, relaxing background music and friendly staff. With a good selection of fresh and tasty dishes, this popular eatery is perhaps best known for its elaborate and well-stocked salad bar.

Grand Gourmet

Location → Grand Regency Hotel Doha · Al Sadd
Web/email → www.grand-regency.com
434 3333
Map Ref → 9-E3

Grand Gourmet serves up an array of contemporary global cuisine from international culinary masters. The food, the surroundings, and the atmosphere are yours to savour all day long in this exquisite buffet and a la carte restaurant.

Whether you want a leisurely breakfast, a power lunch or a candlelit dinner, with friendly staff and faultless fare you'll find the experience as grand as the restaurant's name.

Mint

The Lagoon

Location ➜ Ritz-Carlton Doha · West Bay
Web/email ➜ www.ritzcarlton.com

484 8000
Map Ref ➜ 4-D2

You will find many buffet restaurants in Doha but this is certainly up there with the best. Open all day and bursting at the seams with so many choices, you will want to try it all and may end up being defeated by the never-ending array of tempting creations. With live cooking stations, the talented chefs will prepare certain dishes freshly to order. As you come to expect from the Ritz Carlton, the food is beautifully presented and the service is impeccable. The Friday brunch is particularly popular, especially with families.

Mint

Location ➜ Al Mouthanna Complex · Salwa Rd
Web/email ➜ na

467 5577
Map Ref ➜ 13-A2

Popular with expats and locals alike, Mint is a visually stunning and ever-so hip hangout, designed by someone with a real eye for art and the aesthetic. The fusion menu features fresh salads, pasta, risotto, imaginative sandwiches, and generous main courses of beef, chicken and fish. The breakfast menu is also tempting, offering both continental and full-English. Their signature drink, 'Lemon Mint, is a surprising discovery, and you may just find yourself hooked. With its long dining table, plush sofas, plasma screen TV and entertainment system, the upstairs private room is definitely worth remembering for your next special celebration.

Richoux

Location ➜ City Center Doha · Diplomatic District
Web/email ➜ na

493 1661
Map Ref ➜ 8-D2

A surprising yet welcome touch of class among the City Center mall's eateries, this Richoux is a franchise of the renowned restaurant brand established in London almost a century ago. The dark woodwork, red leather seats and gold-coloured railings and light fittings are a world away from the shops just outside. One side of the menu features breakfast, drinks, pastries, and a full traditional afternoon tea for two (QR110). Flip the menu over and you'll find a comprehensive choice of sandwiches, starters and mains, featuring dishes such as fillet mignon steak and wild mushroom pasta. There's terrace seating out front, but it may be a little noisy for some.

The Palms

Location ➜ Doha Club · Al Khulaifat
Web/email ➜ www.qnhc.com

441 8822
Map Ref ➜ 11-B4

The candelabras, crisp table linen, and shiny silver cutlery announce that the Palms is smarter than your average Doha restaurant, although if you stare too long at the clashing carpet and curtains you may come over a little dizzy. The menu offers classic international dishes; nothing too adventurous but all cooked to perfection and served by faultless waiting staff. A table by the window affords views over the pool area. The restaurant, also known by the name Al Nakeel, is open to non-members and features occasional themed weeks offering cuisines from around the world.

Italian

Other options → Mediterranean **p.196**
Pizzerias **p.198**

Ciao

Location → Haya Complex · Al Mirqab Al Jadeed | **468 9100**
Web/email → na   Map Ref → 13-A2

If you want to experience a fully homemade Italian meal, then Ciao is the place to be. This centrally-located independent restaurant goes the extra mile to provide a true taste of Italia, right down to having its cheeses flown in specially. The pizzas and calzones are cooked in an open oven on the main level of the restaurant. When it comes to deserts the tiramisu cannot be missed, although it faces stiff competition from their homemade gelatos.

Il Rustico

Location → Rydges Plaza · Al Bidda | **438 5444**
Web/email → www.rydges.com   Map Ref → 10-C3

This low key restaurant is not necessarily intimate, secluded or romantic (the decor won't fool you into thinking you're in a quaint Italian taverna), but it is a popular venue offering great, mainly Mediterranean fare in pleasant enough surroundings. The menu is good for meat, pasta and pizza lovers, but vegetarians may be a little disappointed. Your meal starts with a DIY garlic bread platter, deliciously tasty but not recommended if you have an early morning meeting the next day. The wine list is fairly substantial, as are the tempting Italian desserts.

Il Teatro

Location → Four Seasons Hotel · Diplomatic District | **494 8888**
Web/email → www.fourseasons.com   Map Ref → 8-E2

Il Teatro is recommended for those who enjoy the pleasures of a fine dining experience with plenty of attention. The menu is full of rich Italian treasures creatively presented and unique to this restaurant. Although not typically Italian in style, the lavish and elegant surroundings ooze class and luxury. As you would expect the service is outstanding, with the staff seeming to anticipate your every

need. Dining here does not come cheap so be prepared for the bill, but for a special occasion it's well worth a visit.

Porcini

Location → Ritz-Carlton Doha · West Bay | **484 8000**
Web/email → www.ritzcarlton.com   Map Ref → 4-D2

Porcini is tucked away below the hotel lobby, and its welcoming ambiance creates the perfect venue for a romantic dinner, a special celebration, or even for entertaining business clients. The decor is rich and warm, and the open show kitchen is framed by a mosaic of handmade coloured glass tiles. With the emphasis on classical Italian cuisine, the menu features fresh bread, homemade pasta, salads, seafood, and meat dishes, plus a devilishly tempting selection of deserts. Wine lovers will also be more than satisfied with the broad range of vintages available by the glass or the bottle.

Porcini

The Italian Job

Location → Ramada Doha · Al Muntazah | **441 7417**
Web/email → www.ramada-doha.com   Map Ref → 13-B2

The Italian Job is something of a hidden-away gem, located outside the hotel beside the swimming pool. This is a wonderful two-floor restaurant that has a distinct Italian rustic feel to it. The open air kitchen allows for all the beautiful aromas to spill into the main dining areas. The menu features the usual Italian treats, and the pizzas (especially the calzones) are particularly recommended. Their unique brand of musical entertainment, where the servers sing to the guests, make this an interactive dinner venue for all to enjoy.

The Italian Job

Za Moda

Location → InterCon Doha · West Bay
Web/email → www.ichotelsgroup.com

484 4444
Map Ref → 6-D3

This modern, Mediterranean styled restaurant is open and welcoming, and the small colourful bar area is ideal for a pre-dinner aperitif or late night cocktail. The dishes are traditional Italian, and the pizza oven visible from the dining area adds another level of authenticity. The service and presentation of the food is excellent, as is the quality and taste. Always leave room for Chef Danny's signature tiramisu, as this is possibly the best dessert you will ever taste! The overall atmosphere is casual and relaxed, with pleasant live guitar music entertaining diners every evening except Fridays.

Japanese

Other options → Far Eastern **p.188**

Sakura

Location → Ramada Doha · Al Muntazah
Web/email → www.ramada-doha.com

441 7417
Map Ref → 13-B2

This Japanese restaurant is dominated by the huge Tepanyaki table in the middle of the room. Sitting on stools around the table is the best way to appreciate the skill of the chefs who put on a real show, juggling knives, eggs, spatulas, and anything else they lay their hands on. The food is excellent, cooked to perfection and really very tasty. If you fancy something a bit quieter there are a couple of small tables away from the cooking area, and two private rooms where you can avoid the embarrassment of chopstick ineptitude! You can also enjoy a cocktail at the bar before or after your meal.

Mediterranean

Other options → Italian **p.195**

Corniche

Location → Doha Marriott Hotel · Al Khulaifat
Web/email → www.marriott.com

429 8888
Map Ref → 11-D4

Mediterranean in style and cuisine, this all-you-can-eat buffet offers a varied selection of freshly prepared delights, but it's speciality would have to be the seafood bonanza available every evening from 19:00. The service is prompt and polite, and there is no hesitation in clearing your plate or filling your glass. Alcohol is available for lunch and dinner. Delicate pastel colours and panoramic views over the pool and gardens give a peaceful ambiance to this restaurant, so you may linger a little longer despite being unable to eat another thing!

La Villa

Location → Mercure Grand Hotel Doha · Musheirib
Web/email → www.mercuredoha.com

446 2222
Map Ref → 10-D4

This spacious, typically Mediterranean restaurant is found on the 12th floor of the Mercure Grand in the

Ramadan Timings

Restaurants change their schedules during the month of Ramadan. They strictly open at "iftar", the break of fast once the sun goes down upon Maghreb prayers. Although the outlets open later in the day, they remain open until approximately 3am. Also, during this period, nightclubs and bars close for the entire month.

heart of the city. It is beautifully decorated in relaxing blue and greens with a real Mediterranean feel. The menu offers a wide choice of dishes, some of which are prepared with a real unexpected twist. All are creatively presented and delicious. The service is friendly, although the staff's knowledge of the wine list can be a little limited. There are great views of the bustling city below and the Doha skyline, and despite some traffic noise this can be a relaxing dining experience.

Seasons

Location → Mövenpick Hotel Doha · Al Salata	**429 1111**
Web/email → www.moevenpick-hotels.com	Map Ref → 11-A3

This restaurant is best noted for its ever-changing theme nights, with Italian Saturdays, Spanish Mondays, Asian Wednesdays and Mongolian Thursdays. The Friday Brunch is also popular, where kids (children under 100cm tall!) are not only welcomed, but also well entertained. The all-you-can-eat buffets are well presented and plentiful, although the food may sometimes fail to inspire. The staff are eager to please but not overbearing, with friendly smiles and competent service. One piece of advice – if you're a non-smoker make sure you sit as far away as you can from the smoking section, otherwise you may as well just light up yourself.

Moroccan

Other options → Arabic/Lebanese p.186

Tangia

Location → Grand Regency Hotel Doha · Al Sadd	**434 3333**
Web/email → www.grand-regency.com	Map Ref → 9-E3

The Grand Regency's Moroccan restaurant invites diners to experience the sights, sounds, smells and tastes of exotic Morocco. The dishes dispatched by the skilled chef contain unique flavours and aromas, and all are artistically prepared and extravagantly served. The scents of coriander, cumin, and saffron, mingling with the stark aroma of olive oil is just one example of how this is an experience for all the senses, making Tangia the jewel of this new hotel.

Tangia

Persian

Other options → Arabic/Lebanese p.186

Ras Al Nasaa

Location → Corniche · Al Kulaifat Al Jadeeda	**441 1177**
Web/email → na	Map Ref → 11-B4

Nestling beneath and beyond the traditional windtowers near Museum roundabout, this is not one restaurant, but a complex of eateries that really has something for everyone. The small coffee shop is pleasant enough, there's a new ladies-only restaurant, and a big family hall with impressive terracotta brick arches. The bachelors hall is reserved just for the boys (think TV, shisha and comfy sofas) and the floating pontoon restaurant offers good views across the water (albeit only as far as the Doha port). The real must-see is the Qasr Al Sahel Iranian restaurant, serving traditional Persian dishes in a cosy setting with interesting tiles on the walls.

Pizzerias

Other options → Italian p.195

Those who enjoy a good pizza will not be disappointed. Although not the most popular cuisine in Doha, pizza parlors are well frequented and found in most areas. You will find two of the largest international pizza chains scattered around shopping malls and on busy streets with the local equivalent in close competition. They all offer a take away service and most will deliver. Don't forget the local Italian restaurants who will also pack you up a pizza to take home.

Pizzerias		
Il Rustico	Rydges Plaza	438 5444
Italian Job	Ramada Doha	441 7417
Little Caesar's	Ramada Junction	444 0033
Pizza Express	City Center	483 9595
	Landmark Mall	488 5067
Pizza Hut	City Center	483 7328
	Hyatt Plaza	469 7354
	Landmark Mall	486 9989
	Ramada Junction	465 7744
Pizza Inn	Airport Road	465 0644
	Hyatt Plaza	469 7665
	Nr City Center	483 5293

Portuguese

Nandos

Location → Salwa Rd · Al Mirqab Al Jadeed | **435 6756**
Web/email → www.nandos.com | Map Ref → 13-A2

Parking

In general there is ample, free parking throughout the city, but if you're running late or just feeling lazy, why not take advantage of valet parking when visiting hotels. You'll pay a few Riyals for the privilege, but it's a small price for the convenience, especially in summer.

This Portuguese-inspired restaurant chain is known for its uniquely flavoured chicken. All their chicken is basted, flame-grilled and then spiced to your liking. You may select from lemon and herb, mild peri-peri, hot peri-peri, or extra hot peri-peri for those with asbestos taste buds. The menu is extensive, covering light appetizers and also featuring a selection for kids. There are some vegetarian options, but you should remember that Nandos is famous for chicken so this may not be a first choice for non-meat eaters. The food is fresh and tasty, so as they say in Portugal, Bom Proveito!

Seafood

Al Sayyad

Location → Diplomatic Club · West Bay | **484 7444**
Web/email → www.thediplomaticclub.com | Map Ref → 4-D4

For a relaxing casual night out of town this seafood restaurant is a good choice. Set just off the beach at the Diplomatic Club, with outside seating for the cooler months, they offer a great choice from the sea. Artfully decorated with fishing nets and a tank full of tropical fish, you can't help but sit back and enjoy the authentic Arabic salads while you take your pick from the menu. If you can't make up your mind the waiters are right on hand with great advice.

Sultan Ibrahim Fish Market

Location → InterCon Doha · West Bay | **484 4444**
Web/email → www.ichotelsgroup.com | Map Ref → 6-D3

With a lovely setting on the edge of the beach, this is THE place to go if you love seafood. The restaurant has a lively atmosphere with good service and nightly entertainment, including a resident belly dancer. You choose your own fish from the displays and the chef will then cook it in your preferred style. Friday night is buffet night, and the rest of the week there is no menu – you simply pick your fish, and help yourself to salad and fresh vegetables. For a romantic evening in the cooler months, sit on the covered terrace and enjoy the sea views and starry sky.

Steakhouses

Other options → American p.182

The Old Manor

Location → Mercure Grand Hotel Doha · Musheirib | **446 2222**
Web/email → www.mercuredoha.com | Map Ref → 10-D4

If you enjoy quality food but don't want to pay a fortune, then this could be for you. A cross between a gentlemen's club and an English pub, the menu offers firm favourites including shepherd's pie, chicken in a basket, and of course steaks cooked to your liking. The cosy little venue is casual and relaxed, with a big screen TV and comfy chairs. The service is close to perfection; quick and efficient but never intrusive. With a great view over the city centre, this is the perfect place to settle down with a pie and a pint.

Tex Mex

Other options → American **p.182**

Amigos

Location → Khalifa Complex · New District 62
Web/email → na

483 7350
Map Ref → 8-B4

For those looking for a lively night out with food, drinks and entertainment all in one place, then Amigo's is a great choice. The food is plentiful as are the cocktails. The Tex Mex menu contains all your favourites and more, and if you over indulge you can always work off the extra calories on the dance floor. Sizzling mexican platters and moreish margaritas are delivered by the ever-busy but efficient staff. The prices are very reasonable, making this a very popular spot, especially at the weekend.

Paloma

Location → InterCon Doha · West Bay
Web/email → www.ichotelsgroup.com

484 4444
Map Ref → 6-D3

A spicy Latino atmosphere awaits everyone at this lively Mexicana restaurant where good food, entertainment and a superb choice of drinks are found in abundance. Inside, an array of brightly decorated tables is served by friendly, well informed but ever busy staff. For those who prefer a quieter setting there is an outside terrace overlooking the pool and beach resort. A live band plays from 21:00 so you can fiesta on the dance floor until the early hours. The portions are certainly generous and the house wine definitely recommended. Pre, post, or mid-dinner cocktails are stirred and shaken to perfection by the spirited and expert bar staff.

Cafes & Coffee Shops

Other options → Afternoon Tea **p.201**

There are few places in Qatar where you will not find a cafe or coffee shop. The malls and streets are full

of them, especially in Doha itself. One of the largest chains you will find is Starbucks, which is very popular with both locals and expats alike. Many an hour is passed sampling the incredible varieties of coffee from all over the world. Ladies' coffee mornings are very popular with the expat community and several can be very informative if you are new to Qatar. In the evenings the shisha cafes come to life. Although most popular with the men, some do offer a family area, and the more local of these will stay open until the early hours of the morning. Food is served at the majority of cafes, with some offering a full menu for breakfast, lunch and dinner. If you prefer you can simply indulge in one of the many delicious cakes or sweets found in abundance. Keeping in touch with home is easy as internet cafes, and Qtel Hotspots catering to wireless users, are ever increasing in Doha.

> ### Local Qatari Coffee
>
> This is generally served in small coffee cups that have no handles nor saucers. The coffee is made of pressed cardamom seeds and is dark yellow in color. When you are served a cup it is just enough for one or two sips. The person serving you will continue to refill your cup endlessly. The key to stopping the server from giving you more is to shake the cup from side to side. This is the local signal for you have had enough and thank you. Several hotel lobbies will serve the traditional coffee or "kahwa".

Caffe Amici

Location → City Center Doha · Diplomatic District
Web/email → na

483 4811
Map Ref → 8-D2

In the midst of the jewellery and perfume shops, but far enough away from the hustle and bustle of the mall, Caffe Amici is a haven of calm. The biggest draw has to be the generously upholstered armchairs in shades of green and terracotta, that encourage you to take the weight off your feet and forget about the shopping for a while. With courteous and polite service, the cafe boasts a fine selection of croissants, sandwiches and cakes – perfect for constructing your own afternoon tea.

Cinnzeo

Location → City Center Doha · Diplomatic District
Web/email → na

483 9990
Map Ref → 8-D2

This worldwide cake and coffee-shop chain, known for their fresh cinnamon buns and sticks, now provides weary City Center shoppers with a welcome respite. Variations on the traditional cinnamon bun include tempting chocolate flavoured and caramel flavoured options. You can enjoy a tasty bun with a freshly brewed cup of American coffee as a treat when you're all shopped out, or as a tasty breakfast to kick start your day.

Cup & Cino Coffee House

Location → Royal Plaza · Al Sadd
Web/email → na

| 436 8324
Map Ref → 12-E1

This intimate cafe has spent much time and effort selecting their furnishings and lighting to provide a pleasant getaway where shoppers (and shopkeepers) can relax and take the weight off their feet. The windows are adorned with simple cherry wood blinds and the outside tables have umbrellas to suggest something of a Parisian cafe experience. The full menu should have something for everyone, whether just stopping by for a coffee or in need of some more substantial sustenance.

Eli France

Location → Salwa Rd · Al Mirqab Al Jadeed
Web/email → na

| 435 7222
Map Ref → 13-A2

Eli France are known for their bakery, but also offer a surprisingly full international menu. They serve sandwiches, snacks, burgers, a selection of main dishes, homemade desserts, and freshly squeezed cocktail juices. They also have a kids menu and are known for hosting birthday parties for the little ones. Groups of 15 or more have the run of their own private area and are provided with a variety of entertainment, games, and prizes, not to mention good value meal packages.

JG Sandwich Cellar

Location → Nr Ras Abu Aboud Flyover · Al Hitmi
Web/email → na

| 435 7559
Map Ref → 11-B4

This is a family operated English cafe that serves traditional English dishes, and for some Brits it may feel as if you have walked straight into your mother's kitchen. Perhaps a welcome antidote to the five-star finery that can get too much at times,

you may be amused to see the staff serve fruit juice at your table straight from the carton. A good place to catch up with the local and international papers over a cup of tea or coffee, it's certainly popular and you can almost guarantee that sooner or later you'll run into someone you know.

La Dolce Vita!

Location → Ritz-Carlton Doha · West Bay
Web/email → www.ritzcarlton.com

| 484 8000
Map Ref → 4-D2

La Dolce Vita coffee shop is an ideal place to meet your friends or business acquaintances for a chat and to treat yourself from the wide selection of coffees, teas and mouth-watering homemade cakes. Mediterranean in style, the small and cosy cafe is tucked away in a corner of the Ritz Carlton with great views of the resort. The shelves are packed with gourmet foods such as caviar, fois gras, oils and teas from around the world, making perfect presents for gastronomic connoisseurs or just as a special treat for yourself.

Lina's Café

Location → Nr Midmac Flyover, Salwa Rd · Al Nasr
Web/email → na

| 436 5488
Map Ref → 12-E3

Lina's Café is a popular chain with outlets in various locations around the world. They are known for their wide selection of hot and cold sandwiches and assorted homemade breads. The restaurant has a simple relaxed feel to it with attentive and efficient staff. It is a great location to keep abreast of world news via the plasma screen TVs, or to catch up on your emails by hooking your laptop up to their Wi-Fi connection. The comfortable seating and well-lit interior make Lina's Cafe quite functional, and an appealing office away from the office!

Opera Café

Location → The Mall · Al Matar Al Qadeem
Web/email → www.opera-qatar.com

| 467 8885
Map Ref → 16-E1

With a number of locations throughout Qatar, Opera Café appeals to wide variety of patrons from all walks of life, including thirsty shoppers and hungry office workers. With their brand of casual dining they offer a full array of sandwiches, soups, entrees, main courses and desserts. For anyone looking for an impressive gift for a special occasion, or just as a self indulgent treat, their cake and pastry take away sections shouldn't be missed. Other locations include Landmark Mall (486 3331), Al Sadd (442 8887), Al Muntzah (431 1363), and Al Khor (472 1608).

Starbucks

Location → Landmark Shopping Mall
Web/email → na

488 0575
Map Ref → 7-A1

No matter where you are in the world you always know when you've entered a Starbucks, and Qatar is no different. Great hot and cold coffee and tea selections and famous jazz background music make this a great getaway. You can enjoy a small sweet or even a savoury bite to complete your experience. This is the spot for a quick break or a fun place to catch up with friends. Other locations: Al Emadi Center (467 1196), City Center Mall Level One (483 9172), City Center Mall Level Two (483 9519), Hyatt Plaza (469 7273), The Mall (467 8689).

THE One

Location → Landmark Shopping Mall
Web/email → na

488 8669
Map Ref → 7 A1

This cafe is a hip getaway situated within THE One store in Landmark Mall. Customers come here to enjoy the soft lighting, great music, and of course the delicious food from the clever and quirky menu. It is a great meeting spot for a quick coffee, a full meal, or even an after-dinner dessert. The staff are friendly and refreshingly knowledgeable about the dishes on offer. An added attraction is that if you like the furniture, silverware, china, or even the background music in the restaurant, it can all be purchased within the store!

Vogue Cafe

Location → City Center Doha · Diplomatic District
Web/email → na

493 0434
Map Ref → 8-D2

Located near the main entrance of City Center, and with the bowling alley on one side and a waterfall on the other, this is hardly a quiet getaway but does provide some respite from the shopping. Quirky posters on the wall provide an illustrated history of mail transport while you wait for your order, but that won't be long because the service is quick, and friendly. The menu is a fairly mixed bag – mainly Mediterranean via Mexico and Arabia, with a spot of the orient thrown in for good measure. The food won't blow you away, but it's fresh and well-presented, and the juices (especially the two-tier banana and strawberry) are certainly worth trying.

Shisha Cafes

Other options → Arabic/Lebanese p.186

It is a common sight in this part of the world to see people both male and female, young and old, relaxing in the evening with a coffee or juice and a shisha pipe. For visitors and residents, even non-smokers, it's one of those must-do experiences and could just become a regular pastime. Many of the Arabic cafes and restaurants around town have shisha available and it makes a perfect end to a meal, especially when seated outdoors in the cooler months. If you fancy buying your own then the souks are a good place to start, but most Arabian souvenir shops sell them, as do the larger supermarkets.

Afternoon Tea

Other options → Cafes & Coffee Shops p.199

Lobby Lounge

Location → Ritz-Carlton Doha · West Bay
Web/email → www.ritzcarlton.com

484 8000
Map Ref → 4-D2

Within the spacious, open lobby area, afternoon tea is served daily in The Lobby Lounge. Quiet piped music is offset by the sumptuous surroundings, with the tea prepared in an almost art deco style recess. Smartly dressed waitresses are polite and not over attentive. There is an impressive variety of global teas and coffees available, all accompanied by an individual cake stand filled with tasty morsels including fresh sandwiches and fluffy scones. The table presentation is especially pleasing, complete with your own individual tea pot warmer! Taking tea at the Ritz really is a very pleasant way to spend an afternoon.

Internet Cafes

Other options → Internet p.69

Whether you want to get online while enjoying a drink or bite to eat, or you just don't have your own connection at home, there are a few cafes and eateries around town with PCs available for customers to use. Qtel is also increasing its network of wireless Hotspots at hotels, restaurants and coffee shops. These allow users with Wi-Fi enabled devices to access the internet for a small fee. Current locations include the Intercontinental Hotel, the Merweb Hotel, both branches of Eli France (Salwa and City Center Mall), La Maison du Café (Salwa and Royal Plaza Mall), Le Notre, Grand Café, Crepaway, Mint Cafe, and Fauchon.

Fast Food

In addition to the restaurants listed in this section, visitors and residents will be more than happy with the range of fast food outlets available in Qatar. Familiar names such as KFC, Pizza Hut, Hardee's, Burger King, Dairy Queen and McDonald's can all be seen, especially in the area around the Ramada Interchange in Doha. Diners in a hurry who are looking for good quality food at reasonable prices will be spoilt for choice.

Fast food

Friday Brunch

As the weekend starts, Friday Brunch is offered at most of the main hotels in Doha, making for a great family day out and also providing a cure for the Thursday night hangover. Some restaurants will even provide entertainment for the children, giving mum and dad a chance to relax and enjoy an extravagant buffet style brunch featuring a wide variety of international cuisines. Buffet style dining is available throughout the week in many hotels and restaurants, but you will always find that an extra special effort is made on a Friday, and the displays can be described as nothing less than spectacular. You usually pay a set price for all you can eat, so for those with a large appetite it definitely provides value for money.

Parties at Home

Caterers

For parties, special occasions, and business lunches or dinners, there are numerous options for arranging outside catering, allowing you to relax and enjoy yourself and concentrate on anything but the cooking. In addition to specialist companies, many hotels and restaurants have catering departments, so pick your favourite and ask if they can help you out. Depending on what you require, caterers can provide just the food or everything from crockery, napkins, tables, chairs and even waiters, doormen and a clearing up service afterwards. Costs vary according to the number of people, dishes and level of service required. Opera (468 8344) and Fauchon (432 4888) are renowned for their off-site catering.

For a list of hotel numbers, check out the table on p.23. For restaurants and cafes, simply browse this section of the book.

On the Town

If you are looking for life after dark in Doha you will not be disappointed. All the large hotels have bars that stay open until 02:00 on weekdays and 03:00 on a Thursday which is by far the busiest night of the week. You may find that the guys will have to pay an entrance fee if not accompanied by a lady, but this does not apply everywhere. As seems to be the case elsewhere in the Gulf, the night does not start early in Doha, with most people venturing out around 22:30. So if you arrive anywhere at 20:00, company will be in short supply but it does mean you'll be able to find a seat while you wait for the party to start!

Hot & Spicy

! ATTENTION
Dangerously Delicious

KFC

Are...Give US A Call

0 410

KFC Delivery
Four Four Ten Four Ten

Ten Four Ten

For Burger Lovers!

SUPER STAR

Hardee's
Where The Food's The Star

30 444
Delivery Service

PEPSI

AMERICA QUALITY

The weekend in Qatar is Friday and Saturday, and although this is not exactly party central, there are many night spots from which to choose, ranging from dance clubs to family orientated social clubs. Most bars allow children until 22:00.

Ladies nights are popular, mainly taking place on Tuesdays and Wednesdays, with some venues giving free drinks to the ladies all night. If you are so inclined you will also find quiz nights and various theme nights, such as eighties music, and full moon beach parties where you can dance under the moon and watch the glorious Arabian sunrise over the sea.

Bars

Other options → Nightclubs **p.206**

Drinking and Driving

There is zero tolerance for drinking and driving in the State of Qatar. If caught driving under the influence, you risk imprisonment and deportation. Instead of taking that gamble, get around using private taxis or limousine services.

Doha has a limited number of bars available to the public. As many long time residents will confess, Doha seems to be quite content in containing its bar scene. That said, there are a number of themed bars for those who enjoy a more casual sports bar set up, or those who enjoy jazz nights. Some bars offer live entertainment as well. In general you must be over 18 to enter a bar, although this is not monitored strictly.

Door Policy

Most of the bars are quite relaxed with their door policies. This is not to say they do not have minders at the entrances. Those in traditional Qatari garb are not allowed into bar establishments. Some of the venues are more particular on the busier nights and some require that you are a member. There are some instances where depending on your nationality, or the people you are with, you may be refused entry. The best way to combat this is to take your custom elsewhere. On most occasions all women are allowed, and often do not need any membership to gain entry to bars and clubs.

Dress Code

Doha's bars and clubs are quite relaxed when it comes to dress code. For the most part you can wear what you please, although some of the trendier places are a bit more particular and may not allow jeans, shorts, or sandals.

Cigar Bars

Habanos

Location → Ritz-Carlton Doha · West Bay
Web/email → www.ritzcarlton.com

| 484 8000
Map Ref → 4-D2

With furnishings of rich reds and dark mahogany, Habanos has a truly intimate and cosy feel. Picture windows provide sea views, and in the cooler weather you can relax outside on the attractive terrace. The cocktails are divine, and little touches like the complementary snacks (including possibly the best stuffed olives in Qatar) add to the experience. Given that this is a cigar lounge, smokers are not forgotten. The bar has its very own 'cigar butler' who will make recommendations and even cut and light cigars for you. One of Doha's favourite hangouts for the in crowd, Habanos makes a good starting point to an evening or a perfect place to end up later.

Habanos

Library Bar & Cigar Lounge

Location → Four Seasons Hotel · Diplomatic District | **494 8888**
Web/email → www.fourseasons.com   Map Ref → 8-E2

Cigars, snacks and a whole lot of luxury are what you will find when you enter the Library Bar & Cigar Lounge. Surrounded by leather buttoned chairs and comfy sofas you can't help but relax, and abstract art hanging from the dark wood walls adds to the ambience of the gentlemen's club setting. Take your pick from the cigar and food menu while enjoying the splendid sea views, or enjoying live piano music every night from 20:00 till midnight.

General Bars

Admiral's Club

Location → Ritz-Carlton Doha · West Bay | **484 8000**
Web/email → www.ritzcarlton.com   Map Ref → 4-D2

Located in an independent building to the north of the hotel just off the marina, this is a popular night spot that seems to pick up around 23:00 and goes on till 03:00. During the cooler months, Admirals has a wonderful outdoor space overlooking the yachts moored below. There are various themed evenings, including the popular Latino night on Wednesday and Arabian night on Fridays. On busier nights men pay QR 100 to enter, which includes two drinks.

Piano Piano

Location → Mövenpick Hotel Doha · Al Salata | **429 1111**
Web/email → www.moevenpick-hotels.com   Map Ref → 11-A3

More of a bar than a restaurant you will find Piano Piano tucked away within the Movenpick Hotel. As the name suggests, entertainment comes courtesy of a live pianist tinkling the ivories for the evening while you enjoy a few drinks, although a DJ is also on hand to entertain patrons on Thursdays and Saturdays. A full international menu is available from the Seasons restaurant, but the setting and atmosphere is probably more conducive to drinking than eating.

Spikes Lounge

Location → Doha Golf Club · West Bay | **483 2338**
Web/email → www.dohagolfclub.com   Map Ref → 4-A2

If you are going for a round of golf then Spikes Lounge will be just what you are looking for when you drop the ball at the 18th. It offers a relaxed and easy atmosphere, with drinks aplenty and a full snack menu that will revive you after a grueling day on the greens. The outside seating overlooks the course so is great for the winter months, but inside is just as good, with comfy sofas to rest your weary bones while you wait for your fish and chips to arrive.

Spikes Lounge

The Library

Location → Ramada Doha · Al Muntazah | **441 7417**
Web/email → www.ramada.com   Map Ref → 13-B2

This quiet hideaway, located on the top floor of the hotel, is a great spot to get your bearings as the location is in the heart of the city. The wall panels are adorned with Egyptian hieroglyphs, and in a nod to the bar's title the quirky bar stools and tables have legs made from stacks of books. Occasionally there is a harpist playing relaxing background music, helping all to unwind and enjoy their drinks even more.

> **In the Mix**
>
> *The Ritz Carlton has monthly classes that teach the art of cocktail and mocktail mixology. Places are limited so book early if you want to learn the secrets of the latest concoctions.*

Sports Bars

Aussie Legends

Location → Rydges Hotel · Al Bidda
Web/email → www.rydges.com

| 438 5444
Map Ref → 10-C3

The mood and atmosphere here vary depending on the clientele and the night of the week. At weekends the place is jumping, a popular spot for expats to socialise, enjoy a few drinks, and groove on down if there's a live band playing. Midweek though it can be a very different story. In what is basically a rectangular room with a few tables and a bar in the corner, you may find yourself surrounded by lone hotel guests supping a pint while watching sports on one of the many big screens. The drinks are reasonably priced and the bar snacks are tasty, but you're recommended to take some lively friends.

Shehrazad

Location → Ramada Doha · Al Muntazah
Web/email → www.ramada.com

| 441 7417
Map Ref → 13-B2

Probably one of the liveliest spots in Doha, although perhaps not one of the most cultured! There is a live band, and once a month the venue hosts a popular comedy night, but whatever the occasion this bar seems to be packed every night. Traditional bar snacks are served, and there are plenty of waiters to keep your glass topped up. For a night out with your mates and a beer or two this is a good choice – wear your jeans, have a dance, and thanks to the reasonable prices you shouldn't even spend a fortune.

Nightclubs

Other options → Belly Dancing **p.140**

When it comes to the nightclub scene in Doha the selection is quite small. With this in mind, when you hit the clubs in the evenings you always seem to run into people you know, lending a certain charm to the clubbing scene that you rarely find in big cities. There are no real standalone nightclubs either. Instead, some bars and restaurants transform late in the evening into lively joints with hopping dancefloors and a great atmosphere.

These include Amigos (p.199), Aussie Legends (p.206) and Shehrazad (p.206). Some evenings revolve around themed music, from Arabian nights to Spanish Salsa nights. Certain clubs can be a bit more picky than others and may require you to leave your jeans at home for the night.

Entertainment

Cinemas

Over recent years Doha has increased its number of movie screens, and the opening of the 14-screen theater at the City Center mall has allowed for a much greater variety of films to be aired in town. Almost all the major western releases make it to Qatar, and there is also a big market for Indian and Arabic films. Unlike some of its Gulf neighbours, Qatar is quite liberal when it comes to film censorship, meaning viewers are able to enjoy the full story line without missing any of the action. New films are often released on the same day as in the west, but sometimes you may have to wait a few weeks for a movie to arrive. The cinemas offer all the comforts of typical movie theaters, from popcorn to soft drinks and the standard junk food that is all part of the movie-going experience. Cinema timings can be found in the daily local newspapers.

> ### Local Cuisine
>
> Most local Qatari cuisine revolves around rice dishes with either meat or chicken. Ouzi, a whole roasted lamb that is slowly cooked to the point that the meat simply falls off the bone like butter, is one of the most traditional meals. It is served on a bed of rice with pine nuts, raisins, and almonds. Hareis, another authentic dish that is similar to a Western oatmeal, is actually wheat and lamb slowly cooked in a pot over low heat. These dishes are fairly common throughout the GCC. A few local restaurants such as Balhambar and Al Majlis allow one to enjoy an authentic meal in equally authentic surroundings.

Cinemas	
Cinema Land	488 1674
Grand Cinecentre	493 4934
Gulf Cinema	467 1811
The Mall Cinema	467 8666

Comedy

The local comedy scene is not that lively, but the regular Laughter Factory night at the Ramada keeps Doha's residents rolling in the aisles. Judging by the popularity of this event, it's possible that other hotels will look at hosting comedy nights too.

The Laughter Factory	
Location → Ramada Hotel · Al Muntazah	441 7417
Web/email → www.thelaughterfactory.com	Map Ref → 13-B2

The Laughter Factory is a comedy promoter based in Dubai. In conjunction with the renowned London club The Comedy Store, they arrange a mini tour each month where three comedians will play a number of dates around the Gulf. The Shehrazad Bar in the Ramada plays host to this comedy event, and it is always sold out. This is a great opportunity to see professional comics at work. Tickets are QR 75, and the show usually starts at 20:00. The Laughter Factory website has details of forthcoming shows and reviews of the featured comedians.

Concerts

The main concert venue in Qatar is the ballroom at the Sheraton Hotel Conference Center. One of the most famous names to grace Doha was Luciano Pavarotti in 2003. The area behind the Ritz Carlton Hotel near the beach has also been used to host open air concerts in the cooler weather, playing host to the likes of Lionel Ritchie. In 2004 Qatar Airways held a private event and hosted the famous Arab singer Nancy Ajram at an open air concert at the Doha Golf Club. The renowned Iraqi

singer Ilham Al Madfai also performed at a more intimate 'invitation only' musical event at the Ritz Carlton Hotel. Around March each year Doha hosts a Cultural Festival where various musicians, singers, and dancers from around the world perform at the Sheraton Hotel Conference Center. Performers who wowed the crowds at the 2005 event included Majida Al Roumi, Kathim Al Sahar, and the Spanish Flamenco dancers.

Fashion Shows

Qatar is not particularly known for hosting big gala events and shows, but as the country grows and continues to nurture its image as a world-class destination this could well change. In terms of fashion shows, there are a couple that are sporadically held during the year by various non-profit organizations such as the American Womens' Association, and Virginia Commonwealth University's School of Fashion Design.

Theatre

Other options → Drama Groups **p.141**

The best-known theatrical company in Qatar is the Doha Players. Made up of keen amateurs and volunteers, for over 50 years they have been staging English-language productions in the capital. As a result of the bombing in March 2005 they no longer have their own theatre, but the company is in the process of securing funding to rebuild. In the meantime, the Doha Players have been using the facilities at the National Theatre where they staged a successful comeback with a production of Cinderella in December 2005. For information on forthcoming productions and details of how to contribute to the rebuilding programme, log on to www.dohaplayers.com.

Le Nôtre

in the UAE since 1976

MAPS geosystems

Spatial Data Acquisition, Processing & Integration

- Aerial Photography
- Satellite Image Processing
- Ground Survey
- Utility Mapping
- Geodetic Network Rehabilitation
- Terrain Modelling
- T3D Vector Mapping
- Orthoimage Production
- Geographic Data Acquisition
- Spatial Data Integration
- GIS Implementation
- Application Service Provision

Master Reseller of QuickBird from DIGITALGLOBE
The market's highest resolution satellite imagery.

MAPS (UAE), Corniche Plaza 1
P.O. Box 5232, Sharjah, U.A.E.
Tel.: + 971 6 5725411
Fax: + 971 6 5724057

Certified to EN ISO 9001:2000

TÜV
CERT
EN ISO 9001 : 2000

Deutscher
Akkreditierungs
Rat
TGA-ZM-30-96-00

www.maps-geosystems.com
info@maps-geosystems.com

Operations throughout Europe, Middle East and Africa with
regional offices in: **Munich, Sharjah, Beirut, Lisbon, Bucharest,
Dubai, Abu Dhabi, Conakry, Dakar.**

Maps

EXPLORER

Maps

User's Guide

To further assist you in locating your destination, we have superimposed additional information, such as main roads, roundabouts and landmarks, on the maps. Many places listed throughout the guidebook also have a map reference alongside, so you know precisely where you need to go (or what you need to tell the taxi driver).

While the country overview map on this page is at a scale of approximately 1:850,000 (1cm = 8.5km) and the Doha city and surrounding area map is at a scale of approximately 1:300,000 (1cm = 3km) all other map pages scale is 1:20,000 (1cm = 200m).

Technical Info - Satellite Images

The maps in this section are based on rectified QuickBird satellite imagery taken in 2005.

The QuickBird satellite was launched in October 2001 and is operated by DigitalGlobe(tm), a private company based in Colorado (USA). Today, DigitalGlobe's QuickBird satellite provides the highest resolution (61 cm), largest swath width and largest onboard storage of any currently available or planned commercial satellite.

MAPS geosystems are the Digital Globe master resellers for the Middle East, West, Central and East Africa. They also provide a wide range of mapping services and systems. For more information, visit www.digitalglobe.com (QuickBird) and www.maps-geosystems.com (mapping services) or contact MAPS geosystems on (+971 0) 6 572 5411.

Online Maps

If you want to surf for maps online, www.qa.map24.com and www.maporama.com are worth a look. Hardcore map fans though are recommended to try Google Earth (http://earth.google.com). This amazing program (you download it from the site) combines satellite imagery, detailed maps, and a powerful search capability, allowing you to fly between various points on the globe and zoom in for incredibly detailed views.

Community & Street Index

The following is a list of the main cities, towns, roads and communities in Qatar, which are referenced on the map pages. Many roads are longer than one grid reference, in which case the main grid reference has been given.

Town/City	Map Ref	Town/City	Map Ref
Al Khor	1-C2	Dukhan	1-A2
Al Wakrah	1-C3	Madinat Al Shamal	1-B1
Al Ruwais	1-B1	Mesaieed	1-C3
Doha	1-C3	Ras Laffan	1-C1

Doha City	Map Ref	Doha City	Map Ref
Abdul Aziz	13-C1	Al Sadd	9-E4
Abu Hamour	15-D3	Al Salata	11-A4
Al Amir	9-A3	Al Salata Al Jadeeda	13-B4
Al Asmakh	13-D1	Al Soudan North	12-A2
Al Bidda	10-C3	Al Soudan South	12-C3
Al Diwan	10-D3	Alwaab	12-A4
Al Doha Al Jadeeda	13-E1	Al Wukair	17-E4
Al Duhail North	5-A2	Bin Omran	9-D1
Al Duhail South	5-A3	Diplomatic District	8-E2
Al Ghanim Al Qadeem North	10-E4	Hamad Medical Corporation	9-E3
Al Ghanim Al Qadeem South	14-A1	Ibn Mahmood North	10-A4
Al Hilal East	14-A4	Ibn Mahmood South	13-B1
Al Hilal West	13-E4	Kulaib	7-D4
Al Hitmi	11-A4	Madinath Khalifa North	7-B2
Al Hitmi Al Jadeed	9-D2	Madinath Khalifa South	7-B3
Al Jasra	10-E3	Musaimeer	17-A4
Al Khulaifat	11-C4	Musheirib	10-C4
Al Luqta	9-A1	Najma	14-A3
Al Maamoura	12-D4	New District of Doha 62 & 63	8-B4,C3
Al Manzoura	13-D3	New District of Doha 64 & 65	8-A3,B1
Al Markhiya	7-D2	New District of Doha 66 & 67	6-A3,5-D4
Al Matar Al Qadeem	17-B1	New Markets	10-E4
Al Messila	9-C2	Qatar University	3-C4
Al Mirqab Al Jadeed	12-E2	Ras Abu Abboud	11-E4
Al Muntazah	13-C2	Umm Ghuwailina	14-A1
Al Najada	13-E1	Wadi Al Sail West	7-E4
Al Nasr	12-E2	West Bay Lagoon	4-B3
Al Nuaija East	16-C2		
Al Nuaija West	16-C2		
Al Rumaila East	10-B2		
Al Rumaila West	10-A2		

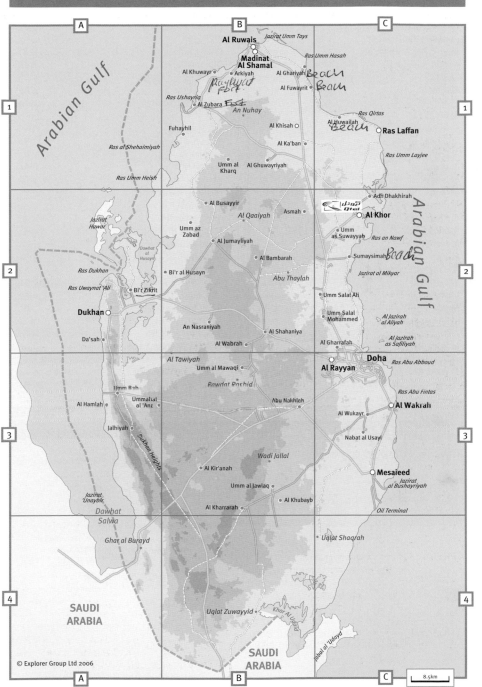

Qatar Overview Map

A · B · C

Al Ruwais
Jazirat Umm Tays
Madinat Al Shamal
Al Khuwayr · Arkiyah
Al Ghariyah · Beach · Beam
Al Fuwayrit · Beam
Ras Ushayriq
Al Zubara · Fort
An Nuhay
Ras Umm Hasah
Ras al Shehaimiyah
Fuhayhil
Al Khisah O
Al Huwailah · Beam
Ras Qirtas
Ras Laffan
Al Ka'ban
Ras Umm Layjee
Umm al Kharq
Al Ghuwayriyah

Arabian Gulf

Al Busayyir
Al Qaaiyah · Asmah
Adh Dhakhirah
Kuwat Qtel
Al Khor
Umm az Zabad
Al Jumayliyah
Umm as Suwayyah · Ras an Nawf
Al Bambarah
Sumaysimah · Beach
Jazirat Hawar
Dawhat al Husayn
Ras Dukhan
Bi'r al Husayn
Abu Thaylah
Jazirat al Mikyar
Ras Uwaynat 'Ali
Bi'r Zikrit
Umm Salal Ali
Dukhan O
Al Jazirah al Aliyah
Da'sah
An Nasraniyah
Al Shahaniya
Umm Salal Mohammed
Al Wabrah
Al Gharrafah
Al Jazirah as Safiliyah

Al Tawiyah
Umm al Mawaqi
Doha
Ras Abu Abboud
Al Rayyan
Rawdat Rashid
Umm Bab
Ras Abu Fintas
Ummaliat al 'Anz
Abu Nakhlah
Al Wakrah
Al Hamlah
Al Wukayr
Jalhiyah
Dukhan Heights
Nabat al Usayl
Al Kir'anah
Wadi Jallal
Mesaieed
Jazirat 'Unaybir
Umm al Jawlaq
Al Khubayb
Jazirat al Bushayriyah
Dawhat Salwa
Al Kharrarah
Oil Terminal

Ghar al Burayd
Uqlat Shaqrah

SAUDI ARABIA
Uqlat Zuwayyid
Khor Al Udaid
SAUDI ARABIA
Jabal al 'Udayd

Arabian Gulf

© Explorer Group Ltd 2006

8.5km

Street Name	Map Ref
22 February St	7-A3, 9-B2
A Ring Rd	13-D1
Ab Hamour St	16-A4
Abdullah Bin Thani St	10-D4
Ahmed Bin Zaidoun St	16-D2
Airport Park St	14-C2
Al Ain St	14-B3
Al Amir St	9-B3, 12-C1
Al Arabiya St	9-B1
Al Bidda St	10-C3
Al Buhaira St	3-E4, 6-B2
Al Bustan St	12-B3
Al Corniche St	10-C2
Al Diwan St	10-C4
Al Istiqlal St	8-A3, 10-A1
Al Jamiaa St	3-E3, 5-1D, 7-E2
Al Khafji St	5-A3
Al Khaleej St	10-B4
Al Madeed St	15-E1, 16-B2
Al Mansoura St	13-E2
Al Markhiya St	8-B3
Al Matar Al Qadeem St	17-C1
Al Matar St	14-A2
Al Muntazah St	13-C1
Al Muthaf St	11-A4
Al Rayyan Palace St	9-A4
Al Rayyan Rd	9-C3, 10-C3
Al Sadd St	12-E1
Al Shamal North Rd	7-A2
Al Waab St	12-C2
Ali Bin Ali Abi Talib Rd	13-B3
Arab League St	3-A3, 5-B2

Street Name	Map Ref
B Ring Rd	13-C1
Bilal Bin Rabah St	16-E1
Bin Mahmood St	10-B4
C Ring Rd	13-B3, 14-A3
D Ring Rd	12-E4, 14-B4, 16-B1
Diplomatic St	8-E1
E Ring Rd	16-B2, 17-C3
Golf Course St	4-A2
Grand Hamad St	10-E4
Haloul St	15-C1
Ibn Seena St	13-C3
Jabel Bin Hayyan St	17-B2
Jawaan St	9-D4
Khalifa St	7-A3, 8-A4
Lusail St	4-C1, 6-C2
Majlis Al Taawon St	8-C3, 10-B2
Makkah St	7-A4
Mesaimeer Rd	15-C1
Mohd Bin Thani St	9-E2
Musaab Bin Omar St	16-C1
Musameer St	15-D2
Najma St	13-E3, 17-A2
Omar Bin Al Khattar St	7-B4
Onaiza St	6-B2
Oqba Bin Nafie St	17-B2
Ras Abu Abboud St	11-C4
Salwa Rd	12-D4, 15-B1
Suhaim Bin Hamad St	10-A4
Wahda St	6-B4, 8-C1
Wholesale Market St	15-B3, 16-A4
Zaid Bin Thabit St	16-B2

Map Legend

E	Embassy/Consulate	**S**	Souk/Shopping Centre	▬▬	Motorway
H	Hotel	**O**	Hospital	═══	Main Roads
M	Museum	**AL SADD**	Area Name		

Map page 1 is at a scale of 1:850,000 (1cm = 8.5km)
Map page 2 is at a scale of 1:300,000 (1cm = 3km)
Map pages 3-17 are at a scale of 1:20,000 (1cm = 200m)

N

A   **B**   **C**

1

Abu Kharaisah
Muaither Rasheedah
Wadi Mahmoud
Ummahat al Has
Wadi al Askar
Sana al Hamaidee
Al Otouriyah
Al Waab
Umm Obairiyah
Al Maslabah al Janoubiyah
Umm Qarn
Abu Husayah
Al Dhaayen

Arabian Gulf

1

2

Al Kharaib
Rawdat Harmah
Abu Fas
Umm al Routh
Umm Salal Ali
Al Hamamah
Umm Salal Mohammed
Al Kheesah
Thuailib
Al Kharaej
Al Khuraitiyat
Doha Golf Club
Qatar University
Pearl Qatar (u/c)
Al Shahaniya
IImm Ghuwailinah
Umm al Afaai
Al Samariyah
Umm al Qahab
Madinat Khalifa
Educational City

Jazirat al Mikyar
Al Jazirah al 'Aliyah
Al Jazirah as 'Safiliyah

2

Al Rayyan
Al Wajbah
Fort
Qtel

Doha
Ras Syhan

3

Abu Janb
Umm al Mawaqa
Muaither
Rawdal Rashed
Al Ghanim al Jadeed
Al Sailiyah
Ain Khaled
Light Industrial Area
Abu Hamour
Doha International Airport
Sewage Works
Ras Kelaib

3

Umm al Zubar al Sharqiyah
Rawdat Mubarak
Al Mashaf
Qtel

Ummahat Owainah
Al Khaldiya
Ummahat Owainah
Al Yawabi
Abu al Sulail
Al Wukair
Al Maamariyah
Al Wakrah

4

Muaither
Beedaa al Qaa
Abu Hasaa
Mazraat al Sheikh Jassim Bin Mohammed
Mazraat Abu Joud
Rawdat Sabt
Wadi Jallal

© Explorer Group Ltd 2006

3km

A   **B**   **C**

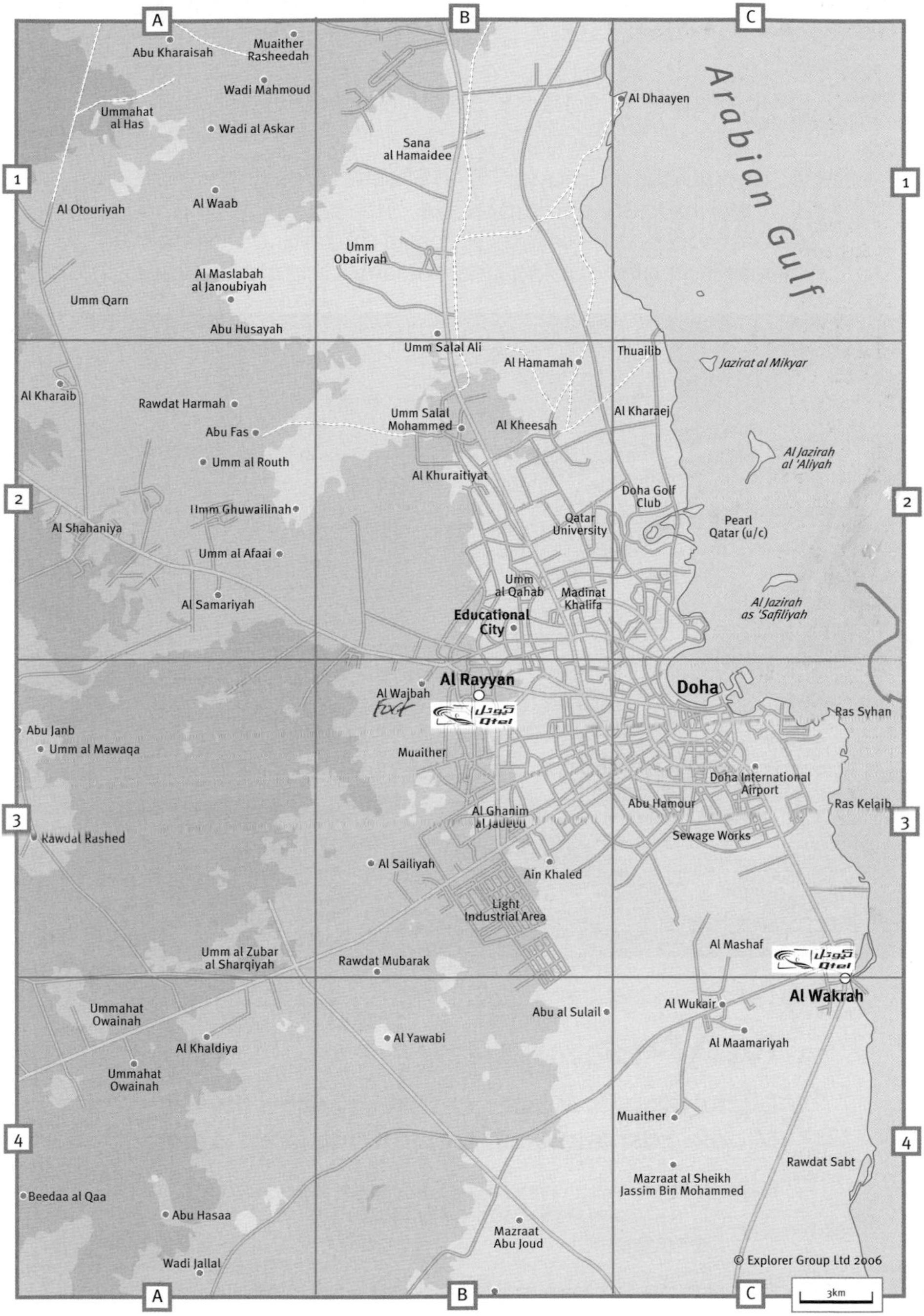

DIGITALGLOBE™

C L E A R L Y   T H E   B E S T

61 cm QuickBird Imagery is the highest resolution satellite imagery available. We offer products and resorces to both existing GIS users and the entire next generation of mapping and multimedia applications.

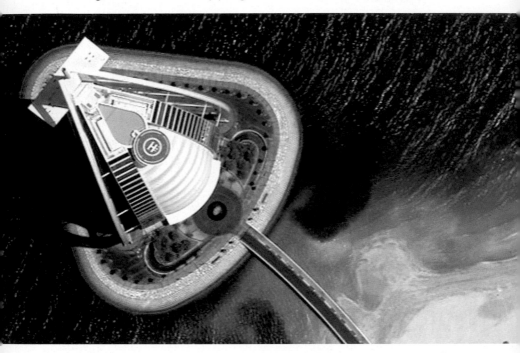

Burj Al Arab, Scale 1:2500, dated May 2003 © DigitalGlobe

MAPSgeosystems

DigitalGlobe's Master Reseller serving the Middle East and East, Central and West Africa

MAPS (UAE), Corniche Plaza 1, P.O. Box 5232, Sharjah, UAE.
Tel : +971 6 5725411, Fax : +971 6 5724057
www.maps-geosystems.com

For further details, please contact quickbird@maps-geosystems.com

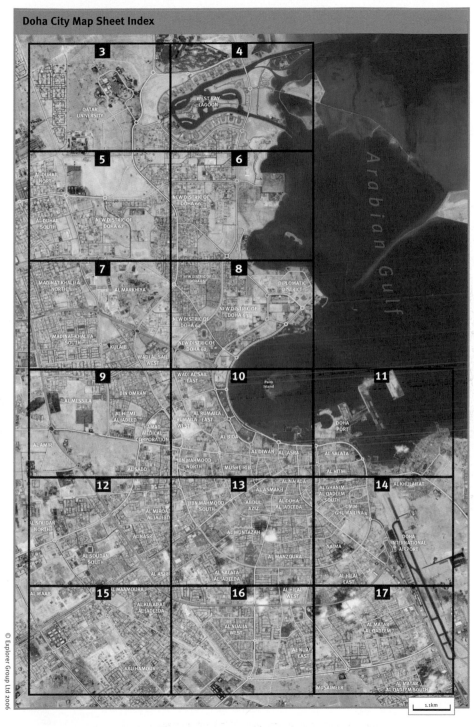

© Explorer Group Ltd 2006

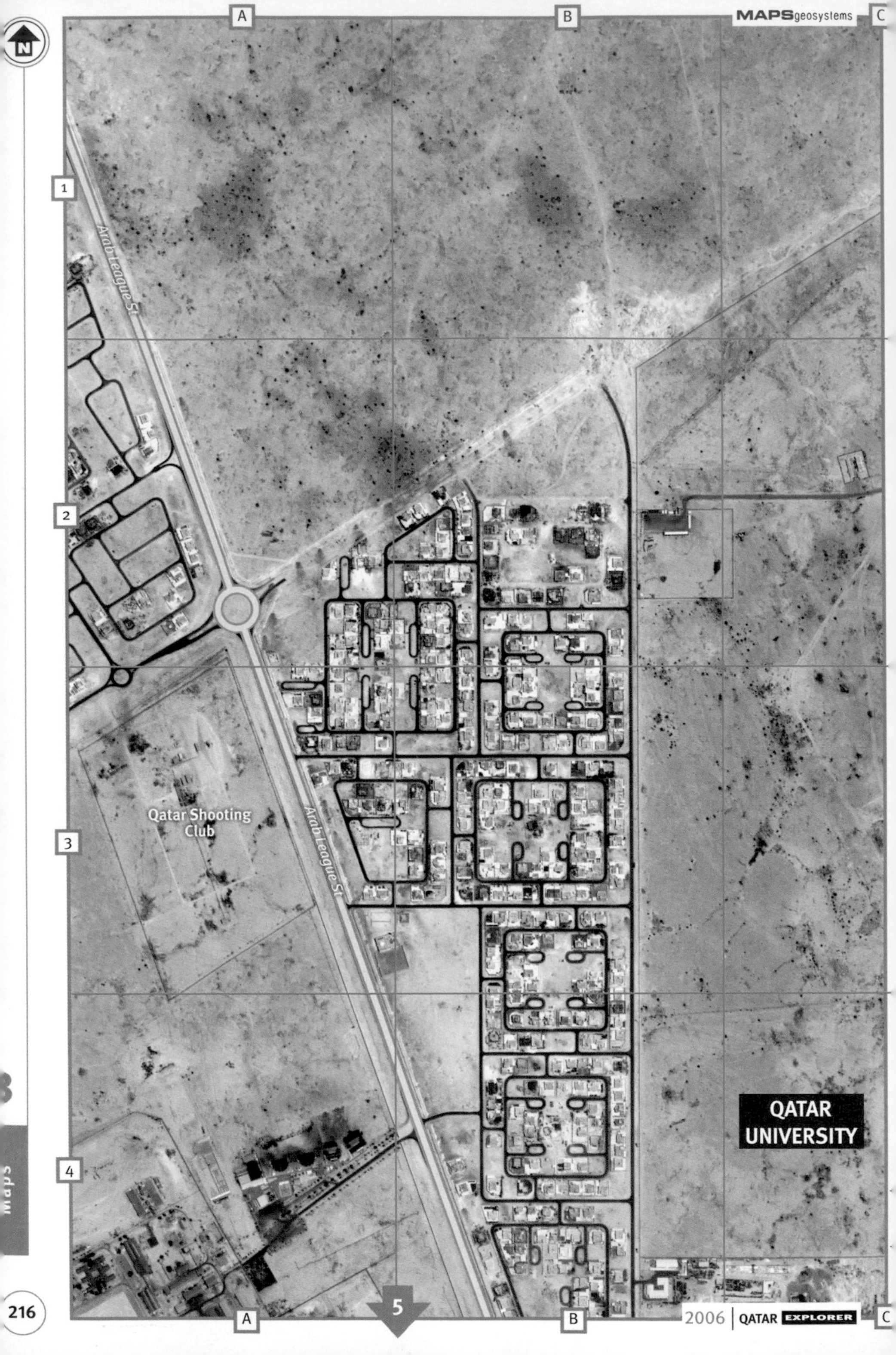

N

Arab League St

Qatar Shooting Club

Arab League St

3

QATAR UNIVERSITY

Maps

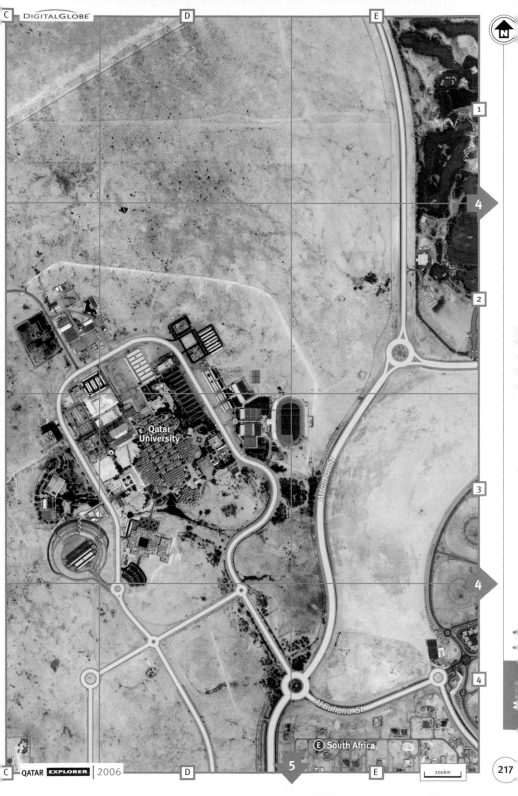

DIGITALGLOBE

Qatar University

Al Jamiaa St

Al Buhaira St

E South Africa

200km

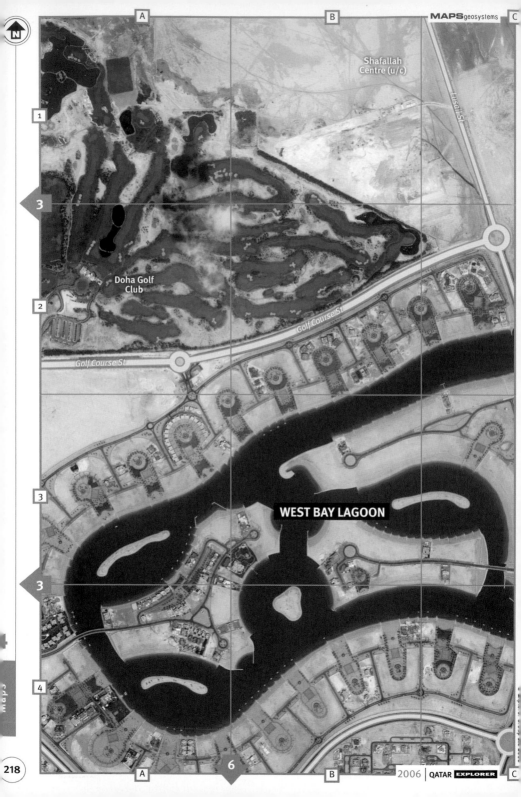

Shafallah
Centre (u/c)

Doha Golf
Club

Golf Course St

Golf Course St

WEST BAY LAGOON

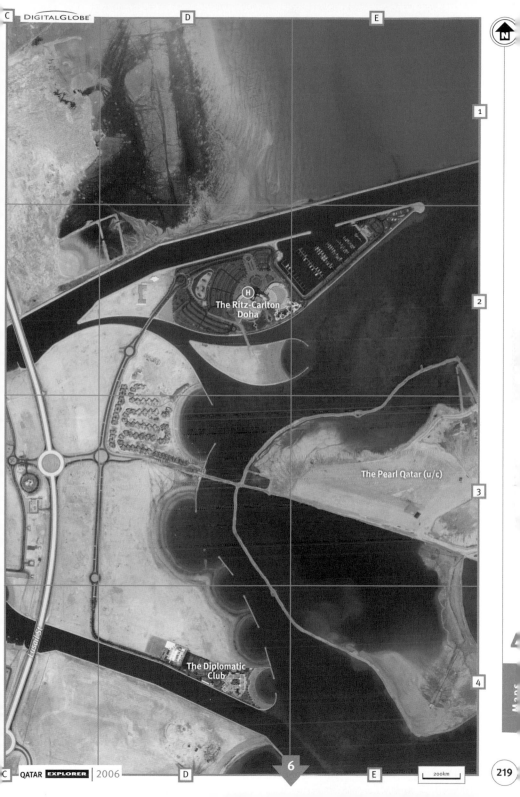

DIGITALGLOBE

The Ritz-Carlton Doha

The Pearl Qatar (u/c)

The Diplomatic Club

Lusail St

6

200km

Maps

MAPSgeosystems

New College of
Technology (u/c)

1

AL DUHAIL NORTH

2

Riviera
Gardens

Arab League St

Al Khafji St

AL DUHAIL SOUTH

3

Arab League St

Al Khafji St

4

maps

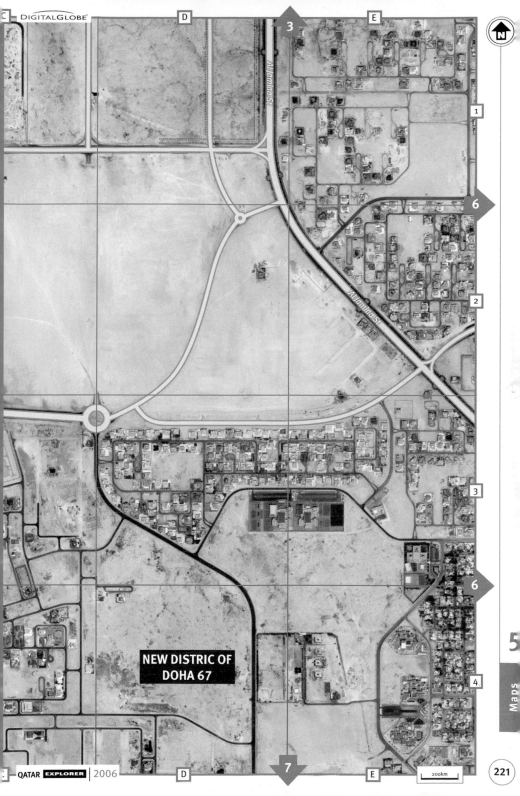

NEW DISTRIC OF
DOHA 67

5

Maps

Al Buhaira St

E Spain

1

5

E Hungary

Intl School
of Choueifat

Onaiza St

Aladdin R/A

Lusail St

2

E Brunei

E Afghanistan

E Venezuela

E Bahrain

**NEW DISTRIC OF
DOHA 66**

3

Lusail St

5

4

Al Hamar St

Wahda St

West Bay

6

Maps

Aladdin's Kingdom

(H)
Intercontinental
Doha

Arabian Gulf

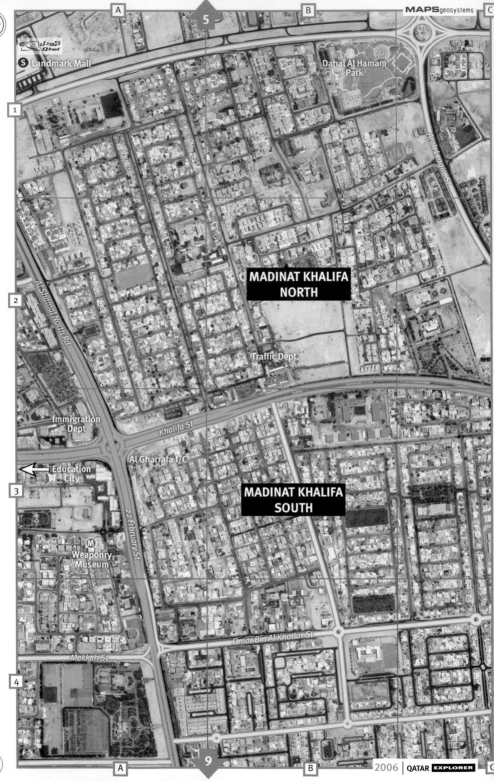

S Landmark Mall

Dahal Al Hamam Park

MADINAT KHALIFA NORTH

Traffic Dept.

Al Shamal North Rd

Immigration Dept

Khalifa St

Al Gharrafa I/C

Education City

22 February St

M Weaponry Museum

MADINAT KHALIFA SOUTH

Omar Bin Al Khattar St

Makkah St

Maps

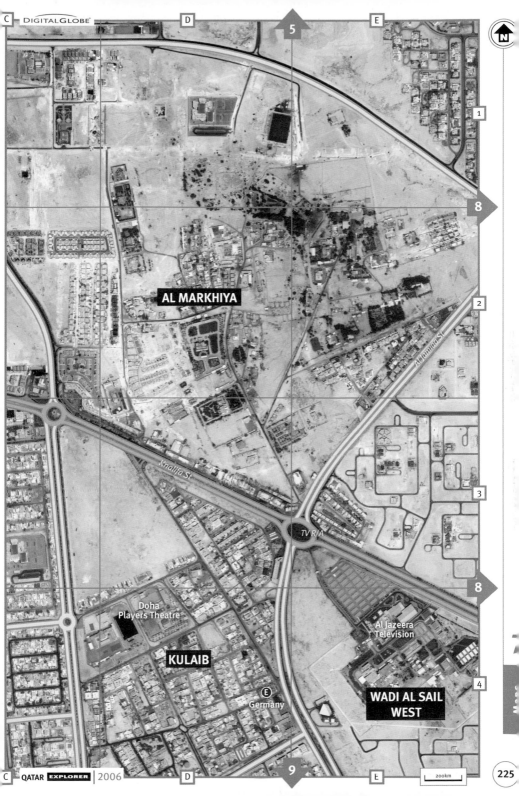

DIGITALGLOBE

AL MARKHIYA

Al Jamiaa St

Khalifa St

TV R/A

Doha
Players Theatre

KULAIB

E
Germany

Al Jazeera
Television

WADI AL SAIL
WEST

1

8

2

3

8

4

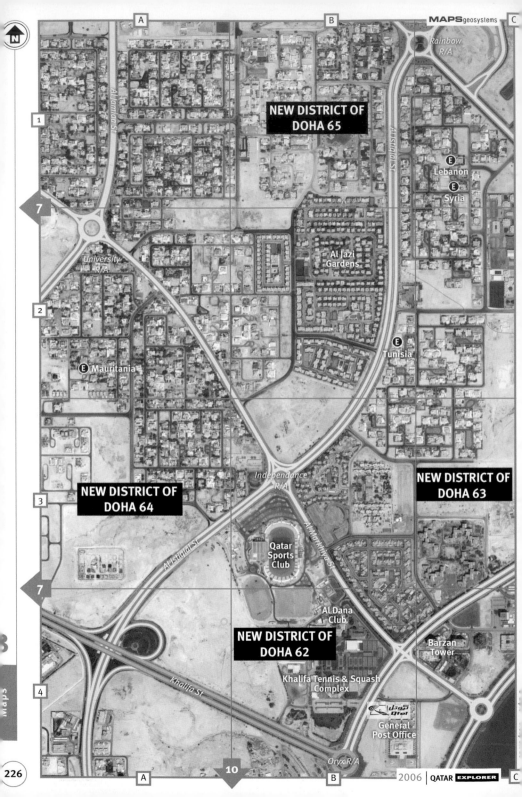

NEW DISTRICT OF DOHA 65

Rainbow R/A

Al Istiqlal St

E Lebanon

E Syria

Al Jazi Gardens

University R/A

E Tunisia

E Mauritania

Independance R/A

NEW DISTRICT OF DOHA 64

NEW DISTRICT OF DOHA 63

Al Markhiya St

Qatar Sports Club

Al Istiqlal St

NEW DISTRICT OF DOHA 62

Al Dana Club

Barzan Tower

Khalifa Tennis & Squash Complex

Khalifa St

Qtel

General Post Office

Oryx R/A

Maps

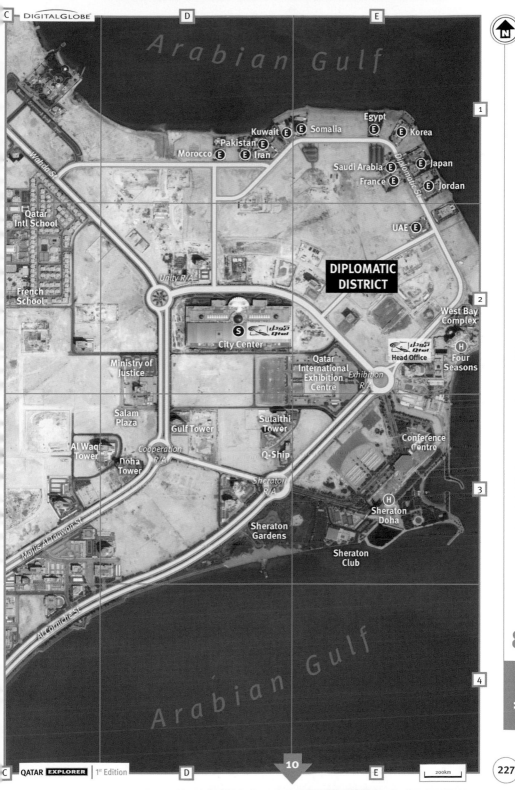

DIGITALGLOBE

Arabian Gulf

1

Kuwait (E) (E) Somalia

Egypt (E)

(E) Korea

Pakistan (E)
Morocco (E) (E) Iran

Saudi Arabia (E) (E) Japan
France (E) (E) Jordan

Wahda St.

Diplomatic St.

UAE (E)

Qatar
Intl School

**DIPLOMATIC
DISTRICT**

Unity R/A

2

French
School

S Qtel

West Bay
Complex

City Center

Qtel
Head Office

(H) Four
Seasons

Ministry of
Justice

Qatar
International
Exhibition
Centre

*Exhibition
R/A*

Salam
Plaza

Sulaithi
Tower

Gulf Tower

Conference
Centre

Al Waqf
Tower

*Cooperation
R/A*

Q-Ship

Doha
Tower

*Sheraton
R/A*

3

(H)
Sheraton
Doha

Sheraton
Gardens

Sheraton
Club

Majlis Al Taawon St.

Al Corniche St.

4

Arabian Gulf

10

200km

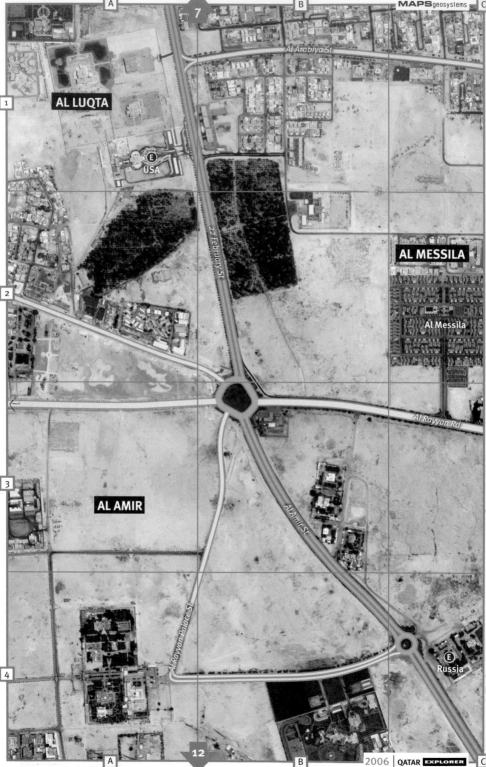

Al Arabiya St

AL LUQTA

1

E
USA

22 February St

AL MESSILA

2

Al Messila

Al Rayyan Rd

3

AL AMIR

Al Amir St

Al Rayyan Palace St

E
Russia

4

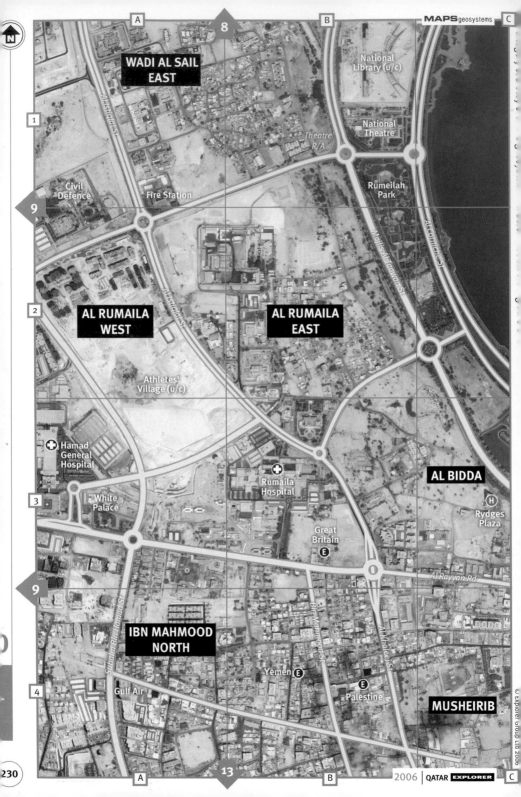

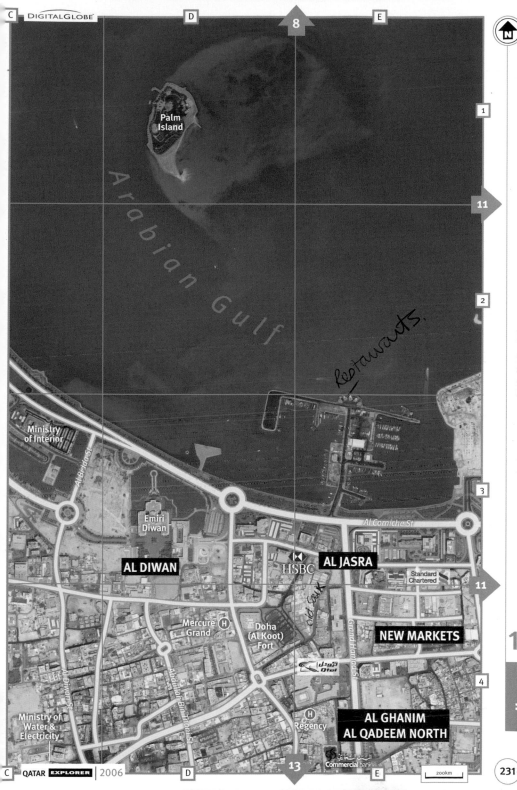

DOHA PORT

Youth & Sports
General Authority

Ⓗ Movenpick

Museum
Park

AL SALATA

Ⓗ Al Bustan

Ⓜ Qatar
National
Museum

Ras Al Nasaa

Al Muthaf St

Doha
Club

AL HITMI

Ras Abu Abboud St

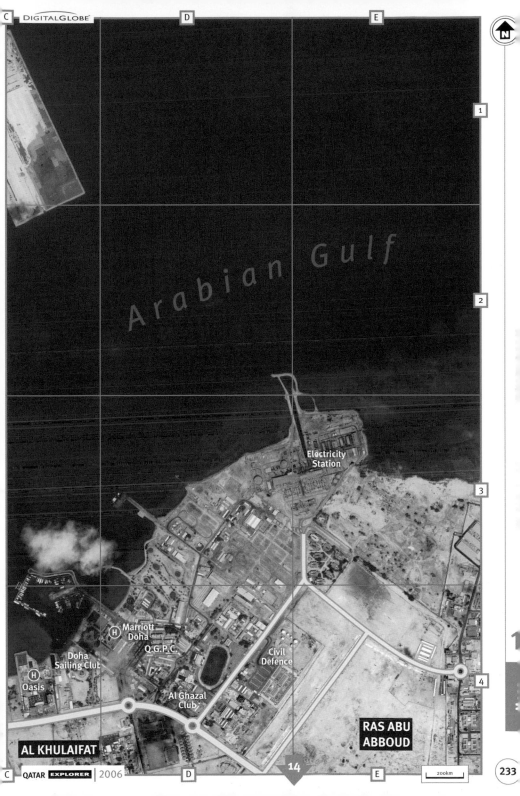

DIGITALGLOBE

N

1

Arabian Gulf

2

Electricity
Station

3

Marriott
Doha

Q.G.P.C.

Doha
Sailing Club

Civil
Defence

Oasis

Al Ghazal
Club

**RAS ABU
ABBOUD**

AL KHULAIFAT

9

1

2

AL SOUDAN
NORTH

Al Waab St

Qtel
Call Centre

Al Busteen St

Al Sadd
Sports Club

3 Khalifa
Sports City

American
School of
Doha

Doha Rugby
Union Football
Centre

Doha
College

S
4 Hyatt
Plaza Mall
Qtel

ALWAAB

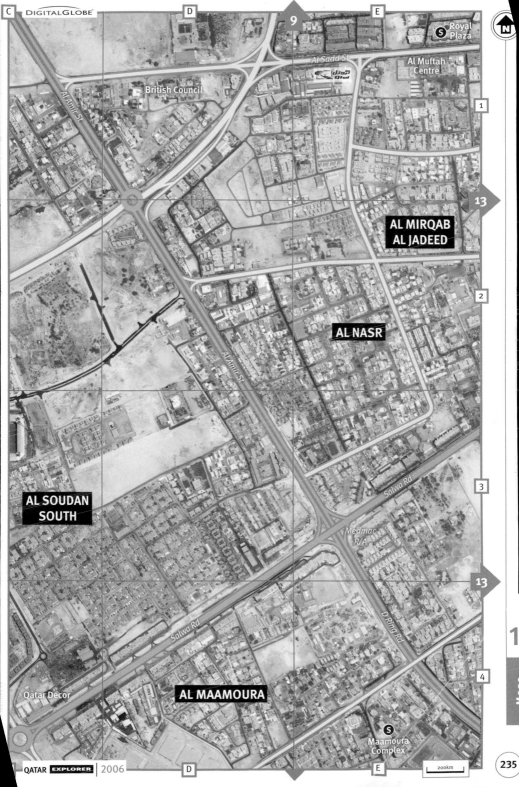

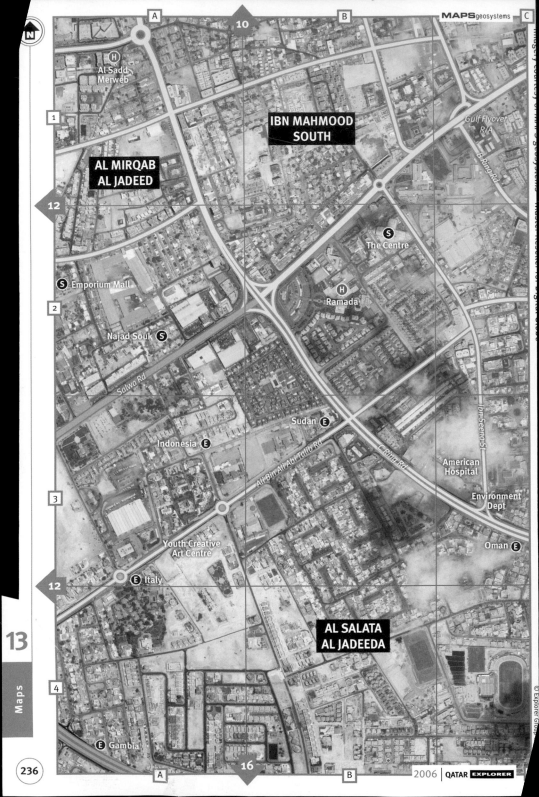

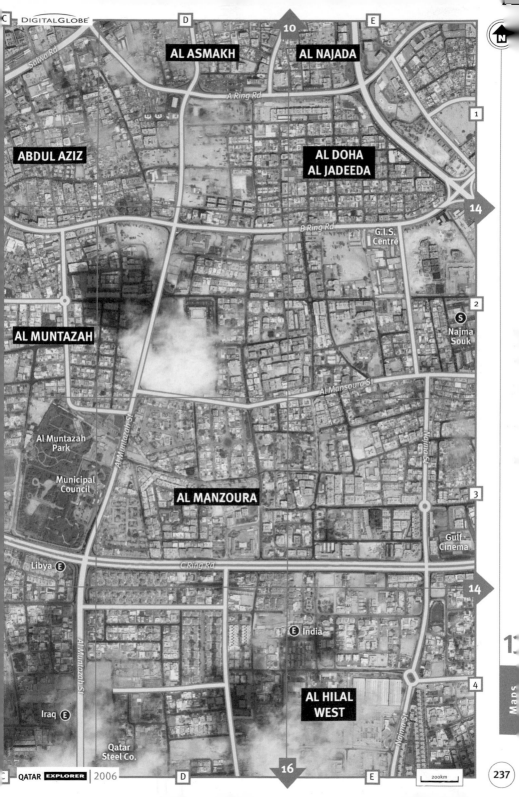

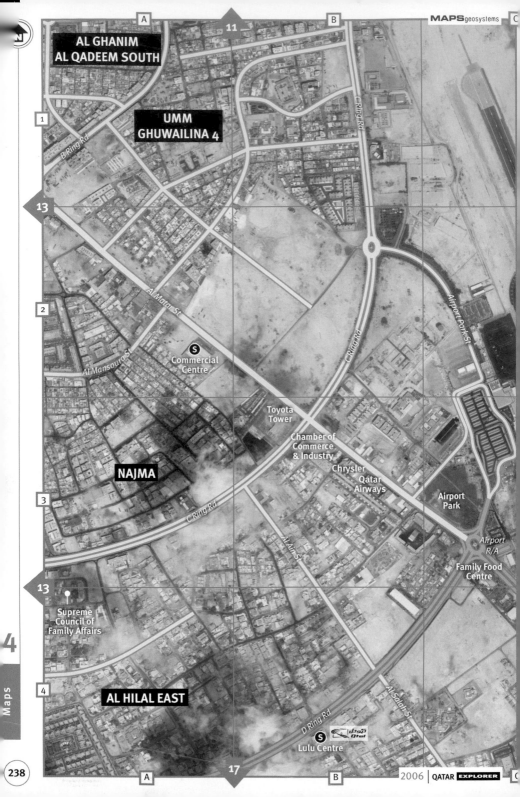

AL GHANIM
AL QADEEM SOUTH

UMM
GHUWAILINA 4

Commercial
Centre

Toyota
Tower

Chamber of
Commerce
& Industry

Chrysler
Qatar
Airways

NAJMA

Airport
Park

Airport
R/A

Family Food
Centre

Supreme
Council of
Family Affairs

AL HILAL EAST

Lulu Centre

B Ring Rd

C Ring Rd

Al Matar St

Al Mansoura St

C Ring Rd

Al Ain St

D Ring Rd

Al Saleh St

Airport Park St

DIGITALGLOBE

Ras Abu Abboud St

DOHA
INTERNATIONAL
AIRPORT

Al Matar St

Maps

Salwa Rd

Ⓢ
Wholesale
Market

Fish
Market

Doha Zoo

Al Maamoura
R/A

Al Naida
Police Station

Thursday &
Friday
Market

Wholesale Market St

Sheep & Bird
Souk

Livestock
Health Section

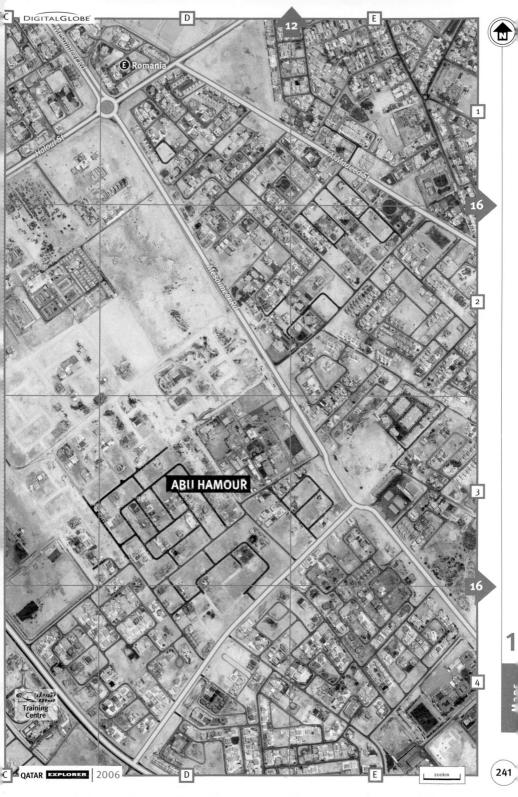

Ⓔ Romania

Haloul St

Mesaimeer Rd

Al Madeed St

Mesaimeer Rd

1

16

2

3

16

ABU HAMOUR

Ⓔ Training Centre

4

1

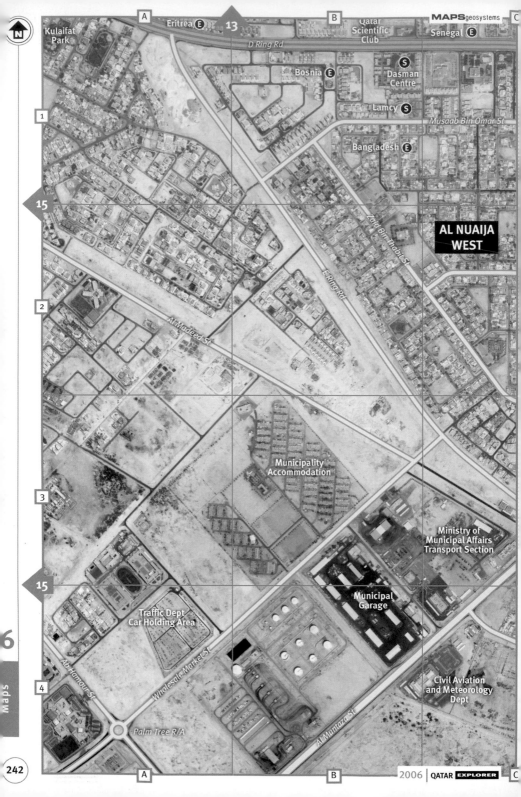

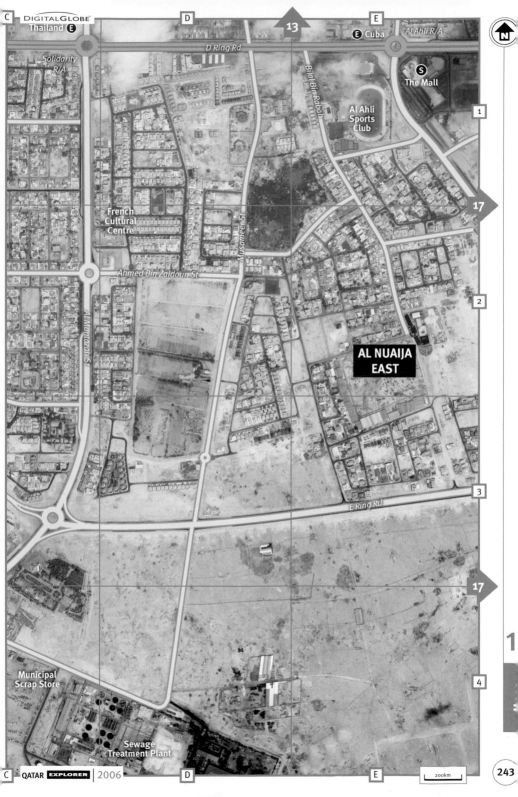

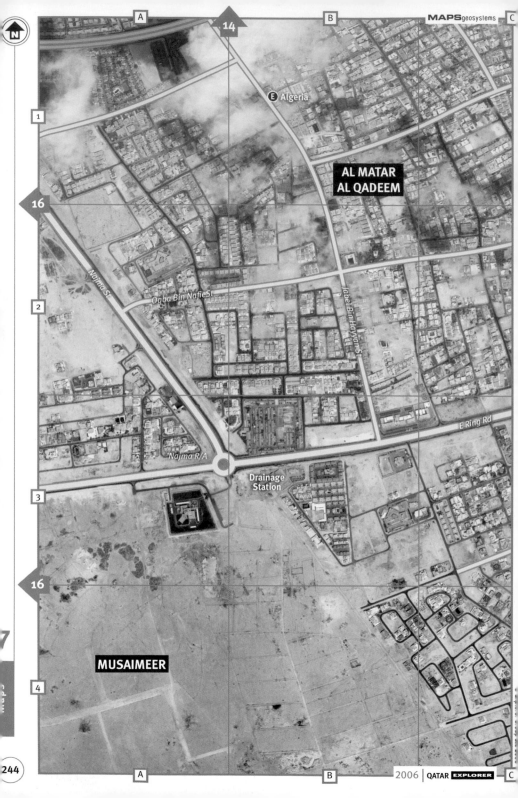

N

A · B · C

14

E Algeria

**AL MATAR
AL QADEEM**

Najma St.

Oqba Bin Nafie St.

Jabel Bin Hayyan St.

E Ring Rd

Najma R/A

Drainage
Station

16

MUSAIMEER

1 · 16 · 2 · 3 · 16 · 4

C · D · E

N

DIGITALGLOBE

Al Matar Al Qadeem St

Al Matar St

Oqba Bin Nafie St

Animal Health Affairs

1

2

AL MATAR
AL QADEEM SOUTH

3

AL WUKAIR

Airforce R/A

4

200km

1

Maps

Made with hand luggage in mind

Don't be fooled by its diminutive size, this perfectly pocket proportioned visitors' guide is packed with insider info on travel essentials, shopping, sports and spas, exploring, dining out and nightlife.

Phone (971 4) 335 3520 · **Fax** (971 4) 335 3529
Info@Explorer-Publishing.com · www.Explorer-Publishing.com
Residents' Guides · Photography Books · Activity Guidebooks · Practical Guides · Maps

EXPLORE
Passionately Publishing